WESTMAR COLLEGE LIBRARY

D0919290

About the author:

W. Lee Humphreys has been a member of the faculty of the Department of Religious Studies at the University of Tennessee at Knoxville since 1970. In addition to teaching courses in ancient Israelite and early Jewish literature and religious traditions and Classical Hebrew, he also teaches an introduction to world religions seminar that studies the relationship of literary study to analysis of the Bible, a course on death and dying and an honors course on the "Sense of Self." Since 1983, Humphreys has also served as director of the University of Tennessee's Learning Research Center, an institute that conducts research on matters related to teaching and learning and also provides support for curriculum, course and instructional design.

Humphreys received a B.A. degree in English and History from the University of Rochester, an S.T.M. degree in Theology from Berkeley Divinity School and a Ph.D. in Hebrew Studies from Union Theological Seminary. He is the author of an introduction to the Hebrew Bible entitled *Crisis and Story* and *The Tragic Vision and the Hebrew Tradition*.

JOSEPH
AND HIS FAMILY

STUDIES ON PERSONALITIES
OF THE OLD TESTAMENT
JAMES L. CRENSHAW, *Editor*

DANIEL IN HIS TIME
by André LaCocque

JOSEPH AND HIS FAMILY: A LITERARY STUDY
by W. Lee Humphreys

JOSEPH
AND HIS FAMILY

A LITERARY STUDY

BY W. LEE HUMPHREYS

UNIVERSITY OF SOUTH CAROLINA PRESS

Copyright © UNIVERSITY OF SOUTH CAROLINA 1988

Published in Columbia, South Carolina, by the
University of South Carolina Press

Manufactured in the United States of America

Library of Congress Cataloging-in-Publication Data

Humphreys, W. Lee.
  Joseph and his family.

  (Studies on personalities of the Old Testament)
  Bibliography: p.
  Includes index.
  1. Bible. O.T. Genesis XXXVII–L—Criticism,
interpretation, etc. 2. Bible as literature.
3. Joseph (Son of Jacob) I. Title. II. Series.
BS1235.2.H86 1988   222′.11066   87-18155
ISBN 0-87249-536-1

To my parents
CECIL and ALBERTA HUMPHREYS

CONTENTS

EDITOR'S PREFACE

Critical study of the Bible in its ancient Near Eastern setting has stimulated interest in the individuals who shaped the course of history and whom events singled out as tragic or heroic figures. For example, Rolf Rendtorff's *Men of the Old Testament* (1968) focuses on the lives of important biblical figures as a means of illuminating history, while Fleming James's *Personalities of the Old Testament* (1939) addresses the issue of individuals who function as inspiration for their religious successors in the twentieth century. Other studies restricted to a single individual—e.g., Moses, Abraham, Samson, Elijah, David, Saul, Ruth, Jonah, Job, Jeremiah—have enabled scholars to deal with a host of themes and questions: psychological, literary, theological, sociological, and historical. Some, like Gerhard von Rad's *Moses*, introduce a specific approach to interpreting the Bible, hence provide valuable pedagogic tools.

As a rule, these treatments of individual figures have not provided books accessible to the general public. Some such volumes were written by thinkers who lacked an expert's knowledge of biblical criticism (Freud on Moses, Jung on Job) and whose conclusions, however provocative, remain problematic. Others were targeted for the guild of professional biblical critics (David Gunn on David and Saul, Phyllis Trible on Ruth, Terence Fretheim and Jonathan Magonet on Jonah). Few such books have succeeded in capturing the imagination of a wide audience in the way fictional works like Archibald MacLeish's *J.B.* and Joseph Heller's *God Knows* have done.

The books in this series are written by specialists in the Old Testament for readers who want to learn more about biblical personalities without becoming professional students of the Bible themselves. The volumes throw light on the imaging of deity in biblical times, clarifying ancient understandings of God. Inasmuch as the Bible constitutes human perceptions of God's relationship with the world and its creature, we seek to discern what ancient writers believed about deity. Although not necessarily endorsing a particular understanding of God, we believe such attempts at making sense of reality contribute something worthwhile to the endless quest for knowledge.

James L. Crenshaw
Duke Divinity School

PREFACE

My engagement with the Joseph material in the book of Genesis has been long standing but intermittent. A substantial portion of my doctoral dissertation, completed some sixteen years ago, treated this material. Since then my interests within biblical scholarship have moved more than once to other units. As they centered on wisdom and Hebraic narrative, there have been periodic returns to the Joseph story. Through much of my work the Joseph material seemed just on or over the horizon, even as it came back into view from time to time. For example, in my discussion of the relationship of the tragic vision with the Hebrew tradition (*The Tragic Vision and the Hebrew Tradition*; 1985), it stood as a counterpoint to the material dealing with the rise and fall of Saul, Israel's first king. Broadly the Joseph material is comic, in that essential tensions and conflicts come to a happy resolution, and at least a glimpse of a divine providential guiding hand is caught behind the toss and tug of human interactions.

I am therefore most appreciative of the opportunity provided by Professor James L. Crenshaw, editor of this series, in his invitation to take up the Joseph material, and to the University of South Carolina Press for their sponsorship of it. When we first discussed the series, Jim suggested that the volumes be aimed at the somewhat mythical and very important figure: the "intelligent lay reader." This is just the sort of reader for whom his own study of the Samsom material was directed, and I have high respect for that work. It is a substantial engagement with the Samson traditions that remains always able to engage both the biblical scholar and a wider audience. I have attempted to keep this wider audience firmly in view, and have not, therefore, either in the text or endnotes, sought to engage in a running debate with other studies of the Joseph material. My debts to many others will be apparent to those in the guild who have worked with this material, but that type of in-house conversation rarely serves those not active within its confines. Notes are generally confined to direct reliance on others or to basic materials in which important themes can be further explored. I have also attempted to refrain from extensive use of transcribed Hebrew text, employing it only where it seemed necessary to make clear a specific point, as in the discussion of repetition or the use of key words in Genesis 37–50.

xi

This study is in two parts. The first takes the material in Genesis 37–50—a unit defined from the point at which we are introduced to Joseph to notice of his death—as a unity. The perspective is synchronic and my interests are literary in the rather traditional sense of attention to genre, plot, characterization, fundamental rhetorical techniques, and the theological perspective that informs the material. Each of chapters 2 through 6 takes the reader through the narrative in a broad way, rather than in a verse-by-verse treatment, with a particular concern or related set of literary concerns in mind. Part II, which is more dependent on some earlier work with the Joseph material, seeks to set out, from a diachronic perspective, a thesis regarding the development of the material into its present form. We trace the hypothetical process through the uncovering of an old kernel in Genesis 40–41, through the construction of the story of Jacob's family around this, to its incorporation into the Torah as an extended bridge between the patriarchial themes of the book of Genesis and the themes of oppression and deliverance in the first half of the book of Exodus. The results of this second part of the study are thereby more hypothetical, not only in that different readings of a text are always possible, but also because we have no form of the text of Genesis 37–50 that reveals earlier stages except as certain critical operations are performed on it.

A third segment might have taken the study of the Joseph traditions on down to the present through treatment of use made of the novella and the figure of Joseph in a wide range of later creative and interpretative efforts. Thomas Mann's monumental *Joseph and His Brothers*, or Freud's treatment of the figure of Joseph, as well as the rock piece on "Joseph and His Technicolor Coat" could claim attention. To give works like these the attention they merit would greatly have extended this volume, and the time involved in its preparation would have been unduly extended.

As it was, the preparation of this volume took longer than anticipated. Both Professor Crenshaw and the University of South Carolina Press, especially editor Kenneth Scott, have been most tolerant of delays caused by unexpected administrative assignments undertaken at the University of Tennessee in Knoxville. I have attempted to combine teaching and writing as a member of the faculty of the Department of Religious Studies with directing the UTK Learning Research Center and coordination of a university-wide transition to a semester academic calendar.

Clearly the support of many people makes this book possible. My gratitude and respect go to my colleagues at the University of Tennessee for their support in providing an academic climate that nurtures both scholarship and instruction. My colleagues in the Department of Religious Studies continue to be a stimulating and challenging group with whom to live. The staff at the Learning Research Center could not be more supportive. Mrs. Tracy Bock has seen this work through several drafts, and her abilities to decipher and make sense of my text is exceeded only by her graceful efficiency and commitment. To her and the others at the center, I express my deepest appreciation.

My wife, Laurey, my daughter, Laurie, and my son, Christopher, continually remind me that there is much more to life than writing and reading, that there is a rich world of human relationships with which what we read and write and teach must relate in ever more enriching ways.

My parents have always supported my work, not least by representing that "intelligent lay reader" who is so essentially our raison d'être as scholars and teachers. In deep gratitude to my mother, Alberta, and in gratitude to and in memory of my father, Cecil, I dedicate this book.

ABBREVIATIONS

AB	The Anchor Bible
AJSL	*American Journal of Semitic Languages and Literatures*
ANET	*Ancient Near Eastern Texts Relating to the Old Testament*, ed. James B. Pritchard
AnOr	Analecta orientalia
BASOR	*Bulletin of the American Schools of Oriental Research*
BDB	Brown, Driver, and Briggs, *Hebrew and English Lexicon of the Old Testament*
BSac	*Bibliotheca Sacra*
BibS	*Biblische Studien*
CBQ	*Catholic Biblical Quarterly*
CBQMS	Catholic Biblical Quarterly Monograph Series
ExpTim	*Expository Times*
FRLANT	Forschungen zur Religion and Literature des Alten und Neuen Testaments
ICC	International Critical Commentary
JAOS	*Journal of the American Oriental Society*
JBL	*Journal of Biblical Literature*
JEA	*Journal of Egyptian Archaeology*
JEOL	*Jaarbericht van het Vooraziatisch-Egyptische Gezelschap*
JNES	*Journal of Near Eastern Studies*
JSOT	*Journal for the Study of the Old Testament*
JSS	*Journal of Semitic Studies*
LXX	Septuagint (Greek Translation of the Hebrew Bible)
MT	Masoretic Text of the Hebrew Bible
NEB	New English Bible
OBT	Overtures to Biblical Theology
OTL	Old Testament Library
RB	*Revue biblique*
RSV	Revised Standard Version of the Bible
V	Vulgate (Latin Translation of the Bible)
VT	*Vetus Testamentum*
VTSup	Vetus Testamentum Supplements
WMANT	Wissenschaftliche Monographien zum Alten und Neuen Testament
ZAW	*Zeitschrift für die alttestamentliche Wissenschaft*
ZDMG	*Zeitschrift der deutchen morgenländischen Gesellschaft*

JOSEPH
AND HIS FAMILY

ONE

THE JOSEPH NARRATIVE AND THE LITERARY REPERTOIRE OF THE HEBREW BIBLE

THE JOSEPH NARRATIVE AND BIBLICAL STUDIES

Analysis and appreciation of classical Hebrew narrative must strive to maintain a balance between the typical and the particular, between that which a particular example shares with other units and that which sets it apart as distinct. In terms of methodologies in biblical studies, the tension must be held between form critical and rhetorical critical concerns,[1] between how a unit exhibits the essential or typical features of a genre and how it stands as a particular example of that genre. Until relatively recently the concerns of the former have dominated critical biblical study; in recent years strong presentations of the latter have made an impact that promises to be the most striking development in study of the Hebrew Bible in the last years of this century. Just as form criticism sought to move behind and therefore overcome the limits of the older literary (source) criticism, so a new sensitivity to the literary qualities of Hebrew narrative has fundamentally changed the meaning of literary study of the biblical traditions.[2]

Form criticism emerged under the guiding hands of H. Gunkel and H. Gressmann as a corrective to source criticism (called literary criticism) and a closely related historical study.[3] As a corrective within a broad movement over a century old, form critical studies were in many ways most typical of the movement that one recent scholar from outside that tradition has characterized nicely as "excavative."[4] The term is of course from archaeology, an additional formative factor that shaped this century and more of biblical study. "Excavative" as here used denotes the attempt to uncover the layered history of a text, to get to its roots or to earlier stages in the development that led to the form now in our hands. The effect was to move the text from the present in a particular confessional context—church or synagogue—in which for centuries the text was cherished and studied in and through the light it cast on larger theological and ethical issues. Jewish study of the Hebrew Bible was a part of the larger study of Talmud. Old Testament and New Testament were the concern of theologians and those who reflected on the life of the church in the world. Since the nineteenth century the disciplines of Old Testament and New Testament study have emerged in seminary and academic curricula as distinct from theological studies, and more and more from each other.

For the older literary or source critic, the Joseph narrative in Genesis proved fertile ground for especially illustrative examples of the sorts of duplications, seams, tensions, and distinct patterns in the use of names, vocabulary, stylistic elements, and point of view that served as evidence of once distinct sources. The contretemps that characterize the removal of Joseph from the pit to Egypt, for example, were nicely treated by the detection of sources only roughly joined in Genesis 37:19–30.[5] More recently, however, the narrative has served as the basis for attack on the traditional source analysis of the Pentateuch. In fact, as the form critic sought to move behind and thereby advance the work of older source criticism, the Joseph narrative suddenly provided less fertile ground. With its particular attraction to shorter units whose roots in oral tradition seemed especially clear, form criticism was drawn to the apparently distinct and brief units that comprise the cycles dealing with Abraham and Jacob, as well as to poetic material that is found elsewhere in the Hebrew Bible. Longer and more tightly interconnected narrative units, such as the Joseph narrative of Genesis, or the accounts of David's rise in 1 Samuel and rule in 2 Samuel, were not as readily analyzed through, nor as inviting to, the methods and perspectives of the form critic. A distinct setting in the life of the nation or people Israel, a clear function amid its varied institutions and customs, a (sometimes overly rigorous) adherence to the typical that defines a given form, anonymity in composition and transmission—all this and more provided a basis for understanding units dealing with Abraham or Jacob and with the early Israelites in Egypt and in the wilderness or in the early days of the federation and its judges. The Joseph material seemed to slip from view.

4

Extended units whose base in an oral tradition seemed less secure and where authorship, in the sense of an individual creative hand giving distinct aesthetic form to a narrative through use of a range of rhetorical techniques, lend themselves rather to a form of literary analysis that comes under the broad heading of "poetics." Such units were neglected by the older form critics or were made to fit their structures with sometimes wrenching effort. The pioneering work of Gunkel on the material in Genesis, as well as that of his student Gressmann, illustrates this. Gunkel, who has done so much in determining the basic forms of the material in Genesis, has noted that large parts of the Joseph narrative cannot easily be fitted into the categories of legend or saga developed on the basis of his analysis of the material dealing with Abraham or Jacob. He continues to speak of legends out of which the Joseph narrative is constructed, but must go on to assert that, unlike the material found earlier in Genesis, those legends dealing with Joseph are "very cunningly blended into a whole."[6] He observes that we get a very complete and consistent picture of Joseph, his brothers, and his father through this careful blending. In other ways as well this extended unit stands apart in its "love of emotions and tears," its interest in the soul-life and in strange customs, its lack of the etiological element, its discursiveness and spun-out style.[7] Only concerning this material does Gunkel speak of "romance," and Gressmann refines this terminology when he speaks not of a *Sagenkranz* but of *Novelle*.[8] All in all, the impression is gained that they are speaking of one type of literary material in terms developed for another type.

While form critical eyes were trained for the typical, it was the particular and the distinctive that leapt to the fore in the Joseph narrative and thereby set this material apart from the fundamental concerns of most methods used in the critical study of the Hebrew Bible. Source analysis had largely run its course, and had reached a point of diminishing returns as well as wide acceptance (new challenges would come only later); form criticism was uncomfortable with extended narratives like that in Genesis 37–50. It is little wonder that for a period of decades (1930–60) precious little significant or memorable critical study of the Joseph narrative emerged.[9] It simply did not fit the interests and perspectives of critical scholarship.

However, fads in critical scholarship change, as they do in almost all areas of life, and by the 1960s and especially the 1970s and early 1980s, new concerns, perspectives, and methodology have led to new analyses of Hebrew narrative material that place the Joseph narrative of Genesis in the very center of our interest. The pendulum had swung from the typical to the distinctive. James Muilenburg coined the term "rhetorical criticism" to describe an emerging interest, not in what characterized a particular unit as an example of a certain type or genre, but in how that unit was uniquely shaped through distinctive qualities and rhetorical flourishes, making it more than just another piece cast from a mold. At the same time literary concerns of a different type (e.g., structuralism) and a related attention to the text in its fuller and final canonical form redirected attention from the small discrete unit to larger expanses of narrative.[10] Renewed attention to the reception of the text in distinct communities, and the competencies readers and hearers brought to the experience of the text as authoritative or canon,[11] has accompanied this shift in perspective. The complex interaction of text, its producer(s), and its readers or hearers is demanding renewed attention. It has become especially fashionable to speak of the final form of the text as the primary object of attention. It is not simply that larger blocks of material exhibit typical patterns and characteristics, although this is now more readily recognized, but a distinct and sometimes arresting artistry is manifest in the design of the larger units (as well as in the composition and combination of smaller units). Approaches that had become commonplace in the study of other literature have found application in study of the Bible as well. And once the polemics of some of the early "new" literary critics against older source and form critics had died down,[12] the newer analysis could be seen as a development out of and built upon earlier work. Just as form criticism was built upon the work of earlier source analysis, avenues toward a more balanced relationship between the several approaches to study of the Hebrew Bible and especially its narrative material could now be developed.

What seems clear is that older "diachronic" approaches, which trace a unit's evolution and growth through time, need to be prefaced and tempered by "synchronic" approaches, which look at the text in and of itself. And, as has recently been argued,[13] priority belongs to the synchronic—if not in absolute terms, at least in order of procedure.

It can be suggested that earlier critical scholarship was too concerned, perhaps under influences coming from Romanticism, with origins, with the "pristine" state of material before it underwent later alteration and was moved from its original *Sitz im Leben* to some place in a literary composition. Certainly this had a fragmentizing effect on our approach to the Bible. Genesis came to seem only a collection of units which individually deserved attention, while the book as a whole or in its larger collections was ignored.[14] Thus Genesis 22—the story of the near sacrifice of Isaac—could be lifted from its context and appreciated in itself even as earlier levels for the text were being proposed in which the story served to legitimize abandonment of the sacrifice of the firstborn son, with an animal substitute provided in his place. The unit became a datum in the history of religious practice. This method came, of course, too often at a cost; in this case in not seeing the story as a particular climax in the overarching pattern in the Abraham material, especially in tracing the trajectory of his movement toward radical faith, and the finely drawn rhetorical qualities of the unit might be neglected as well. But that there was genuine gain cannot be denied.

Elements of the Joseph story in Genesis, however, could not be so readily abstracted from context. Its scenes became pale when lifted from the whole drama and considered apart from their larger context. The composition was, as a whole, usually pronounced to be later in origin than the other material dealing with Israel's fathers and mothers in Genesis—an assessment that in a time of high valuation of original and early material was more than simply chronological. At best the historical roots of the Joseph material, and the earlier blocks used in its later composition, were but dimly perceived in their wholly reworked later form with all its own particular features. Certainly for the Joseph narrative, and perhaps for all other material as well, it seems best to begin not with the parts or pieces, the episodes as separate blocks, but with the whole, with the cake as baked and decorated and ready to eat and not the distinct ingredients. In the language of recent scholarship, "synchrony" should now come before "diachrony." The whole commands attention before its parts. The text as we have it before us takes priority over the history of its development, before a reconstruction of its growth into its present form. "Priority" denotes here at the outset a matter of procedure. And if in the past the Joseph narrative has suffered from neglect in the face of overarching interest in origins and in the distinct pieces comprising larger units, it may well be that in the context of these more recent concerns with the distinctive, with larger narratives, and with the text as we now have it, as well as an attention to the reception of the material by the reader, the Joseph narrative will come into its own and have its special day.[15]

Indeed, especially in Pentateuchal studies, the Joseph narrative promises to occupy a distinct and informative place. That earlier modes of analysis could too readily slight it, or only with some violence fit it into their perspective, is a statement of the limitations of those methods. That more recent methods lead us to a renewed appreciation of the Joseph narrative may serve to legitimize them in the eyes of many—but not in place of, but as a valuable supplement and balance to, earlier work. The fact that Genesis 37—50 has been used both as a source of telling illustrations by the earlier source critic and as a launching pad for fundamental criticism of that enterprise must not be overlooked; it suggests that we should give careful attention both in its unity and in its parts to the text as we now have it and to a reconstruction of its growth into that form.

THE JOSEPH STORY AND HEBREW NARRATIVES

What sort of material have we in this final segment of Genesis? How are we to read it?[16] At heart this is a question of genre, of literary type, and thus of reader expectations; it will be considered more systematically in the next chapter. Yet some preliminary assessment of the relation of the Joseph narrative to other material in the larger Hebrew Bible is in place as a first step.

The neglect of the Joseph material in Genesis is confined to the restricted context of historical critical study of the Bible. The striking and complex ways in which Thomas Mann, at a critical junction in his own life in exile, could build an elaborate and extensive work upon this part of Genesis is compelling testimony to its powerful attraction for the creative imagination of an artist whose medium is narrative fiction.[17] It is just these sensitivities that are more recently informing critical study of biblical narrative as well. There is little doubt that, second only to the account of creation and its aftermath in the fall, the Joseph material is popularly the best known segment of the book of Genesis—even if with a sometimes skewed focus on Joseph's encounter with Potiphar's wife.

As an artfully designed complex and as extended narrative the last chapters of Genesis do stand apart from what has come before. Its parts are clearly interlocking scenes of a larger whole. They appear to be designed first and foremost to take their place in that whole (except maybe chapters 48, 49, and possibly chapter 39). Each is essential, and none can really stand alone as a significant whole. In this the Joseph narrative has always stood apart from the stories about Abraham and Jacob in Genesis as well as the later materials in Exodus and Numbers. If these latter are to be denoted as legends or sagas, the Joseph narrative is clearly something different.

Within the Hebrew Bible attention then turns most readily to narratives dealing with Saul and David in the books of 1 and 2 Samuel. For here, in the story of the rise and fall of King Saul, and of the rise and the rule of David, a similar interlocking of scenes is found in the construction of extended narratives with clear overarching designs and emphases. In all of these units the hand of a particular author seems more in evidence, and the poetic concerns of a literate culture that values the refined use of written words and forms are apparent. From the perspective of this material we can return to the cycles dealing with Abraham and Jacob and detect overarching patterns there as well, even if the units that make up the cycles are more discrete and able to stand on their own. Abraham's trajectory toward faith is just not as finely developed as that which traces Joseph's growth or the restoration of harmony to Joseph's shattered family. Of course, many units that comprise the extended narratives in 1 and 2 Samuel seem quite discrete as well. We might best define a continuum in which we move from cycles of what appear once to have been discrete units now gathered in a loose, overarching design, through enhancement of that design, until finally the units no longer appear as distinct but as episodes or scenes created simply as part of an extended drama. On this continuum we move from one who compiles tradition materials with more or less of a controlling vision of some sort; to one who, in the service of a vision, may rework as well as arrange the material utilized; to one who may draw on certain broad traditional figures and relationships, and even motifs and themes, but who forms his or her material whole cloth, as it were. On one end of the continuum we have the cycles of material in Genesis dealing with Abraham and Jacob; on the other the narrative of Joseph. In between stand the story of the rise and fall of King Saul (1 Sam. 9–31),[18] the story of David's rise (1 Sam. 16–2 Sam. 5), and, more integrated and closer to the Joseph narrative, the so-called "Succession Narrative" (2 Sam. 6–20; 1 Kgs. 1–2). For roughly comparable material we turned first to these units in 1 and 2 Samuel because there we find extended and relatively integrated narratives. We also find stories of families torn by discord. Form and content guide this initital selection. We also find in these units well-constructed and engaging plot lines built around figures drawn from Israel's history and utilizing significant events in that history. We also meet in these extended units complexly etched characterization.

9

We can also seek more widely for other material that is in some respects even more closely related to the Joseph narrative. In terms of style we have the narratives that comprise the books of Ruth and Esther. In terms of content we again turn to Esther, as well as to the shorter units collected in the first six chapters of the book of Daniel. Content and form can also lead us further afield in the ancient Near East to consider certain literary works from ancient Egypt, such as the stories of Sinuhe and Wen-Amon, and from ancient Mesopotamia such works as the story of Ahiqar. All of these extrabiblical materials deal with the adventures of men and women in royal courts. The stories of Esther and Daniel, like that of Joseph, are also set in foreign courts, and their stories relate their successes against various odds or forms of opposition.

In terms of literary type we are dealing with extended narratives in which the several scenes are artfully interwoven, in which there is the development of a distinct plot, in which characterization is often complex, and in which a host of rhetorical and poetical techniques are employed. All this clearly indicates that the material is artistic fiction. Good stories well told mark each as entertainment, even if other purposes or thrusts can be detected in them as well. In terms of content we can note that a number of the materials mentioned—Esther, the material in Daniel 1–6, Ahiqar, Sinuhe, Wen-Amon—are all set in some fashion in royal establishments and deal with the adventures of a courtier as hero or heroine. At issue often is royal favor and the power, prestige, and wealth that come with it. Sometimes (Joseph, Esther, Daniel 1, 2, 4, 5) royal favor is to be won in a contest in which the hero (often an alien) finally is shown to be superior to all rivals (usually natives); sometimes (Daniel 3, 6) it involves the schemes and devices that pit courtier against courtier, one bent on the destruction of the other, with the prize going to the survivor; sometimes it may also involve questions of royal misunderstanding or misapprehension of the true state of affairs with regard to the hero (Ahiqar, Sinuhe).

Considering the Joseph narrative in relation to these court tales will allow us to attend to important dimensions in the story dealing with the rapid rise of Joseph from slavery in prison to a position of authority second only to that of Pharaoh over all of Egypt. This is accomplished through the hero's abilities as an interpreter of dreams, especially the king's dreams, a task at which he succeeds only after all the wise men and magicians in Egypt fail. Genesis 40–41 presents the tale of a court contest in which the hero triumphs through his ability to build upon his acuteness as dream interpreter and is able to show himself a shrewd adviser as well. The larger

Joseph narrative is also set in the context of the Egyptian royal court, with periodic reminders of this lavish setting provided at critical points in the narrative (Gen. 43:23, 32–34; 44:17; 45:16–20; 47:1–10). At the heart of the Joseph narrative stands a kernel (chs. 40–41) that has an almost Horatio Alger quality—a poor boy rises from the pit to undreamed-of success and substance. Around this kernel the larger story develops.

As we consider the larger Joseph narrative, a return to the earlier-cited material will show comparable themes. For overall it is first and last the story of a family, a family apparently determined to self-destruct, a family rent by bitter strife, deceit, jealousy, and blindness. In this regard the narrative recalls the Succession Narrative of 2 Samuel and 1 Kings 1–2, as well as elements in the story of King Saul. Set in the courts of David and the political and international strife of that time, this is the story of David's family. It too is a story of strife: father against son, son against son, son against father. The very fascination of this Succession Narrative is found in the manner in which it weaves the public with the private, David the king with David the father and husband. The two cannot be divorced, of course, and success on one level seems only to spell disaster on the other. The man who could mold an empire could not shape and maintain harmony in his own family. The conquerer of nations could not control his sons. In David's story we also have an account of a strife-torn family; and if in this case the family seems unable to come together in the end, a comparison with the story of Jacob's family in Genesis 37—50 can provide mutual enlightenment.

The Joseph narrative is set in the royal establishment of Egypt; it is in part a courtier's story. But only in part, for it is in essence a family's story. Broadly then, we find here a story of a family rent by strife and deceit that only over time and in the face of all obstacles is reunited in harmony, of hatred that finally gives way to reconciliation. At the heart of this story stands another, which tells of the remarkable rise from rags to riches of the young Joseph in the royal court of Egypt. The Succession Narrative, as well as material that precedes the Joseph narrative in Genesis, also alerts us to another theme, that of the supplanting of elder brothers by the youngest. Here, as with the broad motif of family strife and court rivalry, we find elements very prevalent in literature. And while they help us get a fix on the Joseph narrative in Genesis, on its broad form and content, we need now give close attention to the type of narrative represented, and again address the genre question: "What sort of thing have we here?"

NOTES

1. Phyllis Trible, *God and the Rhetoric of Sexuality*, ch. 1.
2. J. Barton, *Reading the Old Testament*.
3. Witness the title of J. Wellhausen's formative study of the sources of the Pentateuch: *Prolegomena to the History of Israel*.
4. Robert Alter, *The Art of Biblical Narrative*, 12–14.
5. See the commentary of Claus Westermann for a recent example of this: *Genesis 37–50*, 40–42.
6. H. Gunkel, *The Legends of Genesis*, 81.
7. Gunkel, *Legends*, 77-117; see also his "Die Komposition der Joseph-Geschichten," *ZDMG* 76 (1922): 55-71.
8. Gunkel, *Legends*, 86; H. Gressmann, "Ursprung und Entwicklung der Joseph-Sage." FRLANT 36 (1923): 2.
9. The work of Gerhard von Rad noted below is an exception.
10. T. J. Keegan, *Interpreting the Bible*, provides a very readable introduction to structuralism, canonical criticism, and reader response criticism.
11. J. A. Sanders, *Canon and Community: A Guide to Canonical Criticism*.
12. Sometimes terms like "excavative" can become almost expletives when used by supporters of "new" approaches, who at times seem compelled to demolish all that came before to stake out their claims. One is reminded of the critique of much contemporary scholarship by E. Becker: "The problem of man's knowledge is not to oppose and demolish opposing views, but to include them in larger theoretical structure" (*Denial of Death*, xi).
13. R. Polzin, *Moses and the Deuteronomist*, 1–24.
14. Could it be that a lexical use of the text and a form of piety that leads to reading and meditating on the Bible in small and often isolated units have informed this approach as well?
15. Consider the central role of the Joseph material in Alter's *Art of Biblical Narrative*.
16. There is an arbitrariness in isolating the Joseph material as an object of study from the material prior to it in Genesis and even from the account of Israel's origins as a whole. The cast of characters has already been introduced in Gen.; Ex. 1:8, e.g., refers to "a new king over Egypt, who did not know Joseph," while Josh. 24:32 mentions Joseph's burial in Palestine by later generations. Justification for attention to Gen. 37–50 is simply that it opens with special attention to Joseph in Jacob's family (37:1-4) and concludes with notice of his death (50:26). Links with the material's larger context will be considered in time.
17. Thomas Mann, *Joseph and His Brothers*.
18. See W. L. Humphreys, *The Tragic Vision and the Hebrew Tradition*, chs. 2–3, and references there.

PART I

THE POETICS OF THE JOSEPH NOVELLA

TWO

THE JOSEPH STORY AS A
NOVELLA

The Joseph narrative in Genesis can be described as a "novella," and viewing it from the point of view defined by the essential features of that genre will underscore several fundamental characteristics of the unit. Of the several genre designations employed in the exegetical study of the Hebrew Bible, "novella" perhaps betrays most clearly its origins in later Western literary history and analysis. In biblical study it is a borrowed term, for novella primarily denotes a narrative type that has developed in the West since the fourteenth century. Yet the term is being used in biblical study, and it has been found most useful. We should begin, however, by considering the genre as defined in recent literary analysis.

NOVELLA IN RECENT LITERARY STUDY

Clearly the word "novella" is linked to the word "novel." In fact, the latter is the English translation of the Italian *novella*. The links between the novella and the novel are twofold. On the one hand, the novel historically developed from the novellas that first took classical shape in the fourteenth century, with Boccaccio's *The Decameron* (ca. 1348) generally cited as the best known and most typical. These short prose narratives provided rudiments of form as well as themes, typical characters, and plot outlines for later novels. On the other hand, novella is currently used in literary criticism to denote a type of prose narrative that stands between the novel and the short story, sharing characteristics of each. Henry James, for example, used the French term *nouvelle* in this latter sense, and others have coined such terms as "novelette" or "short novel."

Because novella denotes a literary form standing between novel and short story, it is best to begin with a brief consideration of what these two have in common and in what ways they are distinct.[1] First, there are several points held in common by short stories and novels.

1) Both are fiction. They do not report events or describe persons as they actually took place or lived in the past. However true to life they must be—and they must be true to life in a fundamental sense—they are not historical. This does not, of course, preclude the appearance in them of historical personages and events. What is reported in them is not designed, however, to meet tests of historical accuracy.

2) Novels and short stories are narratives built around a plot that follows a trajectory from the establishment of a tension or initial complication through further complications to a resolution and denouement. The plot will contain one or more stressful situations or events. We find here more than mere description of places or persons; novels and short stories are distinct from essays on some topic or situation.

3) They are prose, not poetry. Poetic units of a variety of types may, however, be utilized in them—as indeed may a wide range of other literary forms (letters, reports, visions, etc.). They are more complex genres that can encompass a number of other more simple genres.

4) Both novels and short stories are the conscious creative work generally of a single author. They are not folk products that evolve over time. Both may draw upon motifs, themes, plots, and characters drawn from the realm of folklore and popular oral and written traditions. Yet they reveal from beginning to end the artful stamp of a single careful, controlling craftsman. They are furthermore designed to be read rather than heard. While having perhaps limited links with oral forms, novels and short stories are artistic written compositions and not simply recorded recitations or summaries of the same. They represent a clear artistic break with oral tradition and are rooted in a life setting characterized by a higher level of literacy.

5) Novels and short stories are literary works submitted to the twin tests of aesthetic success and imitative accuracy or truth. They intend to entertain, and this is accomplished, in part at least, by holding out to the

reader an aspect of life as it really is. Unlike a historical record or narrative, they depict not so much what *happened* as what *happens* in life. Even when they are set in the distant past or exotic contexts, it is our world and a humanity we recognize that we meet as we read them. We find in them a truth, even if it didn't happen.

This is what the novel and short story have in common, and the novella, standing between them in length, is characterized by these features as well: it is an artfully crafted piece of prose fiction that entertains and seeks to give an accurate depiction of life.

There are differences between short stories and novels as well, and a review of them will help define the unique place of the novella.

1) Most obvious, of course, is length. Short stories are just that: short, easily read in one brief sitting. Novels can range over many hundreds of pages.

2) The number of characters and events encompassed in a short story is limited. One, or at most a very few, characters are depicted, and usually in a single or a very limited chain of events or situations. Generally the time frame for the short story is brief. Novels may have so many characters that readers need a chart to guide them through. A complex and extended chain of events or situations characterize the novel; in fact, there may well be more than one such chain with varied degrees of interrelatedness. The time frame can range from a few hours to centuries.

3) An essential distinction is that the short story tends to *reveal* the nature of a character or a situation while a novel *develops* characters or situations. James Joyce spoke of the "epiphany quality" of the short story, its quality of revelation. Through a single or compact series of events or situations a character becomes clear and distinct to the reader, or a situation's true quality is revealed. By contrast, over a much wider range of events and situations the characters of a novel change as they grow or deteriorate. The characters in a novel are not seen in a single snapshot but as they evolve and shape, and are shaped by, events and situations.

At this point the novella can be brought into sharper focus as falling between these two types. Of course, boundary lines that are too sharp must not be drawn between short story, novella, and novel, for they clearly shade into each other. But genuine differences are apparent. The novella shares all that the novel and short story have in common. Longer than the short story, it nevertheless also has a compactness with regard to both the number of characters and the range of events. Generally but one chain of events is followed and usually over a limited time frame. Yet, like the novel, its primary emphasis is on the development of—and not simply the revelation of—characters and/or situations. Within a compressed time frame and limited events, characters evolve. Along with the oft-cited *Billy Budd* by Herman Melville, *The Turn of the Screw* by Henry James, and *Heart of Darkness* by Joseph Conrad, John Steinbeck's *The Pearl* represents the novella in recent literature.

NOVELLA AND THE JOSEPH MATERIAL

Turning to the Hebrew Bible, we must at least acknowledge questions as to the suitability of a genre term so rooted in later Western literary history and criticism for analysis of ancient Hebraic material standing worlds apart from the examples just given. There is no comparable term in the Hebrew language for a type of literature akin to the Western novella. But then, with quite limited exceptions, there is little in the way of genre terminology in the Hebrew Bible, and most of the designations used in form critical and genre analysis come from other areas and periods. The essential issue is not the presence or absence of genre terms in the Hebraic tradition, but of material that essentially fits the descriptive criteria that define a specific genre designation.

Clearly there are no novels in the Hebrew Bible. The extended works contained therein are either collections of materials of varied types or have a style and thrust not in line with the novel—e.g., the extended historical corpora of the Deuteronomistic circle or the Chronicler. On the other hand, there do appear to be short stories. Genesis 24 and Ruth would fit this category, and the stories of Daniel 1–6 and Jonah might be noted as well. Jonah with its great fish and rapidly growing plant also has elements characteristic of fables, and this element of the miraculous is even more pronounced in Daniel 1–6. Each of these units is brief and reveals the quality of a situation and/or character. Jonah, Ruth, and even Daniel and his companions are essentially the same at the end of each story as at the outset; they do not grow or develop before us. We just recognize with greater clarity the character of each as the story progresses. They have that 'epiphany quality" of which Joyce spoke.

There seems to be a limited range of novellas or novella-like material as well in the Hebrew Bible. The stories of Samson in Judges 13–16, Esther and Mordecai in the book of Esther, and especially Joseph and his brothers in Genesis 37–50 seem primary examples; one could also take note of Judith and Tobit in the Jewish and Protestant Apocrypha (elements of the fable appear in the latter). These units are longer than the short stories, and they depict the clear development of central characters or situations rather than simply revealing them. Units like the Succession Narrative of 2 Samuel 7–20 and 1 Kings 1–2, and the story of Saul in 1 Samuel 9–31, reveal characteristics of the novella and, being also rooted more in Israel's particular history, might therefore be called "historical novellas." While offering what is claimed to be an account of public events that altered the course of Israel's history and dealing with significant historical figures, they depict Saul and David as evolving through time and are reflective not just of what happened, but of what happens to human beings. They may attempt to meet the standards of historical truth for their day, but they clearly betray novella-like characteristics as well.

At this point we are in position to consider in overview the Joseph narrative in Genesis in relation to the novella. We will see that it provides an apt genre designation for the material, and as such alerts us to dimensions of the work to be considered in the following chapters.

The Novella as Fiction

The novella is the creative product of an artist's imagination. It is not an account of events and persons that bears the stamp of historical reporting and interpretation. The novella gives an account, not of what happened, but of what happens. One comes to it expecting not information about what once occurred on the stage of history, but entertainment and insight into what happens to men and women when faced with certain events or situations.[2]

This does not mean that there may not be links between the novella and the historical narrative. The novella, like the historical report, is generally set in the past, in a particular time and place, and may well give an account of a series of events as if they had occurred. But it is the essence of the novella that it is not confined to public events available for others to witness and assess. The novella moves easily into the private and personal, reporting intimate conversations and often even the thoughts of the characters in a detail that would be available to no one but their creator. Thus in the Joseph material we find not only events of a public nature recalled, such as Joseph's successful audience before Pharaoh and his promotion to high office (Gen. 41), but also private encounters between Joseph and his brothers, between the brothers and their father, and even insight into the private thoughts of the brothers as they plot Joseph's destruction (37:18–20), unsuccessfully seek his release (37:21–22, 26–27), later realize their guilt (42:21–22), and fear revenge on his part (50:15).

The major characters of a novella may be historical figures, and events from history may be incorporated into the plot. But it must be stressed that the intent is not to report historical activity. The historical figures and events are caught up into an imaginative fabric produced by the creative activity of the author. Thus, Joseph and the other sons of Jacob may have been historical personages, and there quite likely was a descent into Egypt by ancestors of those who in time came to be the nation Israel. But simply to read the Joseph narrative as an account of the lives of those persons and as a description of events in the prehistory of Israel—or even, as some suggest, as a reflection of the history and interrelationships between the several tribes represented by Jacob's sons—is to miss the potential impact of the story and risk misuse of the material.[3] Indeed, for all its specificity, a historical inexactness pervades the Joseph narrative just at the points of its possible linkage with the history of Egypt. Neither the specific pharaoh nor even the ruling dynasty is named, nor are events dated relative to known persons or events. Some familiarity with Egyptian custom and practice is reflected in the narrative, lending it a touch of verisimilitude, but it is not possible through what is presented to root the story in any of the reasonably well documented periods of the history of Egypt. On the other hand, these Egyptian traces in the story serve literary ends as they set the stage and advance the plot.

Just as in recent Western literary study it is possible to qualify the term "novel" with the designation "historical," so it is possible to speak of a "historical novella" in the Hebrew Bible. Again the lines cannot be sharply drawn between the two; the Joseph narrative and the Succession Narrative would seem to be illustrative of each. In the former there is little that is clearly historical; the latter seems much more firmly rooted in the public events of Israelite history. Yet there is a marked quality of the private and interior that pervades both works, reflective of the creative imagination of an author, and the latter seems also designed both to entertain and mirror or inform about life as well as report events important in the development of the nation and people of Israel.

It is indeed possible for later generations to treat a novella as history, as a report of what happened, and to utilize it in this way. Thus the Joseph narrative, once an independent composition, was in time utilized within the larger narrative framework of the Torah, effecting the transition from material about the three patriarchs in southern Palestine (Genesis) to that dealing with the tribes in bondage in Egypt (Exodus).[4]

The Novella as Prose

The novella is prose rather than poetry. It is a prose that not only describes events but depicts conversations between characters. The extended interchanges between Joseph and Pharaoh in Genesis 41 and between Joseph and his brothers later are examples of a developed narrative art. Dialogue generally dominates in Hebrew prose fiction.

While the novella is a prose composition, it may contain a number of other literary forms as well. The Joseph narrative has set within it several reports of dreams and their interpretation (Gen. 40, 41); a formal courtly speech (44:18–34); and, perhaps as secondary additions brought into the narrative in its later use in the larger Torah, genealogical lists (46:8–27), blessings (48:15–16, 20), and ancient tribal poetry in the form now of a patriarch's last words (ch. 49).

Setting—Time and Place

The events of a novella are set in a particular time and place that is defined with enough specificity to locate the action. However, we have also seen that often there is not the specificity of detail that allows the events to be as firmly rooted as we would demand of a historical report. In the Joseph narrative the time for the story is, from the perspective of author and reader, the distant past of the patriarchal ancestors of Israel. The narrative's time frame takes in a number of years as Joseph is transplanted from Palestine to Egypt and transformed from a youth to a mature man of stature and with a family of his own. Often gaps of several years are traversed without effort (e.g., between chs. 37 and 39 or the end of 41 and beginning of 42). The most specific descriptions of the passage of time are the seven good and seven lean years and the notice of "two full years" between chapters 40 and 41. The passage of several years linking the events of chapters 42 and 43 is noted with less precision.

The setting moves from the land of Canaan to Egypt and then back and forth several times, as first Joseph and then his brothers and father move from Canaan to Egypt. These movements are accomplished with minimal notice and with ease. As we have noted, the author enters into some detail in presenting the Egyptian setting of the story in an attempt to provide verisimilitude for his work. This ranges from the use of Egyptian loan words and names through the mention of several customs and practices characteristic of what for him and his reader seems to be an exotic, if sometimes ominous, land. The details of the dreams and of the protocol of the royal court (Gen. 40–41) seem generally accurate with regard to what we know of Egypt, even if they are not specific enough to permit the events to be located in a particular period in its history. In a few instances, however, especially the author's notice about Egyptian distaste for shepherds and their unwillingness to dine with Hebrews (46:34; 43:32), we move beyond the verifiable and even the plausible in the service of a good story. These notices serve a narrative function—allowing the brothers to be alone with Joseph at a critical moment and permitting their settlement in Goshen—and they contribute to a sense of wonder at the strange land of Egypt. But if pressed, they would make the position of Joseph, who is always known to be of Hebrew origin (40:15), quite impossible. A number of these "Egyptian" elements in the material will be considered in some detail in the second part of this book.

Plot

The essential skeletal framework of the novella is provided by the plot. The series of events that make up the plot is not an accidental collection of happenings but a carefully woven fabric, extended over time and set in a distinct locale. The novella has a beginning, in which a complication or tension is set out; a middle, in which there are further complications; a climax, in which the tension is resolved; and a denouement, in which the complications vanish. All this is bracketed by a formal opening exposition and a brief conclusion. While separated sometimes by large blocks of time and expanses of space, the events that comprise the plot are carefully integrated, growing out of and leading into each other. They do not stand alone as distinct and complete stories, as might, for example, the several distinct units that make up the cycles of material dealing with Abraham and Jacob. Each of the latter has its own beginning, middle, and end, and most can stand alone. They are but loosely bound into a cycle. Only in rare instances is information contained in earlier units essential for the development of a later saga.

In the Joseph narrative the several units are more akin to the scenes of a play, interlocked with and evolving into and out of each other. They cannot stand alone. The basic complication is set at the outset when we are introduced to a family split by hatred and seemingly intent on its own destruction. Older brothers are jealous of their youngest sibling and more than willing to act on their hatred to rid themselves of this thorn in their lives; the youngest is a spoiled brat, telling tales on his own brothers and boasting of dreams that set him over them and their parents; an old and doting father sparks and feeds the flames of jealousy through favoritism shown the much-loved youngest son. The brothers do act and apparently rid themselves of their youngest brother; all that remains is cruelly to deceive their father. Genesis 37 sets the narrative in motion; the complication is defined and the main characters carefully sketched.

Then for a time the story leaves the family in Canaan and in an interlude follows the adventures of the youngest son as he moves, in the best rags-to-riches tradition, from Egyptian slavery and the depths of obscurity in a house of detention to a position second only to Pharaoh in power over all the land. By the end of Genesis 41 Joseph has become vizier over Egypt, has married into the family of the priest of the Sun God, is busily implementing his strategy to meet the crisis of famine, and is thoroughly Egyptianized. It would appear at first glance that we have abandoned the complication set out in the beginning (with the intrusion of the distinct and complete story in chapter 38 reinforcing this impression) to take up a new story. In fact, it has been suggested that we find in Genesis 39–41 (with 47:13–26 and 50:20) an old and distinct story of the remarkable rise of a Hebrew lad into the Egyptian royal establishment, with its own beginnings, middle, and end; its own complexity, further complication, and resolution.[5] No clear links bind chapters 39–41 with chapter 37, and none is needed. Genesis 37 does, however, explain how the young man came to Egyptian slavery (cf. 40:15), and the famine of chapter 41 is said to afflict the whole earth, bringing many people to Egypt for relief. This once possibly independent story of Joseph's rise and success in Pharaoh's court is a kernel at the heart of the larger family story into which it is now bound.

Suddenly Joseph's brothers reappear after many years, and the complications set out in Genesis 37 are recalled. Soon further complications unfold. Driven by famine from Canaan to Egypt, the brothers encounter only trouble, as this high official takes such ominous interest in their lives and family situation. He makes wild and unfounded charges against them and jails them all for a brief period. Simeon is held for a longer time while the others are sent home with provisions, their money secretly returned, and instructions not to appear again without their new youngest brother (who was born in the intervening years, during which Joseph's mother apparently died, since she is not mentioned after chapter 37). A second trip to Egypt some years later further complicates the family situation. The second reception seems at first the antithesis of the first, but the brother's brief respite leads in the end to further accusations and the gravest of dangers to Benjamin, the father's latest favorite. A number of links bind this scene with what has come before. Only as the tension becomes unbearable is resolution attained. Joseph reveals his true identity—which at first can only spark terror—and then makes clear that he, like the brothers, has changed, and forgives all. He then uses his position of power in Egypt to resolve a subtension introduced by the famine and the danger it poses for the family of Jacob. All are brought to Egypt and settled in Goshen. In time Jacob dies with *all* his sons about him, and before Joseph's own death the brothers are again reconciled (50:15–21). A family that once seemed clearly doomed to self-destruction has been preserved.

This plot will receive detailed attention in the next chapter. It is complex in its movement through time and over great expanses of space. A subplot deals with the remarkable rise of Joseph in Egypt, facilitating the transformation of the hero from an abused youth into a powerful official. This subplot is integrated into the larger story through the motif of the famine and the danger it poses for all the earth; the position Joseph attains in Egypt permits both the complication and final resolution of the tension set out at the beginning. Each scene or episode has its own complication, sometimes further complication, and resolution. Yet each scene builds on what came before and grows naturally out of it. Each opens upon what follows. The scenes cannot stand alone; prior material is assumed, and expectations are raised that demand resolution in what follows. Even when the family is set aside for a time and we follow Joseph through his adventures in Egypt, the larger complication remains in the background; we know the brothers are not rid of this rival for their father's affections; for while he is seemingly lost to them, he is in Egypt, alive and growing in power. Is it possible they will meet again? Earlier tensions linger in the reader's mind and leap back to center stage with the notice of the world-wide famine and the fact that people from all corners of the earth are coming to Egypt for relief (Gen. 41:54, 57). The subplot is artfully integrated into the larger narrative.

Characterization

As the plot evolves, the characters of a novella develop. It is this development of character that essentially sets the novel and novella apart from the short story. Human beings grow and disintegrate before our eyes as the plot runs its course. The figures we meet at the outset are not the same at the end, and more than outward circumstance is altered (contrast, for example, the figures in Ruth). The characters of a novella can range from agents who function as stereotypes to full-bodied and complex individuals, and it is the latter who show real development. Thus Joseph, the spoiled and boastful brat of Genesis 37, becomes a powerful official, able and skilled in his new position, but still ruthless in his treatment of his brothers and father. Whether or not his treatment of them in chapters 42–44 is designed as a test, he toys with them over a span of many years, arbitrarily detaining and releasing them, accusing them unjustly. Yet through it all he changes, and this is made clear as he responds to changes in them. At first overcome as he overhears their self-accusations (42:24; 43:30–31), he later reassures them of his compassion and care. The feared official, who so long toyed with their deepest feelings and lives as a cat with a mouse, allowing even his old father to believe him dead for many years, finally acknowledges that he is not godlike (50:19)—the posture he assumed for so many years.

The others change as well. The bitter brothers are humbled, and show themselves able in a crisis to take action to save a younger brother when again they might forfeit him and escape from a difficult situation. Genesis 44 nicely parallels Genesis 37 in this respect. They are no longer the jealous men of the opening scene, even if to the very end they still entertain some uncertainty regarding Joseph (50:15–18). Jacob also evolves from a man who loves too much and not wisely, who is all too prone simply to surrender to seeming tragedy (37:34–35; 42:35–38), to one who can take charge of a situation (43:11–14) and demonstrate a dignified self-restraint as an honored old patriarch who meets even Pharaoh as an equal (47:7–11).

It is around these figures that the story evolves, and they evolve with it. The remaining characters, ranging from Pharaoh through the chief butler and chief baker, and even Potiphar and his wife, to Joseph's steward, facilitate the action but remain somewhat flat by contrast and certainly unchanging. The central figures, the family of Jacob, are multifaceted, however, and this story is theirs. Our perspective on them is complex. We can feel sympathy with the brothers' outrage at Joseph's tale-bearing and boastful recounting of his dreams. Our feelings go out to them, but their actions cannot be condoned. We can also sympathize with an old father's doting on the youngest of his children, the only sons of his beloved wife. We understand his fierce attachment to Benjamin as a replacement for the lost Joseph. But this single-minded attachment to Joseph and Benjamin can only result in rending the fabric of family harmony, and this we must recognize as well. No doubt this collection of figures was drawn from the older folk traditions of Israel, and the reader was probably acquainted with them and their relationships. But with the sure hand of a fine literary artist, this particular author has shaped them into a set of distinct and complex individuals.

The Creative Work of an Author

Hermann Gunkel, the father of form critical analysis of the Hebrew Bible, described the novella as an expansion of a form called the saga.[6] It was largely his study of Genesis that led him to this understanding of the origin of the novella. It was clear to him that if the very brief individual units dealing with Abraham and Jacob were sagas, the much longer and more complex Joseph narrative could not be so classified. Yet he believed the latter to be rooted firmly in, and an outgrowth from, the former. The Joseph narrative was too multifaceted in its integrated fabric of episodes and range of characters to qualify as a saga. He rightly defined it as a novella. However, his conclusion that it was thus a development of an older saga—for example, through multiplication of episodes, addition of long speeches, an increase of characters—goes beyond the evidence and seems contrary to the basic characteristics of the novella. Sagas are rooted in the folk levels of a people or tradition and have behind them a long history of oral recitation. They are the product of a community, even if their transcription into their present written form is the work of one person. That person stands at the end of a long process of creative adaptation and transmission; and while they may engage in some shaping of the material, it seems inappropriate to speak of such persons as authors.

The novella is defined as the literary creation of an individual, an artfully crafted piece from the hands of an author. The complexity of characterization, the extended and integrated series of episodes that comprise the plot of the Joseph narrative are better comprehended as the work of a literary artist; thus the narrative is best seen as a written composition from the outset, rather than the expansion of brief units of the sort that comprise the Abraham or Jacob cycles. Motifs may be borrowed from folklore in the composition of a novella. The motif of the vengeful rejected woman of Genesis 39, or that of the younger brother who rises above his older siblings, for example, can be found in the folk traditions of many peoples.[7] Clearly the characters of the Joseph narrative are drawn in part from the folk traditions of Israel. As they appear in the narrative in Genesis, however, they are the creation of the author of that novella.

Intention

It is always difficult to attempt to divine the intention of an author, and from one perspective finally just not possible. Yet certain literary forms lend themselves to certain purposes, and rhetorical or poetic techniques are designed to attain distinct ends. The author of a novella seeks to entertain: a good story is told and told well. Characters that engage the interest of the reader initiate, pass through, and react to a series of events that may amuse, excite, or frighten the reader. We are caught up in and awed by the prospects of a family that seems about to self-destruct. We marvel at the sudden rise of Joseph in the alien land of Egypt; are intrigued by the first reunion of the brothers when only one side recognizes the other; share the discomfort of the brothers when wrongly accused and jailed by the one they wronged; are amused by the irony of the brothers being believed when they lie (Gen. 37:31–33) but treated as liars when they speak the truth (42:7–14); are ready to explode, like Joseph, with the tension at the end of the second meeting; and are relieved at the climax as the complications are resolved. In fact, the reader's enjoyment is heightened by knowledge not shared by all the characters: we know who this strange official is whose interest in their family is so ominously intense; we know that Joseph's enquiry about Benjamin is enquiry about his full brother, that his interest in their father is concern for his own. Only the reader can participate with Joseph in the irony of the brothers' self-incrimination in the presence of the one they so wronged and who seems now in complete control of them. Furthermore, the author demonstrates a fine control of narrative pace and a hold on the emotional reactions of the reader; for example, suspension is prolonged when Joseph is summoned from prison and we are made to wait through a second telling of Pharaoh's dreams before we find out if Joseph will succeed in their interpretation after all the wise men of Egypt have failed. At other points, as when Joseph deals with a famine or arranges for his family to come to Egypt, the narrative moves with a sharp dispatch that mirrors Joseph's efficiency.

In all this the novella seeks to reflect life, to present the truth in life: not what happened once in the past, but what happens. This is how people act, and will act again and again. Not all families are so self-destructive, but the potential is there in all, and too often it is realized. Life is like this, the author wishes to say; people behave like this in these circumstances, and these are the results. There is an element of chance in the story, especially in the remarkable rise of Joseph in a single day (and at this point the novella shares characteristics of the fairy tale) and the extreme unlikelihood of a small band of starving Asiatics meeting with the vizier of Egypt. Yet the unexpected does happen, for good or ill, in life, and the matter of fundamental concern is how these characters respond to it. The events of the story are set on a scale larger than most of life; the stage is vaster than that on which most of us play out our roles. This simply serves, however, to magnify life and show all of us more fully and clearly what human beings are really like.

There may be lessons for the reader as well, even sometimes a moral, to be found in a novella. Certain types of behavior are shown to bring certain results; patterns become apparent. Unwise demonstrations of love can only sow discord; vengeance sometimes recoils back on the one who seeks it; deceit comes to haunt the deceiver; power can easily be abused; risking one's life for another can bring life and peace to all. Larger patterns shape the novella and gradually emerge. Joseph's brothers do indeed bow down before him as his dreams foretold (42:6, 9; 50:18). Joseph's remarks to his brothers when he first reveals his identity and again as he reassures them after Jacob's death point to a hidden and unobtrusive divine providential pattern operating in the course of human events (45:5; 50:20). However, it is a providential ordering that permits freedom, within limits, for genuine human decisions and actions as well as responsibility for them. Limits are placed on human initiative (50:20).

Mortals are not gods; they can only cause havoc when they believe and act as if such power were theirs. These and other lessons are to be gained from this novella, and they are underscored in some cases (42:9; 45:5; 50:19–20). But they are not preached in a heavy-handed manner. The story is generally told on its own human terms as the events flow into and out of each other with little overt comment from the author (an exception being the several notices that "Yahweh was with Joseph" in ch. 39). This is a story that holds itself up to the test of truth, truth in life, and final judgment as to its success is left to each reader.

Setting in Life

It is not possible to define the life setting of the novella with as much precision as with more restricted genres in the Hebrew Bible such as the hymn, wedding song, work song, priest's blessing, or even the saga. Broadly, a novella is a consciously crafted piece of literary artistry composed by a single author for the enjoyment and edification of others. The novella therefore presupposes a literate audience, a level of society with the ability, leisure, and interest to enjoy a work of this type. In the case of the Joseph novella, middle- to upper-class circles in the Jerusalem of King Solomon, especially those within the effective reach of the court schools, have been proposed as the audience for which it was first composed. In fact, in this regard the novella has historical value in that it reveals the literary tastes and styles of the period in which it was produced, as well as concerns faced by circles in that world. The Joseph novella may tell us very little about the forefathers of Israel; it can significantly reveal the tastes, interests, concerns, and developing literary forms of Solomonic Jerusalem and those who looked to it as a "golden age."

In time this novella was taken up into the larger Pentateuchal narrative, possibly in a revision of the Yahwist's epic, to provide an extended transition between major themes in the Torah story. In this context it has taken on added functions, possibly received additional material (Genesis 38, 48, and 49), and attained new links with Israel's ancient traditions regarding its ancestors. Yet even in this context, it stands apart as a clearly distinct type of literary material. And as such it has continued to entertain and edify its readers as the premier example of the genre novella in the Hebrew Bible.

In the next four chapters of part I of this study we shall consider the Joseph novella as it now appears in the Book of Genesis, expanding on characteristics noted in this chapter. Our approach will be synchronic as we give greater attention to the central aspects of it that mark the Joseph material as a most characteristic example of Hebraic novella. We shall give attention to those basic rhetorical dimensions of the work that, in the language of literary study adopted from Aristotle, can broadly be termed "poetics." First we attend in more detail to the plot of the Joseph novella, then to its levels, types and manner of characterization, next to additional rhetorical aspects of the novella, especially the use of narrative perspectives or point of view, the many uses of repetition, and the effective employing of a disparity of knowledge and irony within the work. Finally we shall consider the theological vision of the novella. In this the characteristics of the Joseph novella, outlined briefly in this chapter, will be discussed more extensively.

In Part II (chapters 7 through 10) we shall consider indications within the novella that permit informed speculation about its growth, the relation of the kernel in chapters 40–41 to the larger family story as well as its own particular qualities, the relation of the novella to its larger context in the Pentateuch, the possibility of later additions to the novella as incorporated into the Torah in chapters 38, 39, 46:1–4, 8–27; 48, 49. Broadly the perspective of this second part of our study will be diachronic as we trace the development of the novella over time.

NOTES

1. A very useful discussion of these genre terms and their use in modern literary analysis is found in Hugh C. Holman, *A Handbook to Literature*; this has informed the present discussion.

2. History, of course, can be well told and entertaining as well.

3. Herman Melville displays a full knowledge of New England whaling practices in *Moby-Dick*, but to read his masterpiece simply as a treatise on that subject would be a distinct failure of imagination. Just so, there may be a residue of historical material in the Joseph narrative, and reflections of relationships between tribes, but to deal with the narrative simply on these terms is to miss the primary thrust of the work. In fact, William McKane, *Studies in the Patriarchal Narratives*, 42–74, 101-3, suggests that much that reflects tribal history (e.g., Gen. 48) is secondary, breaking the flow of the narrative.

4. In this I differ with George W. Coats (*From Canaan to Egypt: Structural and Theological Context for the Joseph Story* and "Redactional Unity in Genesis 37–50," *JBL* 93 [1974]: 15-21), who stresses the links between the Joseph narrative and its context and suggests that "the

transition is fundamental for the narrative of the story. . . . The Joseph story was created from the beginning to serve this function" (*Canaan*, 77). See below, pp. 204–205.

5. See W. Lee Humphreys, "Joseph Story, The," *Interpreter's Dictionary of the Bible, Supplementary Volume*; George W. Coats, "The Joseph Story and Ancient Wisdom: A Reappraisal," *CBQ* 35 (1973): 285–97.

6. Hermann Gunkel, *The Legends of Genesis*.

7. See Donald B. Redford, *A Study of the Biblical Story of Joseph (Genesis 37–50)*, 87–100.

THREE

THE POETICS OF THE
JOSEPH NOVELLA

PLOT

Every story has a trajectory. The outline of the Joseph novella at the end of this chapter demonstrates that both the novella as a whole and many of its constituent elements follow the same broad pattern. For the novella as a whole this trajectory can be depicted in the following manner:

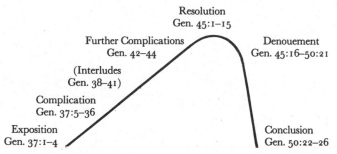

Resolution
Gen. 45:1–15

Further Complications
Gen. 42–44

Denouement
Gen. 45:16–50:21

(Interludes
Gen. 38–41)

Complication
Gen. 37:5–36

Exposition
Gen. 37:1–4

Conclusion
Gen. 50:22–26

A brief exposition provides minimal information needed to define both characters and situation as well as the formal and psychological relationships between them. This is followed by the initial episodes in which the fundamental complication of the narrative unfolds. Further complications follow (only after an important interlude in 39–41) that take us to a peak of tension calling for resolution. The relatively brief resolution is then followed by a more drawn-out denouement, in which the implications of the resolution are depicted. A formal conclusion brings the novella to a close.

As is characteristic of Hebrew narrative material, this trajectory is made up of distinct episodes or scenes with brief transitions between them. We move from one intense burst of activity and dialogue to another, with the sometimes extensive time and space that separate these focal moments covered with short notices ("After two whole years . . . " 41:1a). The effect of this is to present us with moments of intense illumination of character and situation rather than allow us to take in the steady flow of life. Within these illuminating episodes a brief exposition leads into dialogue, usually between two figures, which often brackets brief narrated reports of action. The center of attention is not on the action in and of itself but on its meanings as revealed through the words of those who initiate or are impacted by it.

An example from what is perhaps the best-known scene in the Joseph novella should make this clear. It takes but one verse to tell of the attempted seduction by Potiphar's wife, from her seizing Joseph's cloak to his flight from it and her into the street (39:12). The repetition of her demand, "Lie with me!" (*šikbāh ʾimmî*, only two words in Hebrew), is sandwiched between the report of her grasping and his fleeing. This brief narrative report is surrounded by fuller speech, first dialogue between Joseph and the seductress, and then her words to the servants followed by words with her husband. Meanings emerge through words spoken by those involved. The servants and Potiphar actually say nothing, which is also very revealing, and Joseph is allowed no defense once charged by his master's wife. The enveloping dialogue is proceeded by an exposition that sets the stage (39:1–6) and followed by a conclusion that brings this episode to an end even as it effects a transition into the next (39:21–23).

These brief observations on narrative pattern will provide a structure for tracing the development of the plot of the Joseph novella. An outline of the novella is given at the end of this chapter.

EXPOSITION (Gen. 37:1–4)

Following the title, "This is the history of the family of Jacob" (37:2a), we meet Joseph. Then, through their relationships with him, both biological and psychological, we meet the other members of this family. Joseph, who is seventeen and on the brink of manhood, is described as

33

shepherding flocks with his brothers. The next line qualifies this in two ways. First, he is only with those half brothers (not named) who were sons of the two maid servants whom Jacob's wives, Leah and Rachel, gave him to increase indirectly their fertility. Next we are told that Joseph is a *naʿar* with them; usually this is translated "lad," but quite possibly here the term bears the extended connotation of "attendant" (see 1 Sam. 9:3, 5, 7). Joseph, the youngest, is singled out for attention by being presented first and by being named. However, he is then described as attending upon those who hold but second rank among the sons of Jacob. Immediately we are told that it was his manner to bring an evil report of these half brothers to their father. Set as it is in the exposition that opens the novella, this additional notice is not just a report of a unique event but an account of the habitual way of things: Joseph would attend his half brothers and then bring an evil report about them to their father.

Tale-bearing is combined with privilege as the biological and psychological relationships within this family begin to form a complex nexus of competing tensions. Israel's love for Joseph, and especially the robe, that outward token that demonstrates it, sparks hatred in the ten remaining brothers. What will be key words throughout the novella,[1] "son/sons" (*bēn, bānîm*) and "brother/brothers" (*ʾāḥ, ʾaḥîm*), appear here in significant juxtaposition. Joseph is the "son of his old age," and therefore the beloved of his father. The others are called sons of their father only when contrasted with this favored son. Otherwise they are Joseph's brothers: "But when his brothers saw that their father loved him more than all his brothers . . . " (37:4a).

From the outset we are presented a family rent by excessive love and hatred, and this is not simply reported directly but demonstrated in the relationships as they are set in counterpoint. The youngest, who first holds the reader's attention and alone of the brothers is named, attends those other brothers of second rank in the family, but carries tales about them and is the object of the father's special devotion. Through the tokens of that devotion he is set above his older brothers. This motif of a reversal in rank, position, or power among brothers is a recurring theme in Hebraic narrative tradition (see Isaac and Ishmael, Jacob and Esau, Moses and Aaron, David and his brothers), and it is often a source of conflict that bodes ill for the family: "They hated him, and could not speak peaceably to him" (37:4b). Through what is said, through allusions to a prevalent motif, and in the mode of narrative presentation, a situation fraught with tension is sketched in a few lines.[2]

34

THE POETICS: PLOT

INITIAL COMPLICATIONS (Gen. 37:5–36)

With the situation set, an initial episode demonstrates just how deep the tensions cut that rend the fabric of this family's life. A brief notice (37:5) tells us that Joseph had a dream and related it to his brothers, further sparking their hatred. The ensuing dialogue (37:6–8) nicely presents this young man's boast and the response of his brothers and father. This first and the paired second dream serve not only to underscore and illustrate the strife within this family, but also introduce another theme that is highlighted by Jacob's more ambivalent response to his son's dreams ("but his father kept the sayings in mind," 37:11b). We are given here hints that the very member of this family who is the focus of excessive love and hatred may be destined for a future that will set him above his brothers, that he could reach heights that will find them prostrate in obeisance before him. These are but hints, only the dreams of a youth who is spoiled by his father; but within the world of this narrative dreams will come to be seen as revealing more than just the psychological state of mind of a dreamer. These dreams will come to be recognized as the first in a series that will to the discerning eye disclose the future. As the episode closes, we are uneasy, concerned about the tension within this family and wondering what the future might bring—a future foreshadowed both in signs of hatred and by hints of grandeur for the hated.

Whatever path Joseph's life is to take, the immediate track is downward, for in the next episode the favored son is sent from his father's love to his brothers' hatred. Opening dialogue between Jacob and Joseph (37:13–14) follows a notice that the brothers are pasturing their father's flocks near Shechem (37:12). The father charges his son to bring a report on the welfare of his brothers. The occasion will now be provided for the brothers to rid themselves of this thorn in their collective flesh. The brief interlude, in which Joseph meets the unnamed man in the fields of Shechem (37:15–17), serves, among other things, to underscore the isolation of the coming encounter between the brothers and to leave Joseph for a time suspended between father and brothers, between love and hatred. Dialogue, this time between his brothers, follows as Joseph approaches them (37:19–22).

Their scheme is hardly hatched before schisms appear in the ranks of the brothers, and these are compounded as they seek to put their plans into action. First Reuben, as firstborn and the one primarily answerable

35

to their father (37:21–22, 29–30), and then Judah (37:26–27) seek to modify the plan, the one to return Joseph to his father, the other to turn a profit. Both plans abort, as the stage suddenly seems crisscrossed by caravans of Ishmaelites and Midianites and by brothers acting at cross purposes. The Ishmaelites acquire Joseph—or so one probable reading of Genesis 37:28b allows, in which "they" refers to the Midianites mentioned in 28a. In part the issue depends on the possibilities for identifying the Ishmaelites of verses 25, 27, 28 with the Midianites of verse 28. If they are to be understood as one and the same, then the subject of the verb "sold" and referent for "they" would be the brothers, acting on the advice of Judah to turn a profit and not shed their brother's blood. In this case the brothers would succeed at least to this extent. However, if Midianites and Ishmaelites are not to be identified, and the only possible indication that they are comes in the last verse of the chapter (cf. Gen. 39:1), then the Midianites seem to appear just in time to steal even this brief success from the brothers: *they* sell Joseph to the Ishmaelites and enjoy the twenty pieces of silver as their profit (the average valuation of a young Hebrew male, Lev. 27:5). In either reading Reuben's plan is thwarted (his reaction shows he would also have had to be absent if the brothers retrieved Joseph from the pit and sold him), and all must face their father. Attempts to explain the condition of the text in terms of the combination of two sources can only tell us how what we have received was formed and not how we are now to read what we have before us.[3] As the text now stands, syntactical ambiguity signals a breakdown in the ability of the brothers fully to shape events.

The token of their father's love for Joseph becomes the vehicle for the brothers' deceit (37:31–32), and when it is recognized and interpreted in the worst possible way by Jacob, it becomes the focus for his extreme grief (37:33–34). The brothers appear rid of Joseph, but they seem also to have lost considerable control of events as divisions appear in their ranks. Reuben and Judah develop their own schemes and both apparently abort. Their father is deceived but his grief is beyond their powers to console (37:35). At the end of the opening episodes that so effectively set out the initial complications of this novella, we sense that the brothers have initiated more than they know or can shape and that Joseph, while taken from the scene to Egypt, may prove to be just what they in their scornful reference to him as "master of dreams" (37:19) did not intend. On one level they appear to have solved their problem, but the last verse of Genesis 37 follows Joseph to Egypt.

Dialogue dominates throughout the opening episodes, and, as is typical of Hebraic narrative, only two figures or groups are on stage at any moment. Joseph relates his dreams, and the brothers respond to the first, his father to the second. Jacob sends Joseph to his brothers; he meets the man in the fields; the brothers discuss his approach and plot against him; one then another steps forth in an attempt to reshape their scheme; they as a group confront their father and then his grief. Brief narrative notices of action are set off by the more extended dialogue that reveals the significance of the events.

INTERLUDES (Gen. 38–41)

Judah and Tamar (Gen. 38)

At this point the plot seems to swerve dramatically from its initial themes, following neither the course of events within the family nor Joseph and his fate in Egypt. As the material now appears in Genesis, it is to events within the family of one of the brothers that we now turn in chapter 38. From a story of men we turn to one that centers on a woman as well.[4] Yet many, and none better than Robert Alter,[5] have pointed out that the effect of placing this story just here is not only to retard the narrative pace and keep us in suspense concerning the fate of both Joseph in Egypt and his family in Canaan. The unit also provides a counterpointing commentary on what we have witnessed of this family and a proleptic look at what is yet to come. The effect for the sensitive reader is to bring to awareness certain critical dimensions and themes in the larger novella, thereby to shape perspectives for reading what is to come. In quiet ways this digression informs our reading of the novella in which it is set.

Deceit plays a formative role in both chapters 37 and 38. Not only does Judah deceive once more as he leads his daughter-in-law Tamar to expect marriage in time to his youngest son, but this deceiver is now deceived in turn by Tamar. Her deceit, however, is clearly in the service of righting a wrong, as Judah himself is willing to acknowledge in the end (38:26). Once more the instrument of deceit is an article of apparel that especially represents its owner. Death is present here as well, the death of both of Judah's sons and then his wife. And Judah's minimal response—at best he seems to have gone through the expected motions of grief for his wife (38:12) and hardly that for his sons—is a counterpoint to Jacob's excessive grief when confronted with the supposed death of his son. In each instance a father is asked to recognize/identify (*NKR*) the item of apparel, and this will not be the last use of the key term *NKR* in the novella. We will pick it up once more at the point at which we again take up the family's story.

This narrative serves as counterpoint to the Joseph novella in other ways as well. Right and wrong are clearly drawn in Genesis 38, and right triumphs in time with due recognition. As the deceiver is deceived and then made to recognize the righteousness of Tamar, a pattern of retribution that pervades the story is made clear. By contrast, the Joseph novella as we left it seems ambiguous at best. Right and wrong are not as clearly apparent, and it will indeed take complex patterns of retribution to set right the competing forces and tensions set out in Genesis 37.

Thus in chapter 38 we find a distinct story that serves as a counterpoint to the larger novella in which it is now placed. It has the characteristic trajectory of Hebrew stories—exposition (38:1–6), complications (38:7–11), further complications (38:12–24), resolution (38:25–26), denouement (38:27–30)—and is a unit unto itself, needing neither what comes before nor what follows. Yet its placement shapes in significant ways the reader's sensitivities to the material that surrounds it, with particular attention to details like apparel, key words like recognize/identify (*NKR*), and fundamental themes like retribution and the triumph of harmony and righteousness.

From the House of Potiphar to the Royal Court (Gen. 39–41)

We next take up what appears to be a subplot within the larger novella, a unit that is complete within itself and that also serves as a kernel around which the larger story of the family is built.[6] First, we have what for the novella's hero is a false start. Joseph is sold to an Egyptian official named Potiphar. Yahweh, we are told, is with Joseph and ensures his success. He is placed over all of his master's estate. Like his father (Gen. 30:25–31:15) before him, he turns to profit all he puts his hand to. As he comes to his master's notice and to ours in this new way—and we must recall his dreams—he also comes to the notice of his master's wife as physically attractive. An attempted seduction leads to false but effective accusations, and Joseph moves from power to prison. The transition notice taking

Joseph from Potiphar's estate to prison tells us once more that Yahweh has ensured his success; but in the next episode, he is found waiting upon two royal officials who have been placed in custody. Exposition and conclusion tell of success because Yahweh was with him and bracket a narrative that tells of apparent defeat.

While Yahweh is mentioned here with a frequency (39:2, 3, 5 [twice], 21, 23 [twice]) that sets this material off from the rest of the novella, the pattern of retribution found in Genesis 38 is not apparent here. Joseph is cast back into servitude, and no further notice is taken of Potiphar and his wife.

Joseph's future fortunes will revolve in part around fortuitous circumstances, especially two additional pairs of dreams, and also around his ability to capitalize upon what fortune brings. The dreams come once more in pairs, the first allotted to the royal officials whom he serves. Narration surrounds dialogue, as the exposition in 40:1–6 sets the stage, and the conclusion in verses 20–23 briefly relates that events transpired just as Joseph in his interpretation stated they would. These second matched dreams in the novella seem to reverse the pattern of the first in their impact on Joseph's fortunes. His own dream in the opening episodes set him on a descent that brought him down to Egypt (the brothers cynically refer to him as "master of dreams"). Joseph grasps the possibility that the dreams of others will be the vessel that brings him release: "But remember me, when it is well with you, and do me the kindness, I pray you, to make mention of me to Pharaoh, and so get me out of this house. For I was indeed stolen out of the land of the Hebrews; and here also I have done nothing that they should put me into the dungeon" (40:14–15). However, the path to release is not uninterrupted, for in spite of his petition following his fortunate interpretation of the chief butler's dream, we are told with repeated emphasis in the final note in this episode that this official did not remember him; he forgot him (40:23). Each official goes forth to his foretold fate; Joseph remains in prison.

The chief butler's lapse in memory and gratitude results only in interruption, however—even if it is for two whole years. A final pair of dreams, this time of Pharaoh, will bring Joseph to mind and hasten him from prison to the center of a state crisis. The rhythms of narrative pace in this extended segment of the interlude reflect the rhythms of Joseph's rise. We linger over Pharaoh's dreams as the narrator recounts them in full, both of them. Their baroque quality understandably triggers Pharaoh's concerns, and the concerns heighten when "all the magicians of Egypt

and all its wise men" prove unable to provide an interpretation. The chief
butler now recalls his lapse, and Joseph is called. It takes but one verse
(41:14) and a burst of verbs—send, call, bring, hurry, shave, clothe,
come—to bring Joseph to his audience with the king of Egypt. Joseph may
linger in prison as we linger over Pharaoh's dreams; but once recalled, he
moves from his cell to the palace with breathless haste. After a brief
exchange with Pharaoh, in which the relation of dreams to the divine is
first made clear, Joseph is able to catch his breath as once more we receive
an account of the royal dreams, this time from the dreamer himself, with
just enough variation[7] to underscore their impact on Pharaoh. Joseph's
interpretation follows and leads directly into advice on how to deal with
the crisis that the dreams foretell. The pace quickens as it is immediately
recognized that only one with Joseph's demonstrated abilities as interpreter and adviser could oversee the execution of the plan of action. We
then linger over Joseph's elevation to the highest office in the land next to
that of the throne, as he is heaped with titles, symbols, privileges, power,
and a wife (41:41–45). After two years, in two bursts of activity (41:14,
37–45) Joseph is transformed from a Hebrew slave waiting on prisoners to
an Egyptian official of highest rank. He even marries into the highest of
Egyptian religious families, taking the daughter of the priest of the Sun
God as wife (41:45). The crisis in Joseph's own life is resolved, and he must
now resolve the crisis facing the land of Egypt.

The final segment of this episode provides a good opportunity to
reflect for a moment on the relationship between narrated and narrative
time. Literature often leaps over extended time periods and over great
geographic spaces as well. The Joseph novella moves back and forth
between Canaan and Egypt. The episodic nature of Hebrew narrative
gives this movement a particular accent as intense scenes covering limited
time frames stand at the center of attention. They are bright spots illumi-
nated in circles of light, held together by comparatively thin threads that
stretch sometimes over years. Time stands at the center of Joseph's interpretation of the dreams in this episode—seven years of plenty will be followed by seven years of severe famine. As the episode comes to a
conclusion, we watch Joseph assume power ("And Joseph went out from
the presence of Pharaoh, and went through all the land of Egypt") as the
years of plenty give way to years of famine. The episode began with the
shortest of notices of a significant time span passing ("After two whole
years")—significant because our hero must languish in prison forgotten;
and now it ends with a longer notice, but one that is still disproportionate

in terms of time that actually passes (it is also interrupted by notice of the birth of Joseph's sons). The notice that Joseph was thirty years old when he entered Pharaoh's service recalls the fact that he was seventeen as the novella opened. Thirteen years have elapsed for him in Egypt, and there are seven more years of plenty before the seven years of famine begin.

By contrast, we find a full narration of the events of the single day that changed the whole course of Joseph's life, and would lead to the salvation of Egypt as well as bring peoples from other lands to Egypt for food. And even within the core of the episode the pace has varied; at points we linger, and at others we rush with Joseph from prison to royal audience, with honors and awards piled upon this new official to underscore his dramatic change of status. The narrative breaks up the measured pace of mechanical clock or seasonal time with its illumination of particular episodes, while leaping over years that must have been filled with other events. As with most literature, we have here not the mechanical day-to-day time of the clock, but time as experienced psychologically, in which some brief moments shape years, while years can pass and be hardly remembered between these bright events. The effect is to underscore significance and patterns in the complex and often apparently unconnected flow of a lifetime.[8]

FURTHER COMPLICATIONS (Gen. 42–44)

The famine, with its grip not only on Egypt but on all the earth, serves to link the extended interlude, in which we followed Joseph to Egypt, with the story of Jacob's family, which we left suspended in his inconsolable grief at the end of chapter 37. The subplot joins the main plot as "all the earth came to Egypt to Joseph to buy grain" (41:57). Joseph's brothers are among those coming for relief. Seeking sustenance, they encounter complications undreamt of in even their wildest fears. The notice in 41:53–57, which serves as a conclusion to the interlude, also forms a transition to and exposition for the next episodes.

These additional complications are set out in carefully matched scenes.[9] Just as paired dreams propelled Joseph from Canaan to Egypt and then from prison to power, now paired journeys will bring ten brothers from Canaan to Egypt and from a simple request for food to a plea for a youngest brother's life and the life of their father as well.

41

A long span of time has passed for the family as well as for Joseph; but whereas Joseph's condition during this period is fundamentally transformed, the family seems unchanged when we once more center on them. As in chapter 37, there are a father, ten sons, and a favored son in 42:1–4. Jacob is abrupt with his ten sons, and he still has a favorite whom he sets apart from the others. He still moves between extremes, setting the crisis posed by famine in stark life-and-death terms. His ten sons seem as powerless to deal with the situation as they were to console him in his grief. Jacob's opening words picture them as we last imagined them: standing around looking at each other. "When Jacob learned that there was grain in Egypt, he said to his sons, 'Why do you look at one another?' And he said, 'Behold, I have heard that there is grain in Egypt; go down and buy grain for us there, that we may live, and not die.' " (42:1–2).

For the brothers the years apparently have passed with little change. They are still "twelve brothers, the sons of one man in the land of Canaan," and, in fact, "the youngest is this day with our father," while in a final oblique notice, "one is no more" (42:13). Their mention of the brother who is "no more," which can mean anything from not present to dead to forgotten, simply underscores with great irony just how much has really changed. Irony builds on disparity of knowledge or meaning, and only Joseph and the reader can enjoy it here. They are indeed "twelve brothers, the sons of one man" as they speak together; and the one is no more is so only in the sense that he is not what he was when they last saw him. They seem unchanged, but everything has in fact changed.

The passage of time now becomes a factor that not only brings change or apparent lack of change; it also links the reader to Joseph and his perspective, serving as an important element of shared knowledge which the brothers and father do not have. As the first journey ends in an uneasy homecoming with supplies and money restored, but one brother absent, we know that the famine is to run a course of seven years and can trust, in the face of Joseph's demand that they are to return only if accompanied by their younger brother, that the supplies will not last out the crisis. They will come back down again to Egypt. In each of the paired journeys the ten brothers come to Egypt to face the unexpected. First coming for supplies, and expecting no doubt to deal with at best a middle-level bureaucrat, they suddenly find themselves in the presence of the highest official in the land. This disjuncture in expectation and actuality sets the stage for the next scene. Requesting supplies, they are confronted by accusations that they have come to spy out the land, to see its nakedness or vulnerability exposed, and they expose their own vulnerability as they blurt out their family's story in disjointed fragments. This elicits a proposal for a "test" after the accusation (42:15). But the reader and Joseph know that any test would demonstrate they are not spies. What then is this "test" all about? After a taste of jail they are offered release and supplies, but on condition that on their next descent to Egypt they bring their youngest brother with them. Simeon is then held as surety. Their self-recriminations, along with Reuben's accusation, provide the occasion for the narrator to inform us that all this time they and Joseph had been speaking through an interpreter (42:23). As Robert Alter notes,[10] this information is effectively withheld until now, allowing the earlier dialogue between brothers an immediacy that the presence of an interpreter would blunt; it also now reinforces the disparity between the power and position of the brothers and what Joseph and the reader know and what the others do not know. As the unnamed man in Shechem's fields mediated a reversal in relationship, so the interpreter now signals an even more dramatic change.

For the brothers, throughout the account of this and the next journey, the unexpected sets a mood of radical disjunction. Seeking relief, they are accused of spying. This elicits their family's story from them, which brings only renewed accusation and imprisonment. Release triggers guilt, and in time they discover their money in their supplies. The second journey will highlight the disjunctions of the first.

As the brothers are sent home with provisions and their money restored, we know that they are the victims of an elaborate game staged by Joseph. Its effect is to set their world upside down. Guilty of a crime committed many years past, they find themselves falsely accused of another crime. In their confusion and confession the two come together, and Alter has nicely indicated that it is on the psychological level of guilt that the two are joined.[11] In fact, it is only on this psychological level that Joseph's repeated accusation that they are spies, following their brief family history, makes sense:

> He said to them, "No, it is the weakness of the land that you have come to see." And they said, "We, your servants, are twelve brothers, the sons of one man in the land of Canaan; and behold the youngest is this day with our father, and one is no more." But Joseph said to them, "It is as I said to you, you are spies. By this you shall be tested: by the life of Pharaoh, you shall not go from this place unless your youngest brother comes here." (42:12–15)

43

On the surface there are gaps in the logic of this exchange, for their family relationships do not lead to or support the charge of spying. But on the psychological level of the tension and guilt that now define those family relationships, the accusation of a crime in which they took advantage of the weakness of the one whom they stripped of his cloak now strikes home. Their self-recriminations following the three days in prison make perfect psychological sense. In fact, this first of the paired journeys, with its links back to chapter 37 (Joseph recalls his dreams, Reuben once more rebukes his brothers) as well as its symmetry with the next journey makes it clear that this novella is plotted essentially in terms of psychological development. Psychological unbalancing moves from moment to moment of dialogue.

We must note here a brief proleptic anticipation by the narrator that binds the brothers' two journeys to Egypt together. Joseph's test and condition are set out in 42:18-20a. They trigger the overheard confession of guilt and recrimination of 42:21–22. Between this psychologically sophisticated linkage of condition and confession comes the brief notice: "And they did so" (42:20b—only two words bound as one in the Hebrew). This narrative glance ahead in time balances the brothers' own look back, and keeps the novella centered on the psychology of the figures even as it lessens doubt about what course events will take.

Important in this development is the absence of a clearly stated motive behind Joseph's staging of this elaborate game. Is it revenge? Is it a test? Of what sort? Is it designed to teach some lesson? Joseph turns away from them to weep as he overhears their guilty recollection of their treatment of him (42:24), but this only suggests that his motives are complex and no more clearly understood than is the course events are yet to take.

The brothers, now nine, return home in a scene that recalls the time many years before when they returned home to their father with one of their number missing. Then they returned only after preparing for the encounter with their father by sending ahead the bloodied cloak. This time they come with the unsettling discovery of their money (are they now to be accused of theft as well?), and its appearance as they empty their sacks triggers another burst of grief in which the fate of Joseph and Simeon, and the anticipated fate of Benjamin, are all linked. Apparent good fortune can only trigger guilt and grief in this family. "As they emptied their sacks, behold, every man's bundle of money was in his sack; and when they and their father saw their bundles of money, they were dismayed. And Jacob their father said to them, 'You have bereaved me of my children: Joseph is no more, and Simeon is no more, and now you would take Benjamin; all this has come upon me'." (42:35–36). Reuben's offer to put his own sons' lives on the line for Benjamin's only compounds the grief—can dead grandsons in any conceivable way make up for lost sons? He is dismissed in words that echo Jacob's last words in chapter 37: "But he said, 'My son shall not go down with you, for his brother is dead, and he only is left. If harm should befall him on the journey that you are to make, you would bring down my gray hairs with sorrow to Sheol'." (42:38).

Time passes, however, and the famine lingers. Time does not heal the torn psychological fabric of this family. A second journey must be undertaken that is constructed as a counterpoint to the first, as these further complications are finely drawn out. Now preparations take more time; no abrupt command from Jacob will do (43:1–15; cf. 42:1–2). For this time the stakes are psychologically immense, and Jacob will accept Judah's terms only after extended dialogue. Then he does all that is possible to ensure success through what he sends with the brothers as they, once more ten in number, go down to Egypt. He recognizes that all the preparations may not prevent disaster; experience has driven this lesson home time and again. His words of dismissal, with their levels of play between "your brother," "your other brother," and "the man" resonate with strains of grief: "Take also your brother, and arise, go again to the man; may God Almighty grant you mercy before the man, that he may send back your other brother and Benjamin. If I am bereaved of my children, I am bereaved" (43:13–14).

In contrast to the preparations, one brief sentence (43:15) takes them from their father to their brother (this time they "stand before Joseph"; last time they "bowed with faces to the ground"). But even that brief transition allows us to picture them as they "took the present, and they took double the money with them, and Benjamin." The "and Benjamin" hangs like the resigned sigh of a father trapped between the need to live and the possibility of a life made utterly empty through another loss.

The encounters in Egypt this time parallel the encounters of the first journey primarily as contrasts. Then they sought food but found accusation, confusion upon confusion, and guilt. Now they come guilty and prepared for accusation, only to be warmly received, reassured by Joseph's steward, and in time they dine with the high official. There are no new charges of spying or of theft. As in the first journey it is dialogue that dominates, for the episode is once more plotted on essentially a psychological

45

level. It is Joseph's surrogate who does most of the talking for him in this second encounter, at least in the first audience, just as it is another surrogate for Joseph (Benjamin) who stands before him. This time inquiries about their family, rather than accusations, come first from Joseph's lips; and as they once more bow before him in an additional fulfillment of the dreams of so long ago (43:28b; cf 42:6b), Joseph is united with his full brother. This encounter between brothers ends not with jailing but with release, and then with a feast in which all are honored and the youngest singled out with a portion five times as large as that of the others. Once more in the theme of reversal, as even now the brothers are not treated with strict equity, we suspect that they are beginning to recognize that this is an inescapable fact of life.

Preparations for the journey home parallel the first trip (44:1; cf. 42:25) with the single addition this time of the silver divining cup in the baggage of Benjamin. This, of course, makes the discovery scene, with Joseph's steward as the discoverer, all the more traumatic. The return home becomes a return to Egypt and a final meeting with this mysterious official. Judah's first plea to place all of them in slavery for Benjamin receives a balanced reply that stresses fairness: only the one who apparently took the cup will be his slave; the others may return in peace. The calm fairness of Joseph's words now contrasts sharply with his accusations and oaths of the first encounter.

> When Judah and his brothers came to Joseph's house, he was still there; and they fell before him to the ground. Joseph said to them, "What deed is this that you have done? Do you not know that such a man as I can indeed divine?" And Judah said, "What shall we say to my lord? What shall we speak? Or how can we clear ourselves? God has found out the guilt of your servants; behold, we are my lord's slaves, both we and he also in whose hand the cup has been found." But he said, "Far be it from me that I should do so! Only the man in whose hand the cup was found shall be my slave; but as for you, go up in peace to your father." (44:14–17)

But nicely balanced fairness is grossly unfair and is impossible at this point; they cannot return without Benjamin. Their confusion is now carried to new heights and to an additional confession of guilt and understanding as well. Echoes of the first meeting are laced through these final moments in the second meeting. Joseph's pretended fairness ("Far be it from me that I should do so!" recalls his earlier pretense of lifting a harsh sentence (42:18–20). His accent on his ability to divine recalls his earlier powers as dreamer and interpreter of dreams (truly a "master of dreams"), and this once more underscores the disparity of knowledge between Joseph (shared with the reader) and the brothers. And Judah's confession of guilt ("God has found out the guilt of your servants") recalls their earlier confession (42:21) regarding their brother, then unintentionally made in the hearing of that brother. Not only has "God found out" their guilt, but Joseph, who stands like a god in power over them, is about to find out about them as well. This whole complex nexus of connections supports a complex psychological development in the novella.

Judah's remarkable speech follows, balancing polity and protocol with a barely contained desperation fueled by empathy for what his father must suffer and recognition that he cannot allow this to happen. The inequities of parental love are accepted by acknowledging the ties that bind father and sons in complex ways, and this is now apparent and understood by Judah, who speaks for all. This father will love some more than others, will love excessively and thus risk suffering in equal measure. It is, and will remain, his way. Throughout this speech Judah hovers between bursting into an overwhelming outpouring of words and emotions and maintaining his poise by use of the proper modes of courtly address by an inferior before one far superior in rank. Nor must we miss the irony in his many polite references to "your servant my father." Through speech within speech the plot of the novella as it concerns the family is rehearsed just before the resolution. In this rehearsal of their past encounter Judah omits reference to anything that might put Joseph in a negative light and thereby displease him. Thus the accusation of spying and the imprisonments are left unmentioned. Furthermore Joseph now discovers just what took place at home after he was taken to Egypt. The anguished cry of his father (37:33) rings out again as it is heard once more in the brothers' recollection: "Surely he has been torn to pieces" (44:28). The use of direct speech within speech here—as Judah uses Jacob's actual words—makes the father's grief and fear all the more present and palpable. Here, in the brothers' fearful anticipation and memory, he is made present to this Egyptian official with immediacy that must hit home:

> My lord asked his servants, saying, "Have you a father, or a brother?" And we said to my lord, "We have a father, an old man, and a young brother, the child of his old age; and his brother is dead, and he alone is left of his mother's children; and his father loves

47

him." Then you said to your servants, "Bring him down to me, that I may set my eyes upon him." We said to my lord, "The lad cannot leave his father, for if he should leave his father, his father would die." Then you said to your servants, "Unless your youngest brother comes down with you, you shall see my face no more." When we went back to your servant my father we told him the words of my lord. And when our father said, "Go again, buy us a little food," we said, "We cannot go down. If our youngest brother goes with us, then we will go down; for we cannot see the man's face unless our youngest brother is with us." Then your servant my father said to us, "You know that my wife bore me two sons; one left me, and I said, Surely he has been torn to pieces; and I have never seen him since. If you take this one from me, and harm befalls him, you will bring down my gray hairs in sorrow to Sheol." (44:19–29)

Judah's outpouring then takes the plot into a future course that he cannot allow to happen:

Now therefore, when I come to your servant my father, and the lad is not with us, then, as his life is bound up in the lad's life, when he sees that the lad is not with us, he will die; and your servants will bring down the gray hairs of your servant our father with sorrow to Sheol. For your servant became surety for the lad to my father, saying, "If I do not bring him back to you, then I shall bear the blame in the sight of my father all my life." Now therefore, let your servant, I pray you, remain instead of the lad as a slave to my lord; and let the lad go back with his brothers. (44:30–33)

He is now willing to give his life in place of Benjamin. His father's terrors and his own merge, and at the climax of his plea "my father" is no longer qualified by the polite "your servant." Jacob is too present in Judah's own terror and grief.

RESOLUTION (Gen. 45:1–15)

Relationships and the complex psychological lines of emotion that bind these relationships together have reached a point that demands resolution. Judah's offer must be accepted or rejected, and the consequences of each course is clear. Judah's speech reveals that profound changes have taken place in the brothers, that they have changed in their very acceptance of what will not change and what they cannot change. Their father will love one son more than the others; love is not nicely balanced, and its disproportions can result in pain and insensitivity. But even one who loves in an excess that must result in imbalances and pain can be understood, and must be loved, for through this love run ties that bind sons to father. Even Reuben in his own crass and ineffective way demonstrated this earlier in his offer of his sons for the life of Benjamin.

The brothers demonstrate this change, but the distance between them and Joseph is immense and now cries out to be bridged. It is a distance in knowledge, a gulf that accents what Joseph and the reader know that the brothers do not know. There is also the distance between what we as readers know now about the brothers—what moves and motivates them, how they are changed—and what we know of Joseph. We have had brief hints in two short balanced notices of his private outbursts of emotion: in 42:24, where he turns away from their sight and weeps, but also in the same sentence throws Simeon into prison before their eyes; in 43:30 the encounter with his full brother leads him quickly to retire and weep, but then to mask all signs of this before his return. Now Joseph weeps a third time (45:2), and this time there is no notice that he removes himself. Indeed, the Egyptians overhear the outburst. Now these distances in knowledge and power are bridged. The first is taken on directly: "I am Joseph; is my father still alive?" (45:3). The first phrase is clear and its impact immediate: "But his brothers could not answer him, for they were dismayed at his presence" (45:4).

The second phrase, the enquiry about his father, is more complex. On one level it is of course natural; but coming as it does, after the earlier enquiry and the assurances (43:27–28), and especially after the long speech by Judah which had their father's feelings as the center of its concern, the question could betray a mistrust that lingers in Joseph's mind. Is it one final test of them? Could he, in spite of his show of emotions, still suspect that they might by lying, that the whole tapestry of their disclosure about themselves and their family was fabricated? To the reader this seems hardly credible. They have dissembled before, but have also shown themselves barely capable of sustaining a single moment of deceit. That they would have the resources to concoct a pattern of deceit as complex as Joseph's question might imply is certainly beyond what the reader would now expect. But then we as readers have followed them home once before to Canaan between the journeys to Egypt. And Joseph has been privy to only a part of their self-disclosure (42:21–23). Of course it is possible that the question he asks may be little more than an indirect affirmation that after all these years my father is indeed alive!

Confronted by their silence and dismay, Joseph goes on, and the second formal introduction to his speech ("So [and] Joseph said to his brothers") suggests the full extent of a pause that leaves them suspended. Moreover, the way he now addresses them is not designed quickly to allay their dismay, even as it is tailored to allow the reader to savor the full impact of the disclosure and to wonder along with the brothers just what this strange Egyptian is up to now. His invitation to them to approach is interrupted by the narrator's statement that they did approach and by still another introduction to Joseph's further words. In but four verses there are three introductions to Joseph's speeches and two narrated interruptions. Even in such a brief span of words the author is able to retard the pace of the story, so that each stroke of revelation is allowed its full impact on the brothers. One can also sense the pauses between each element in what comes next:

> So Joseph said to his brothers: "Come near to me, I pray you." And they came near. And he said, "I am your brother . . .
>
> Joseph . . .
>
> whom you sold into Egypt . . . .
>
> And now do not be distressed or angry with yourselves, because you sold me here; for God sent me before you to preserve life."
>
> . . . .
>
> "So it was not you who sent me here, but God; and he has made me a father to Pharaoh, and lord of all his house and ruler over all the land of Egypt." (45:4–5, 8)

The resolution now becomes in effect one long outpouring of information by Joseph. His brothers are silent, just as he was silent in the opening episode as they spoke and acted against him. Only now his words are of actions and intentions that are not directed against him. He speaks, in fact, on so many levels that it is no surprise that the brothers are here left speechless. He speaks of both past and future, of their past actions and what he will do for them in the future. He speaks of death and life. He speaks of famine and of his position in Egypt. He speaks of them as a family and of their families. He speaks of what they have done and must now do, and of what God has done. In this last he sets the family's story in a context of which there had been only hints to this point, but nothing more than hints: in the three sets of dreams, in the recollection of them by Joseph when his brothers first appear, in the brothers' first words of self-recrimination, in Judah's confession of guilt. Now it is boldly stated: their story is part of a larger story scripted by God. Of this, much more will be said.[12]

We must especially note that the resolution of the complications in this novella involves the final coming together of what have been disparate levels of knowledge, as well as placing the family's story in a larger context shaped by a providential understanding of what God is doing. The brothers are reunited as they come to know what Joseph and the reader have known for some time. And all the brothers come together as they and the reader come to understand that finally Joseph's designs are not malevolent—or at least are so no longer. Perspectives are joined as the brothers join in embrace, and as preparations are made to tell their father what they now know and to reunite him with all his sons: " 'You must tell my father of all my splendor in Egypt, and of all that you have seen. Make haste and bring my father down here.' Then he fell upon his brother Benjamin's neck and wept; and Benjamin wept upon his neck. And he kissed all his brothers and wept upon them; and after that his brothers talked with him" (45:13–15).

"His brothers talked with him"—finally, after so much talk that seemed at cross purposes, so much talk that was not really "with" him. This counterbalances as it rectifies the notice of the opening exposition to the novella that they "could not speak peaceably to him" (37:4). Moreover, as the brutes at the outset tore Joseph from their father, so now they will arrange for the reunion of Jacob with Joseph in Egypt. The wound they caused, they will heal.

The last statement by the narrator describes the brothers talking with Joseph, but their words are not reported. Reunited in recognition and shared understanding they can talk together. However, we find no report of any actual words to Joseph until much later, long after their father has been reunited with Joseph, and after they have together buried their dead father in the homeland of Canaan. When the brothers finally speak with Joseph in words reported by the narrator, we have moved from climax through to denouement. However, we encounter a striking scene that can be paired with the resolution just experienced. The pattern of pairs that has shaped the plot of the novella to this point—Joseph's paired dreams, the paired occasions for his interpretation of dreams, the pair of journeys by his brothers to Egypt, paired confessions—meets us again in resolution and denouement.

When Joseph's brothers saw that their father was dead, they said, "It may be that Joseph will hate us and pay us back for all the evil which we did to him." So they sent a message to Joseph, saying, "Your father gave this command before he died, 'Say to Joseph, Forgive, I pray you, the transgression of your brothers and their sin, because they did evil to you.' And now, we pray you, forgive the transgression of the servants of the God of your father." Joseph wept when they spoke to him. His brothers also came and fell down before him, and said, "Behold, we are your servants." But Joseph said to them, "Fear not, for am I in the place of God? As for you, you meant evil against me; but God meant it for good, to bring it about that many people should be kept alive, as they are today. So do not fear; I will provide for you and your little ones." Thus he reassured them and comforted them. (50:15–21)

Just as in the earlier pairs the elements served to reinforce and/or provide counterpoint to each other, so 45:4–15 and 50:15–21 reinforce through repetition of a basic theme. Once more past intention and present reality are contrasted, as again human design and divine direction are set in counterpoint. But whereas in chapter 45 Joseph's words centered on his own power and position in Egypt and were at the heart of his words about divine design, this time he clearly acknowledges that he is not in a position he has appeared to assume for some time. He is not in the place of God. Genesis 50:19–21 is more than simple repetition of his assurances in chapter 45. Joseph at the very last fully assumes his place within his family. From this assurance we move into his concluding words in 50:24–25 that link the novella to the larger story of the Torah. Joseph is wholly joined with his brothers as even his fate after death is linked to the future of his family. Before this, however, and between chapters 45 and 50, stands a full account of the denouement of the novella.

DENOUEMENT (Gen. 45:16–50:22)

The resolution is relatively brief, but carefully paced. The denouement, the working out of the many implications of the revelatory and resolving speech of Joseph, takes some time and assumes an added layer of complexity as Jacob comes back into the story not only as a father reunited and reconciled with his sons but as the patriarch and bearer of the name of the nation and people of Israel. The modern reader may find the denouement drawn out, being accustomed to a rapid wind-up once the climactic resolution of a story is reached. Here we are allowed to savor the reconciliation of Joseph with his brothers, of the father with his sons, and especially the reunion of Joseph and Jacob after so many years.

Preparations seem almost to tumble over each other as both Pharaoh and Joseph make provisions for the family to come and settle in Egypt. The pattern of pairs is augmented once more as Joseph provisions the brothers for a return to Canaan. As before, they carry a special gift, and Benjamin is given an extra treasure (45:22; cf. 42:25; 44:1–2). But this time the gifts and treasures are not hidden, awaiting later discovery. No further blows await them on the way back to Canaan. The brothers depart finally with special provisions for their father and with telling admonition, "Do not quarrel on the way" (45:24). In a single verse (45:25) the distance between Egypt and Canaan is traversed, and in a very few verses the greater distance this symbolizes, the distance in knowledge, is overcome as well:

> "And they told him, 'Joseph is still alive, and he is ruler over all the land of Egypt.' And his heart fainted, for he did not believe them. But when they told him all the words of Joseph, which he had said to them, and when he saw the wagons which Joseph had sent to carry him, the spirit of their father Jacob revived; and Israel said, 'It is enough; Joseph my son is still alive; I will go and see him before I die' " (45:26–28).

The next journey is preceded by a night vision in which God legitimizes the descent of Jacob and his extended family into Egypt. One suspects that here concerns of the larger context of the novella within the Torah are present. This family on the road to reunion and reconciliation is also the family of promise, the seed of Abraham and of Isaac, the roots of the nation that will emerge from slaves freed in time from bondage in Egypt. In the larger patriarchal tradition departure from the land of promise is generally signaled as appropriate by some encounter with the deity (Gen. 28:10–17; contrast Gen. 12:10–20). The journey is then covered through a list of those who made it as well as others who also comprise this family. Through this list of "the names of the descendants of Israel, who came into Egypt" (46:8) we glimpse this family united again. The actual reunion follows. The joining of father and lost son is presented in comparatively simple terms after the years of grief and earlier extremes of emotional outburst: "Then Joseph made ready his chariot and went up to meet Israel his father in Goshen; and he presented himself to him, and fell on his neck, and wept on his neck a good while. Israel said to Joseph, 'Now let me die, since I have seen your face and know that you are still alive' " (46:29–30).

Joseph then arranges for the audience his brothers and his father will have with Pharaoh. The family attains land in Goshen, the patriarch blesses Pharaoh, and Joseph provides for his family. Joseph's provisions for his family are balanced and contrasted by his manner of providing for Egyptians. They too receive food, but in the process they and their land are acquired for Pharaoh, and the double tax instituted at the outset of the years of plenty now becomes a permanent feature of Egyptian life.

> So Joseph bought all the land of Egypt for Pharaoh; for all the Egyptians sold their fields, because the famine was severe upon them. The land became Pharaoh's; and as for the people, he made slaves of them from one end of Egypt to the other. Only the land of the priests he did not buy; for the priests had a fixed allowance from Pharaoh, and lived on the allowance which Pharaoh gave them; therefore they did not sell their land. Then Joseph said to the people, "Behold, I have this day bought you and your land for Pharaoh. Now here is seed for you, and you shall sow the land. And at the harvests you shall give a fifth to Pharaoh, and four fifths shall be your own, as seed for the field and as food for yourselves and your households, and as food for your little ones." And they said, "You have saved our lives; may it please my lord, we will be slaves to Pharaoh." So Joseph made it a statute concerning the land of Egypt, and it stands to this day, that Pharaoh should have the fifth; the land of the priests alone did not become Pharaoh's." (47:20–26)

The juxtaposition of Genesis 47:1–12 and 13–26 produces one more nice counterpoint in the novella. Joseph and Pharaoh freely provide for the Canaanite family of Jacob. Joseph's provisions for the Egyptians cost them their freedom as they are bought for Pharaoh. Land and privilege gained balance land and freedom lost. This contrast is all the more effective in the larger context, in which it is the descendants of Jacob and his family who will become slaves in Egypt. This Pharaoh offers the family more than they request.

The death of Jacob brings together once more the family's story with the larger story in Genesis of the roots of the nation Israel. We have had anticipations of Jacob's death from the outset; the novella necessarily leads to his death, but the manner and context is not that feared by him and others for so long (37:35; 42:38; 43:27–28; 44:22, 29–31; 45:3, 28; 46:30). In chapter 48 a grandfather who believed that he had lost his son now blesses this son's sons, and the future relationship of significant units within Israel represented by Ephraim and Manasseh are fixed and made legitimate. Again there is the theme of reversal as older gives way to younger. A pattern of deathbed testimonials by significant figures in the history of Israel is established in Genesis as Jacob provides a brief and sometimes cryptic sketch of each of his sons as progenitors of the tribes of Israel (cf. Deut. 33 and, more broadly, all of Deuteronomy; Josh. 23–24; 1 Sam. 12:2; 2 Sam. 22:1–23:7). In Jacob's burial in Canaan we see the brothers united in action. Their father's love had once separated them; his death unites them as they fulfill his wishes, journeying together now from Egypt to Canaan and back again. They are then brought once more together in Genesis 50:15–21, the encounter that we treated as a pair with the resolution in 45:4–15. Joseph once more reassures them of his good intentions and sets their story in the context of God's providential care. Resolution brings reassurance and comfort in this story of a family whose potential seemed for so long to produce nothing but discord, deceit, and strife.

CONCLUSION (Gen. 50:22–26)

As the outline of the Joseph novella makes clear, both the work as a whole and many of the episodes that comprise it are bracketed by brief opening expositions and conclusions. The conclusion to the novella as a whole both looks back to the opening exposition of 37:1–4 and on ahead to what will come next in the larger contextual Torah story in which the novella is embedded.

"So Joseph dwelt in Egypt" (50:22) stands in balance with the opening of the exposition, "Jacob dwelt in the land of his father's sojourning, in the land of Canaan" (37:1). The movement from Canaan to Egypt is now complete. Within the larger Torah story this is not the final movement, as Joseph's words to his brothers and his oath he has them take make clear. The movements of this particular family are complete, but the larger family of which they are the roots had many twists and turns yet before it.

Next comes the notice of Joseph's age at his death. We met him first as a lad of seventeen (37:2), and he passes from our sight as a man who has

55

reached the Egyptian's ideal age of 110 years (50:22, 26). The exposition moved from Jacob to his sons and their interrelations and back to Jacob in his relations with his sons. The movement produces a picture of discord, the potential for bitter strife that is soon realized. The conclusion traces a briefer but contrasting peaceful moment from Joseph to his sons to their sons to the third generation on Ephraim's side (50:23), back to Joseph in relation to his grandsons and also in relation to his brothers. "And Joseph saw Ephraim's children of the third generation; the children also of Machir the son of Manasseh were born upon Joseph's knees. And Joseph said to his brothers, 'I am about to die; but God will visit you, and bring you up out of this land to the land which he swore to Abraham, to Isaac, and to Jacob' " (50:23–24). He has seen his future in the sons of Ephraim and Manasseh, and he binds his future to the future of the family. His burial in Canaan will await God's future action in the life of this family, and it is tied to the brothers in oath. This unifying oath is a final note of concord in the story of the family that began in such discord. From Canaan to Egypt, from tale-bearing and hatred to harmony in oath-taking, and from settlement in Egypt to a brief look into a future movement from Egypt to Canaan, with a glimpse into future generations: in all this the conclusion balances the opening exposition and strikes the note of peace that winds up a carefully plotted novella.

NOTES

1. See pp. 93–95 below.

2. The author assumes that the reader will recognize these figures as drawn from the traditional lore of the Hebraic heritage and know some fundamental things about them.

3. Claus Westermann, *Genesis 37–50*, 40–42.

4. See Phyllis Trible, *Texts of Terror*, ch. 3, for another Tamar's story.

5. Robert Alter, *The Art of Biblical Narrative*, 3–12.

6. See ch. 7 and 8 below for a full discussion of this "kernel." The term was first used by Gunkel.

7. See pp. 74–75 below.

8. See W. L. Humphreys, *Crisis and Story: Introduction to the Old Testament*, 1–13.

9. See pp. 108–16 below.

10. Alter, *Art*, 167–68.

11. Alter, *Art*, 163–75.

12. See pp. 108–16 below.

I.   Exposition (37:2–4)

    A.   Jacob dwells in Canaan: link with larger Torah story (37:1)
    B.   Title (37:2a)
    C.   Introduction to Joseph (37:2b)
    D.   A father's love for his favored son (37:3)
    E.   Brothers' hatred of their brother (37:4)

II. Initial complications (37:5–36)

    A.   Joseph's dreams (37:5–11)

        1.   Exposition (37:5)
        2.   First dream related (37:6–7)
        3.   Reaction of brothers (37:8)
        4.   Second dream related (37:9–10a)
        5.   Reaction of father (37:10b)
        6.   Concluding summary of reactions (37:11)

    B.   Strife and deceit in Jacob's family (37:12–36)

        1.   Joseph sent to his brothers (37:12–17)

            a)   Exposition (37:12)
            b)   Father's commission (37:13–14)
            c)   Shechem interlude (37:15–16)
            d)   Concluding transition (37:17)

        2.   The brothers' plot (37:18–22)

            a)   Exposition (37:18)
            b)   The plan (37:19–20)
            c)   Reuben's plan to save Joseph (37:21–22)

        3.   Execution of the plot (37:23–30)

            a)   Joseph stripped and put in a pit (37:23–24)
            b)   Ishmaelite caravan (37:25)
            c)   Judah's scheme (37:26–27)
            d)   Midianites take Joseph and sell to Ishmaelites (37:28)
            e)   Reuben discovers Joseph gone (37:29–30)

        4.   The brothers deceive their father (37:31–35)

            a)   Bloodied cloak sent to Jacob (37:31–32)
            b)   Jacob recognizes the cloak (37:33)
            c)   Jacob's grief (37:34–35a)
            d)   Concluding notice (37:35b–36)

III. Interludes: Judah and Tamar; Joseph in Egypt (38–41)

    A. Judah and Tamar (38:1–30)

        1. Introduction (38:1–5)

            a) Judah' marriage (38:1–2)
            b) Birth of his sons (38:3–5)

        2. Introduction of Tamar (38:6–11)

            a) Her marriage to Er (38:6)
            b) Death of Er (38:7)
            c) Sin and death of Onan (38:8–10)
            d) Tamar sent to dwell with her father (38:11)

        3. Judah deceives Tamar (38:12–19)

            a) Death of Judah's wife (38:12a)
            b) Judah's journey to Timnah (38:12b)
            c) Tamar's disguise (38:13–15)
            d) Judah's proposition (38:16a)
            e) The affair concluded (38:16b–19)

        4. Judah seeks to pay his debt (38:20–23)

            a) Friend's failure to find harlot (38:20–21)
            b) Report to Judah (38:22–23)

        5. Trial of Tamar (38:24–26)

            a) Tamar accused (38:24a)
            b) Judah passes sentence (38:24b)
            c) Tamar's defense (38:25)
            d) Judah affirms Tamar's innocence (38:25)

        6. Birth of Perez and Zerah (38:27–30)

    B. Transition from Canaan to Egypt (39:1, cf. 37:36)
    C. Joseph in the house of Potiphar (39:2–20)

        1. Exposition: Joseph appointed over Potiphar's estate (39:2–6a)

            a) Notice of Yahweh's favor (39:2–3)
            b) Appointment as overseer (39:4, 6a)
            c) Yahweh's blessing of Potiphar's estate (39:5)

        2. Joseph and Potiphar's wife (39:6b–20)

            a) Notice of Joseph's appearance (39:6b)
            b) Attempted seduction (39:7–12)

                (1) The proposition (39:7)
                (2) Joseph's refusal (39:8–9)

      (3)   Renewed proposition (39:10–12a)

      (4)   Joseph's flight (39:12b)

    c)   Joseph accused by Potiphar's wife (39:13–18)

      (1)   Report to servants (39:13–15)

      (2)   Report to Potiphar (39:16–18)

    d)   Potiphar's response (39:19–20)

      (1)   Notice of Potiphar's anger (39:19)

      (2)   Joseph imprisoned (39:20)

D.   Joseph in prison (39:21–40:23)

    1.   Conclusion and transition: Joseph appointed overseer of prison (39:21–23)

      a)   Notice of Yahweh's favor (39:21)

      b)   Appointment as overseer (39:22–23a)

      c)   Yahweh's blessing of all he does (39:23b)

    2.   Joseph interprets the dreams of the butler and baker (40:1–23)

      a)   Exposition: Imprisonment of butler and baker (40:1–4)

        (1)   Pharaoh's anger (40:1–2)

        (2)   Imprisonment (40:3)

        (3)   Joseph attends them (40:4)

      b)   The dreams and their interpretation (40:5–19)

        (1)   Dreams and distress (40:5–6)

        (2)   Joseph's offer to interpret (40:7–8)

        (3)   Butler's dream and interpretation (40:9–15)

          (a)   The dream related (40:9–11)

          (b)   The interpretation (40:12–13)

          (c)   Joseph's plea (40:14–15)

        (4)   Baker's dream and interpretation (40:16–19)

          (a)   The dream related (40:16–17)

          (b)   The interpretation (40:18–19)

        (5)   The outcome (40:20–23)

          (a)   Pharaoh's birthday feast (40:20)

          (b)   Restoration of butler (40:21)

          (c)   Execution of baker (40:22)

          (d)   Joseph forgotten (40:23)

E.   Joseph in the court of Pharaoh (41:1–57)

    1.   Transition: Passage of two years (41:1a)

2. Pharaoh's first dream (41:1b–4)
   a) Two sets of cows (41:2–3)
   b) The second eats the first (41:4)

3. Pharaoh's second dream (41:5–7)
   a) Two sets of ears of grain (41:5–6)
   b) The second eats the first (41:7)

4. Pharaoh's distress (41:8a)

5. Failure of Egyptian interpreters (41:8b)

6. Joseph interprets Pharaoh's dream (41:9–32)
   a) Butler remembers Joseph (41:9–13)
   b) Joseph summoned (41:14)
   c) Preliminary exchange (41:15–16)
   d) First dream recounted (41:17–21)
      (1) Two sets of cows (41:17–19)
      (2) The second eats the first (41:20–21)
   e) Second dream recounted (41:22–24a)
      (1) Two sets of ears of grain (41:22–23)
      (2) The second eats the first (41:24a)
   f) Failure of Egyptian interpreters recalled (41:24b)
   g) Joseph interprets the dreams (41:25–32)
      (1) Opening statement of the interpreter (41:25)
      (2) Symbols of good years (41:26)
      (3) Symbols of lean years (41:27)
      (4) Notice of divine intent (41:28)
      (5) Interpretation (41:29–31)
      (6) Notice of divine determination (41:32)

7. Joseph offers advice on meeting the crisis (41:33–36)
   a) Need for an able administrator (41:33)
   b) Impose a double tax in good years (41:34–36)

8. Elevation of Joseph (41:37–52)
   a) Recognition of Joseph's abilities (41:37–39)
   b) Installation of Joseph into new office (41:40–45)
      (1) Pharaoh's words of installation (41:40–41)
      (2) Symbols (41:41–43)
         (a) ring (41:42a)
         (b) linen garment (41:42b)
         (c) gold necklace (41:42c)
         (d) chariot (41:43a)
         (e) command (41:43b)
         (f) summary (41:43c)

(3)   Pharaoh's final words of installation (41:44)
(4)   Joseph's Egyptian name (41:45a)
(5)   Joseph's Egyptian wife (41:45b)
(6)   Notice of Joseph's age (41:46a)

  c) Initial action to meet crisis (41:46b–49)

(1)   Survey of land (41:46b; cf. 41:45c)
(2)   Years of plenty (41:47)
(3)   Gathering for famine (41:48–49)

  d) Joseph's sons (41:50–52)

(1)   Birth notice (51:50)
(2)   Naming of Manasseh (41:51)
(3)   Naming of Ephraim (41:52)

9. Conclusion and transition: Famine arrives (41:53–57)

IV.   Further complications (42:1–44:34)

A. First Journey to Egypt (42:1–38)

1. Jacob sends the ten brothers (42:1–4)

  a) Commission (42:1–2)
  b) Execution (42:3)
  c) Exception of Benjamin (42:4)

2. Journey (42:5)
3. The brothers' first audience with Joseph (42:6–17)

  a) Introduction to Joseph (42:6a)
  b) Brothers bow before him (42:6b)
  c) Initial recognition and accusation (42:7–8)

(1)   Recognition (42:7a)
(2)   Accusation (42:7b–8)

  d) The dreams recalled by Joseph (42:9a)
  e) Additional accusation (42:9b)
  f) Protests of innocence (42:10–11)
  g) Additional accusation (42:12)
  h) Additional protests of innocence (42:13)
  i) Joseph's offer of a test (42:14–16)
  j) Brothers imprisoned (42:17)

4. Second Meeting with Joseph (42:18–25)

  a) Joseph sets a second test (42:18–20)
  b) Recriminations (42:21–24)

(1)   General confession (42:21)
(2)   Reuben's response (42:22)
(3)   Joseph's reaction (42:23–24a)

        c)   Simeon bound (42:24b)

5. Departure (42:25–28)

        a)   Joseph gives orders for departure (42:25)
        b)   Notice of departure (42:26)
        c)   Discovery of money (42:27–28a)
        d)   Reaction (42:28b)

6. Homecoming (42:29–38)

        a)   Appearance before Jacob (42:29)
        b)   Recounting of what happened in Egypt (42:30–34)
        c)   Discovery of money (42:35)
        d)   Jacob's reaction (42:36)
        e)   Reuben's offer (42:37)
        f)   Jacob rejects Reuben's offer (42:38)

B. Second journey to Egypt (43:1–44:34)

   1. Jacob sends the ten brothers (43:1–14)

        a)   Exposition: The famine continues (43:1)
        b)   Jacob's commission (43:2)
        c)   Judah recalls Joseph's warning and conditions (43:3–5)
        d)   Israel's protest (43:6)
        e)   Brothers' defense (43:7)
        f)   Judah's offer (43:8–10)
        g)   Israel's instructions for journey (43:11–14)

            (1)   Present (43:11)
            (2)   Money (43:12)
            (3)   Commission with mention of Benjamin (43:13)
            (4)   Prayer (43:14a)
            (5)   Acceptance of fate (43:14b)

   2. Journey to Egypt (43:15a,b)

   3. Brothers' first audience with Joseph (43:16–25)

        a)   Joseph first sees Benjamin (43:16a)
        b)   Charge to steward (43:16b)
        c)   Execution of charge by steward (43:17–25)

            (1)   Brothers brought to Joseph's house (43:17)
            (2)   Brothers' fears (43:18)
            (3)   Brothers' defense (43:19–22)
            (4)   Steward's response (43:23a)
            (5)   Return of Simeon to brothers (43:23b)
            (6)   Preparations for the meal (43:24–25)

4. Brothers' second audience with Joseph (43:26–34)

    a) Brothers come into Joseph's presence and bow down (43:26)

    b) Joseph inquires about father (43:27)

    c) Brothers respond and bow down (43:28)

    d) Joseph takes note of Benjamin (43:29)

    e) Joseph exits and weeps (43:30)

    f) Joseph returns and orders the meal (43:31)

    g) The meal (43:32–34)

        (1) Notice about Egyptians (43:32)

        (2) Seating by rank (43:33)

        (3) Portion reserved for Benjamin (43:34a)

        (4) Concluding notice of the meal (43:34b)

5. Departure (44:1–13)

    a) Joseph orders money and cup put with food (44:1–2)

    b) Brothers depart (44:3)

    c) Joseph commands steward (44:4–5)

    d) Steward executes command (44:6)

    e) Brothers protest innocence and request search (44:7–9)

        (1) Statement of innocence (44:7)

        (2) Recollection of earlier money returned (44:8)

        (3) Offer of search and penalty for guilty (44:9)

    f) Steward accepts and modifies offer (44:10)

    g) Search (44:11–12)

    h) Return to Egypt (44:13)

6. Third audience with Joseph (44:14–34)

    a) Brothers enter and bow before Joseph (44:14)

    b) Joseph's accusation (44:15)

    c) Judah's confession (44:16)

    d) Joseph's offer (44:17)

    e) Judah's plea (44:18–34)

        (1) Introduction (44:18a)

        (2) Opening request to speak (44:18b)

        (3) Review of past experience (44:19–29)

        (4) Future anticipated (44:30–32)

        (5) Petition (44:33–34)

V. Resolution (45:1–15)

    A. Joseph's first self-disclosure (45:1–3)

        1. Notice of Joseph's emotions (45:1a)
        2. Command to clear room (45:1b)
        3. Command executed (45:1c)
        4. Joseph weeps (45:2)
        5. Joseph reveals his identity (45:3a)
        6. Brothers' reaction (45:3b)

    B. Joseph's second self-disclosure (45:4–15)

        1. Joseph invites brothers to him (45:4a)
        2. Joseph identifies himself (45:4b)
        3. Joseph offers reassurance (45:5a)
        4. Joseph's explanation of divine guidance and will (45:5b–8)
        5. Joseph gives orders for brothers' return to father (45:9–11)
        6. Joseph's final reassurance (45:12)
        7. Command to bring father down to Egypt (45:13)
        8. Reunion of Benjamin and Joseph (45:14)
        9. Concluding notice of reconciliation (45:15)

VI. Denouement (45:16–50:21)

    A. Brothers' departure (45:16–24)

        1. Pharaoh makes provision for family in Egypt (45:16–20)
            a) Report to Pharaoh (45:16)
            b) Pharaoh's command to Joseph (45:17–20)
        2. Commands executed (45:21–24)
            a) Execution notice (45:21)
            b) Gifts to brothers, Benjamin, and father (45:22–23)
            c) Joseph sends brothers to Canaan (45:24)

    B. Brothers arrive in Canaan (45:25–28)

        1. Arrival notice (45:25)
        2. Brothers report that Joseph is alive (45:26a)
        3. Jacob's response (45:26b)
        4. Notice of brothers' further report (45:27a)
        5. Jacob's response (45:27b–28)

    C. Jacob and family journey to Egypt (46:1–27)

        1. Night vision at Beer-sheba (46:1–7)
            a) Arrival and sacrifices at Beer-sheba (46:1)
            b) Israel's night vision (46:2–4)

64

           (1)   Notice of vision (46:2a)

           (2)   Call (46:2b)

           (3)   Response (46:2c)

           (4)   Divine self-identification (46:3a)

           (5)   Assurance and announcement of future (46:3c–4)

       c) Concluding notice of journey to Egypt (46:5–7)

  2. List of descendants of Israel who came down to Egypt (46:8–27)

      a) Introduction (46:8a)

      b) List (46:8b–25)

      c) Summary of list (46:26–27)

D. Family's arrival in Egypt (46:28–47:27)

  1. Jacob sends Judah before him (46:28)

  2. Joseph reunited with father (46:29–30)

      a) Notice of reunion (46:29)

      b) Israel's words (46:30)

  3. Joseph presents family to Pharaoh (46:31–47:10)

      a) Joseph prepares brothers for audience (46:31–34)

      b) Audience with Pharaoh (47:1–10)

           (1)   Joseph announces family's arrival(47:1)

           (2)   Joseph presents five brothers to Pharaoh (47:2)

           (3)   Pharaoh addresses brothers (47:3)

           (4)   Brothers respond (47:4)

           (5)   Pharaoh allows them to settle in Goshen (47:5 6)

           (6)   Joseph presents Jacob to Pharaoh (47:7–10)

               (a) Opening notice of Jacob's blessing (47:7)

               (b) Pharaoh addresses Jacob (47:8)

               (c) Jacob responds (47:9)

               (d) Concluding notice of Jacob's blessing (47:10)

  4. Family settled in Goshen (47:11–27)

      a) Joseph executes Pharaoh's command (47:11–12)

      b) Joseph's organization of land of Egypt in famine (47:13–26)

           (1)   Opening summary of famine (47:13)

        (2)   Joseph collects all monies for Pharaoh (47:14)

        (3)   First petition by Egyptians (47:15)

        (4)   Joseph's reply (47:16)

        (5)   Egyptians comply (47:17)

        (6)   Second petition by Egyptians (47:18–19)

           (a)   Statement of condition (47:18)

           (b)   Request (47:19)

        (7)   Joseph acquires land for Pharaoh (47:20)

        (8)   Joseph enslaves Egyptians (47:21)

        (9)   Priests excepted (47:22)

    (10)   Joseph sets conditions (47:23–24)

    (11)   Egyptians comply (47:25)

    (12)   Concluding summary (47:26)

      c)   Concluding notice of settlement (47:27)

E.   The last days of Jacob (47:28–50:14)

    1.   Notice of Jacob's age (47:28)

    2.   Joseph's oath to bury Jacob in Canaan (47:29–31)

    3.   Blessing of Joseph's sons (48:1–22)

    4.   Blessing of Jacob's sons (49:1–27)

    5.   Charge to sons to bury him at Machpelah (49:28–32)

    6.   Death of Jacob (49:33)

    7.   Burial of Jacob in Canaan (50:1–14)

      a)   Joseph's grief (50:1)

      b)   Jacob's body is embalmed (50:2–3)

      c)   Joseph seeks Pharaoh's permission (50:4–5)

      d)   Pharaoh assents (50:6)

      e)   Jacob buried in Canaan (50:7–13)

      f)   Return to Egypt (50:14)

F.   Brothers' final audience with Joseph (50:15–21)

    1.   Brothers' fear (50:15)

    2.   Brothers' preparation for audience (50:16–17a)

    3.   Joseph's reaction (50:17b)

    4.   Brothers' audience with Joseph (50:18–21)

      a)   Brothers bow before Joseph (50:18)

      b)   Joseph's reassurance (19–21)

VII.   Conclusion: The last days of Joseph (50:22–26)

A.   Joseph and family live in Egypt (50:22a)

B.   Joseph's age at death (50:22b)

C. Joseph's descendants (50:23)
D. Joseph's words to brothers about future (50:24)
E. Joseph takes oath of brothers (50:25)
F. Joseph dies (50:26a)
G. Joseph embalmed (50:26b)

FOUR

CHARACTERIZATION

The Joseph novella tells the story of a family. It is the members of this family whose characters are most distinctly and sharply drawn. Praise for the author's skill in depicting the central characters is not uncommon. Indeed, Joseph, his brothers, especially Reuben and Judah, and Jacob all emerge not only as finely drawn figures but as men undergoing profound development over time. In important ways the novella is a character study: a depiction of how human beings interact and change through that interaction as they encounter situations laced with danger and keen stress.

It is important to note at the outset that these family figures, who command center stage, occupy an arena filled with a number of other figures who are significant in moving along the plot as they initiate, facilitate, or frustrate action. These additional figures are not as fully drawn; in particular they do not undergo the profound transformations seen in the central family members, transformations in character that are characteristic of the genre novella. A. Berlin has suggested that in biblical narrative characters can be classified under three broad headings or types defined in terms of the extent of their development and the role they play in the story: "Agent," "Type," and "Full Character."[1] Jacob, Joseph, and his brothers fall into the third (with the significant exception of Benjamin) and will command most of our attention in this chapter. But the other categories demand some consideration at the outset. It is, of course, necessary to keep in mind that these three categories describe overlapping fields on a spectrum rather than closed and sharply distinguished boxes.

AGENTS

In many stories there appear a number of "agents" who facilitate action but to whom minimal attention is otherwise drawn. Dramas have always had their messengers, guards, troops, courtiers, servants, and other attendants whose absence would be noted but whose quiet presence is designed only to direct attention elsewhere. In the Joseph novella these include the unnamed man whom Joseph encounters on his way from his father to his fateful meeting with his brothers (37:15–17); Ishmaelite and Midianite caravans (37:25–28, 36; 39:1); the servants in Potiphar's house (39:11, 14) whose absence is as timely as their presence; the Egyptian jailor (39:21–40:4); the magicians and wise men of Pharaoh's court (41:8); the retainers in Joseph's own establishment (42:23, 43:32; 45:1); Joseph's Egyptian wife (41:45) and his sons (41:50–52). Their functions are several in the novella.

The man encountered in the fields outside Shechem serves to redirect the action and our perspective as he directs Joseph to Dothan and his brothers (37:15–17). Many believe this figure unnecessary, and that no clear purpose is served in moving the brothers from Shechem to Dothan. For some this is only an elaborate device to transfer the brothers from the potentially dangerous Shechem area (given the events of Genesis 34) to the safer regions of Dothan.[2] The encounter serves primarily to stay the action of the story at a critical point at which Jacob unwisely—he seems willfully blind to the dynamics of his sons' interrelationships—thrusts the defenseless Joseph toward the group of embittered brothers in a setting far removed from any checks he might have on his sons. Not only is the reader delayed in finding out what will happen when the brothers encounter their youngest sibling, but the isolation of the coming encounter is keenly felt. Moreover, as we shall see, the reader's perspective on Joseph is transformed from that of the father who sends his son to that of the brothers about to receive this favored one into their power.

Other agents play a more apparent role. The servants in Potiphar's house are first conveniently offstage, then present to hear the lies of their master's wife, and serve thereby to underscore her treachery and the dan-

69

ger to Joseph. The jailor places Joseph in attendance on the chief butler and chief baker, a role in which he can soon demonstrate his abilities as "master of dreams" and dream interpretations that will eventually result in his rise. The courtiers of Pharaoh—the magicians and wise men—underscore through their failure the extraordinary skill of Joseph (and his God) in interpreting Pharaoh's dreams. Their wonder at his sound advice on how to meet the danger to which the dreams point serves to reinforce the wisdom of his appointment to power by Pharaoh (41:37–38). They too find Joseph's advice sound, and Pharaoh's question to them in 41:38 is clearly rhetorical, leading straight to his action. Joseph and the Egyptian courtiers appear as rivals only in that he is successful where they fail (41:8). In this we have what I have elsewhere called a tale of court contest, rather than one of conflict.[3] And even as a contest the elements of the motif are here attenuated. There is, for example, no mention of a dire penalty from which the hero's success saves all others (cf. Dan. 2) and himself, nor is there a reward offered at the outset to the one who succeeds (cf. Dan. 5). The point here is simply to underscore Joseph's remarkable skill and move him and the narrative along to his triumph. The Egyptian courtiers are simple foils for Joseph. Notice of Joseph's marriage to Asenath,[4] her pedigree as daughter of the high priest of the Sun God (41:45), and in short order the birth of sons (41:50–52) serve fully to integrate this new vizier into the highest circles of the Egyptian royal, social, and religious establishments.

Also serving as an agent in the novella is Benjamin, the last son born to Jacob and the full brother of Joseph. The first notice of him comes as something of a surprise, both to the reader (42:4) and quite likely to Joseph (42:13). Joseph covers his surprise nicely by going ahead with his accusations in this first encounter with his brothers after the famine. But the mention of "twelve" and then of the "youngest" who is "with our father this day" is most effective, not only in calling up an earlier time when the "youngest" was with their father, and then was not. An important new element now enters the story: Joseph makes the presence of this new "youngest" a condition for future ventures to Egypt by the family. Benjamin becomes a focus of concern for both father and brothers when a second journey to Egypt becomes necessary, and he is the pivot around which action, accusation, and plea revolve. He is even distinguished by Joseph's reversed protocol at table (43:33), and as the one with whom the silver cup is found. Benjamin is the center of a great deal of attention, but he never defines the reader's point of view. Attention to him is directed through and by others; we see him from their perspectives but never them from his. He never speaks. He is the subject of no verb of action. Placed in danger, he is allowed no cry of distress, no personal statement of innocence, no plea. No spotlight is allowed to isolate him as a center of our attention for long. He is an agent in the action and in the complex conditions set by Joseph, and in the unfolding development of the other characters as well. He is finally a cherished prop. It is a sure sign of the control exercised by the author of the Joseph novella that the depiction of Benjamin remained under such restraint. Had we been allowed even brief moments in which the events and other figures were seen from his point of view, it would have been a quite different experience. However, the intense focus on a very limited range of figures under extreme stress was not to be diffused in any way; this is in no way Benjamin's story.

TYPES

Occupying a sort of middle ground between the agents and the full characters are what Berlin calls "types." More attention is drawn to them, and more is reported of what they do and say. Yet they too demonstrate little development over time and seem primarily to represent a particular sort of person or office. The type can become a stereotype. In the Joseph narrative one finds Potiphar and his wife, the chief butler and chief baker, Pharaoh himself, and the steward in Joseph's own court. Each of these figures acts or speaks; attention is drawn to each. In more or less stereotypical ways they represent distinct sorts of human beings in particular positions or offices.

In Potiphar we have the unobservant husband—taking no care not only for his affairs but for the potential affairs of his lustful wife. The story itself is one example of a motif found in literature elsewhere, including especially the literature from ancient Egypt.[5] Each figure in this odd couple is nicely and economically drawn. The husband's position allows him all authority to act, even on impulse; yet he never speaks. In biblical narrative, in which speech carries such an important burden in the development of character and of narrative, a speechless character is something of a brute. We can compare Nabal in 1 Samuel 25, who has but one short and intemperate speech (vv. 10–11). He is easily controlled by the words of others. We have here the stock figure of a man with all formal power and authority in his hands, who is actually a pawn in the hands of others. Another comparable example is the king, Ahasuerus, in the book of Esther. It is generally women who finally control these men, for good or ill, and in this the irony of the tension between real and apparent power is graphically etched.

Like the wife of Nabal, Potiphar's wife says a great deal; unlike her, she fails to attain all upon which she sets her designs. At first Potiphar's wife appears remarkably blunt in her words. We are told that she spoke "day after day" in her effort to seduce Joseph, but her actual words are few and could not be more to the point: "Lie with me!" (39:7, 12). Joseph's elaborate protestations, as they are sandwiched by her commands, underscore her bluntness. But what more need she say to an underling? Only when Joseph flees from her, leaving his robe, does she command more words, and reveals a very subtle command of them at that. Her recounting of Joseph's "outrage" to the servants clearly sets the blame for the supposed assault upon her husband, who "brought among us a Hebrew to insult us" (39:14). But her words to her husband shade into an ambivalence that allows the earlier implication but need not be so taken: "He came to me (bā' 'ēlay, 39:17; cf. Judah's "Let me come to you," hābāh-nā 'ābô' 'ēlayik, in 38:16), the servant, the Hebrew (finally we learn just who came), who you brought to us to insult me" or "whom you brought to us, to insult me." Both the change in pronoun—from "us," including the servants along with herself as objects of the insult, to "me" when just the two of them speak—and the ambiguous relationship of the last clause to the whole—demonstrate her effective tailoring of her words to her audience. Does she mean to say the Hebrew servant, whom he brought to them, came to insult her? Or does she say that he brought the Hebrew servant to them to insult her? It is a shrewd speech that can imply the latter but can also mean the reverse if she is confronted about her meaning by her impulsive husband. Anger, urged on by implied guilt, triggers harsh action in this man who seems neither to stop nor speak nor even think. Remarkably, but necessary for the story, Joseph is only placed in prison rather than summarily executed.

While the impulsive Potiphar, urged on by his shrewd wife, spirits Joseph off to prison, the Pharaoh's chief butler and chief baker serve each in his own way to reverse Joseph's fortunes in time. At least they provide the opportunity for this when they give Joseph a chance to demonstrate that he is not only a dreamer but also master of the dreams of others as well (cf. 37:19). In these figures we have vignettes of typical courtiers.

Joseph is appointed to attend them while they are in detention, apparently while some unspecified charges against them are investigated by Pharaoh. All we know is that they have angered Pharaoh for having "offended" him (40:1). Already uneasy, and in one case possibly knowing reasons to fear the worst, each has an ominous dream during the same night. These dreams are in fact relatively clear, if more complex than Joseph's two dreams of Genesis 37, and seem to be literary constructs designed for this story. However, an interpreter is provided, and the occasion provides Joseph a chance to demonstrate his skill. As figures who move the story along the butler and baker also provide brief sketches of typical courtiers, and so help set the stage for Joseph's appearance in court.

Both officials are remarkably self-centered, looking out for what may advance their cause. Thus the chief baker seizes the favorable interpretation of the chief butler's dream as indication that fortune may await him as well: "Also, *I*, in *my* dream" (RSV "I also had a dream," 40:16). He is, of course, disappointed. The chief butler thinks no more of Joseph once he is restored to office—as Joseph indicated would happen. Only after two full years and a new crisis that demands the services of one skilled in dream interpretation does he recall Joseph and set him on the path to position and power. In fact, the narrative stresses the chief butler's neglect of Joseph through a double statement cast in both negative and positive terms: "Yet the chief butler did not remember Joseph, but forgot him." (40:23).

Of the remaining types Pharaoh himself demands attention. He appears as a powerful but benevolent ruler, needing interpretation of his dreams, but also able to recognize and act on sound advice. He dispatches matters with few words, be it the sudden elevation to highest rank of an obscure foreigner, or the arrangements for that man's family to settle in Egypt (47:5–6). When on stage he is in command, and all defer to him. The contrast with Ahasuerus in the book of Esther could not here be more marked. Pharaoh has and wields power, and in ways that are creative. Ahasuerus has the trappings of great power (Esth. 1:1), but is totally impotent in that he exercises no real power except as shaped by others. And too often he serves their destructive ends. Above all, the depiction of the pharaoh reminds the reader that this family's story is also a story set in court, in that context where apparent absolute power is wielded by the ruler and by those who can capture the favor, trust, and respect of the ruler, those who serve him well.

Yet even this ruler has limits. A man of power, he remains mortal. Not only is he unable to interpret his dreams, but they seem to grow more ominous as the delay in finding an interpreter up to the task leaves him wondering about their impact. Thus in his recounting of them to Joseph there are subtle but telling alterations when compared to the prior relating of them by the narrator. This is an effective literary move, as the reader first encounters the dreams from the perspective defined by the narrator—that is, what actually appeared in them—and only later from the point of view of their impact on the one whose dreams they were but who cannot divine their meaning. Thus Pharaoh's description of the second set of cows to emerge from the Nile in 41:19 is augmented in several ways when compared to 41:3. There is the addition of $m^{e\jmath}\bar{o}d$ as emphatic in the description of their bad shape $(t\bar{o}\jmath ar$; cf. $mar\jmath eh$ in v. 3) and the addition of the phrase "meager of flesh" $(raggôt\ b\bar{a}\acute{s}\bar{a}r)$, absent entirely in the narrator's words. Finally Pharaoh adds: "I have not seen as bad as they in all the land of Egypt" (41:19b, author's translation). This is then followed by a further addition. After stating that the second group eats the first, Pharaoh goes on: "When they had eaten them no one would have known that they had eaten them, for they were still as gaunt as at the beginning" (41:21). In this story even Pharaoh broods over what puzzles him, and this is nicely depicted in his own account of his dreams.

The story of Jacob's family is set in the context of the Egyptian royal court, and it is especially in the person of Pharaoh that we find that context defined as one that can shape lives for good or ill (courtiers can be reinstated or dispatched and no reasons given) and in which the skilled and shrewd can achieve position and power. But it is as well a context defined by limits, limits on the knowledge and therefore the power of Pharaoh. On one level Joseph's words about God giving Pharaoh a favorable answer (41:16) and dreams and their meaning being fixed by God (41:25, 28, 32) serve as polite discourse, a protocol in dream interpretation that separates the interpreter from the interpretation, the messenger from the message.[6] But on another this protocol defines a context of knowledge and power transcending that of even the god-king of Egypt. This family story is set in a context defined by external royal power, but that royal power is set in a larger theological context as well.

We must also note that through the benevolent intention of Pharaoh this foreign court never becomes the setting for genuine danger, like the royal courts in which Esther and Mordecai and then Daniel and his companions must work out their fate. This king is neither crass, stupid, nor impotent. Indeed, there is a nice transformation of expectations here as one reads the Joseph narrative within the larger context defined by the normative Hebraic religious traditions, which define Egypt as the land of danger and Pharaoh as archvillain. Egypt was the place and symbol of slavery and death. It was Yahweh's deliverance of his chosen from bondage in this land and his dramatic defeat of Pharaoh, climaxed at the Sea, that shaped the myth that provided the basis for the covenant that molded the Israelite and early Jewish experience of God and his action in human affairs and that determined the relationship they would have with that God. Egypt is death, and flight from it is a journey to new life in freedom. A journey back to Egypt is a flight from Yahweh and freedom back to death (Jer. 42–44). Here, however, Egypt is the land of life and space for living. It is the setting for reconciliation as well as relief from famine. For Joseph in the hands of his brothers, and for his family in grip of famine, Canaan is the land of death and alienation. New life and unity are found in Egypt. This reversal of usual expectation and experience is depicted in the character of Pharaoh as a benevolent, effective, if human, ruler (cf. Gen. 12:10–20).

Finally there is the brief sketch of the steward over Joseph's own establishment, a model of the faithful official who is able so fully to stand in and speak for his master that the two seem to merge into extensions of each other. Indeed the brothers address him as a surrogate for his (and their) master (43:19–23). As an extension of Joseph he is able to play a critical role during this second journey to Egypt, first in lulling the brothers into a false sense of security and then in confronting them with the renewed danger sparked by Benjamin's apparent theft of Joseph's silver divining cup. As does Joseph in the first encounter with his brothers, his steward now skillfully creates a context defined as ambiguous and arbitrary, shaped by fits and starts and changes in tenor that constantly keep the brothers off balance. Guilt and confession are met by reassurance and feigned ignorance of any offense (43:23); protests of innocence are met with accusation (44:6–12).

In all these sketches of types in the novella we find that the persons take on tone and substance that lead them to be viewed as more than agents. Yet they remain part of the situation and event-shaping context in which the full characters must play out their story. We are not allowed to center attention on any of these "types" for more than an episode or so, and are not permitted to follow their own stories to resolution. What ever became of Potiphar and especially his wife? Did he ever discover her deceit, and was she appropriately punished as the motif demands and as she is in other forms of the story? On what grounds were the two officials whose dreams Joseph first interpreted dealt with as each was? Who was this particular Pharaoh who knew Joseph so well? Types significantly define context and set the tone; they are more than props. They do not, however, take over a story and become the focus for the reader's attention.

FULL CHARACTERS

This novella provides a restricted but richly hued set of full characters drawn wholly from within the family of Jacob. As we can expect in a novella, these central figures are shown to develop in the course of the story; indeed, they undergo profound transformation.

Jacob

In the figure of Jacob (Israel) we watch a man of passion transformed into a man of controlled dignity, a dignity gained through extended suffering. A man of excesses becomes in time a man of reserve. Pouring forth words of love and grief and issuing abrupt commands in the opening half of the novella, he measures his words and actions with careful deliberation in the concluding sections. Insensitive to the impact of his words and deeds on those around him, he will become one well attuned to his place and position. It is appropriate that his first speech in the novella strikes a balance of apparent genuine wonder that stands midway between excessive assertion and sheer puzzlement. He rebukes Joseph, but "kept the saying in mind" (37:10–11). His reaction to Joseph's dreams is as telling of his character as the reactions of his sons are revealing of theirs. He wonders at these dreams; the ten dismiss them with cynical question. In each case we have here the first direct speech of these figures, and it is especially revealing of character.[7]

In the exposition that sets the stage for both the first episode and the whole novella we are told that Jacob loved Joseph as his youngest (and presumably only son of the beloved Rachel) more than he loved his other sons, and that this love was demonstrated through the gift of a special long-sleeved or colorful robe. This notice of Jacob's love follows immediately on the notice of Joseph bearing a malicious tale about his half brothers. The mix of tale-telling and exceptional love naturally sparks discord. A volatile setting is defined that might explode at any time without special care and balance demonstrated by the head of this family. Hints of such balance appear in the father's rebuke of his son's reports of his second dream, but we remain uncertain when we learn that the father kept (guarded) these words of his son. Was this because he saw portents in them or the potential for danger in this family situation? Or is this one more sign of a doting father who cherishes every word and even the fantasies of his favored son?

Jacob seems all business in sending Joseph to bring a report about the brothers to him. Yet he ignores the fact that his emissary is the one whose earlier tales and reports of his dreams will have made the brothers less than receptive to this younger brother, who was also kept at home with his father and spared having to tend the herds in the field. Even a minimal awareness of the feelings of the brothers would suggest prudence before sending Joseph to bring word on the "peace" (šālôm) of those who could not speak "peacefully" (šālôm) with him (37:14, 4), and in a setting where there can be little to hold their actions in check. While we have had narrative notice that the brothers were aware of their father's feelings for Joseph, and we are told of their own feelings (37:4, 5, 8), we have not had any objective notice that Jacob is aware of his sons' reaction to all that he has done to manifest his love for Joseph. The brothers seem transparent; their words and what is said about them by the narrator fit. Jacob seems in some ways opaque, as his actions do not fit what should be clear to him. His treatment of Joseph would suggest a dangerous level of insensitivity, an insensitivity of one who is turned inward.

Jacob next appears in grief that is expressed with a flair for the dramatic gesture and word. He is all too ready to be duped by his sons: upon sight of the bloodied cloak, the special token of his love for Joseph, he declares rather than enquires, assumes rather than probes. No denial here; excessive in love, he is primed for grief: "And he recognized it, and said, 'It is my son's robe; a wild beast has devoured him; Joseph is without doubt torn to pieces' " (37:33). Three short phrases: the third with the reinforcing infinitive (ṭārôp ṭōrap), the first in Hebrew simply binding the critical nouns "robe" and "my son." And then the outpouring of grief, an excess that is once more insensitive to the others around him. As Alter has pointed out, there is a pronounced touch of the dramatic here that suggests that Jacob may in some ways love mourning,[8] as earlier he seemed not only to love Joseph but to love loving him through the external show of it. Jacob's last words in this episode ("Certainly, I shall go down (*ʾērēd*) to my son, mourning, to Sheol") are nicely balanced, first by the factual and objectively dry notice that the Midianites sold him in Egypt (37:36) and then by the opening of chapter 39 (the next scene of the novella after the interlude of the episode about Judah and Tamar): "and Joseph was brought down (*hûrad*) to Egypt." There is irony in Jacob's words that the sensitive reader will not miss. Joseph has indeed "gone down," and in time Jacob will be "brought down" (45:13, again the verb *yārad*) to him, to Egypt if not to Sheol. We have already noted that Egypt in the Hebraic tradition is overwhelmingly the symbol of bondage, of death; it is in many ways Sheol. Yet in this narrative it is the land of provision in time of famine, of new beginnings, of reunion and reconciliation, of life.

But that is still far in the future. Now Jacob is condemned—better, condemns himself—to years of extreme grief. He appears in the novella, in his own eyes, and in the fears of others as a man moving to the brink of death. It is so often in his words (37:35; 42:38) and in those of others concerning him (43:27-28; 44:22, 29-31, 45:3). He is on a move toward death, even if it finally will come about in a way that is the reversal of all he feared (45:28, 46:30). In the period between initial grief and reunion with his son, Jacob will be shown more than once as alternating between a man tossed by emotion and one who is all business. When dealing with the crisis at hand and with his other sons, he is blunt and practical. When the memory of Joseph intrudes, the reversal is pronounced.

Thus as we make the transition back to the family in Canaan, from the adventures of Joseph in Egypt, it is the practical Jacob we meet, dealing with famine and apparently inept sons: "Why do you look at one another?" (42:lb). He sees a way to deal with the crisis and orders them into action. But Joseph is not forgotten: "But Jacob did not send Benjamin, Joseph's brother, with his brothers, for he feared that harm might befall him." (42:4). The words "lest harm befall him" (*pen yiqrāʾenû ʾāsôn*) are echoed at the end of the chapter: "and harm befall him" (*uqᵉrāʾāhû ʾāsôn*) in 42:38. Only the slow realization through the pleading of his sons brings Jacob in time to allow Benjamin (the surrogate Joseph) to accompany his brothers on a second journey. Jacob's words on this occasion are a fine blend of the practical and a dramatic resignation filled with excess of emotion:

> Then their father Israel said to them, "If it must be so, then do this: take some of the choice fruits of the land in your bags, and carry down to the man a present, a little balm and a little honey, gum,

myrrh, pistachio nuts, and almonds. Take double the money with you; carry back with you the money that was returned in the mouth of your sacks; perhaps it was an oversight. Take also your brother, and arise, go again to the man; may God Almighty grant you mercy before the man, that he may send back your other brother and Benjamin. If I am bereaved of my children, I am bereaved." (43:11–14) Whatever mercy God Almighty is to grant to the brothers on their delicate and dangerous mission is translated into the release of Simeon and the safe return of Benjamin. Actually, only Benjamin is named; the phrase "your other brother" linked with the name of Benjamin also recalls Joseph, and would betray the deeper hope beyond the expressed hope of this still bereaved father. On whatever level, it is understood this must be left to God Almighty. As far as negotiations for food and dealing with the potential danger resulting from failure of payment on the first trip, Jacob has arranged for them himself. It is the Jacob of extreme love and grief who will now occupy the brothers in this second trip. It is their fear of what the loss of Benjamin will do to him that shapes their perceptions of all that takes place.

By the way he attributes motives to others Jacob serve to place himself at the center of all that is harmful, attributing to all that happens an intentionality that is akin to paranoia. As the brothers empty their sacks on the return from the first journey to Egypt and discover to their dismay their money, Jacob's response is revealing: "And Jacob their father said to them, 'You have bereaved me of my children: Joseph is no more, and Simeon is no more, and now you would take Benjamin; all this *has come upon me*'" (42:36). In one of the few instances where he is identified as "their father" he seems starkly insensitive to what they might feel, as all is centered on him. When the next journey is imperative, and Judah recalls "the man's" conditions, Jacob replies, "Why did you treat me so ill as to tell the man that you had another brother?" (43:6). In trouble, the focus is on Jacob, self-directed and shaping the perspectives on what will follow. Thus when Judah makes his last plea before Joseph to stand in the place of Benjamin, the events that have transpired are recalled from the perspective of their impact on Jacob, and the future Judah fears is one that centers wholly on his father: "Now therefore, when I come to your servant my father, and the lad is not with us, then, as his life is bound up in the lad's life, when he sees that the lad is not with us, he will die; and your servants will bring down the gray hairs of your servant our father with sorrow to Sheol" (44:30–31).

We next meet Jacob when he is told by his sons that Joseph lives. The hope beyond hope is realized. His first reaction—"his heart fainted" (45:26)—is not unexpected. He has so immersed himself in grief for his lost son that he is indeed in no way prepared to receive news that he is alive and in power in Egypt. Denial is here the natural reaction to news that is a shock. His next words are more of a surprise, however. When convinced by the testimony and evidence presented by his sons, he states: "It is enough; Joseph my son is still alive; I will go and see him before I die" (45:28). This *rab*, "enough," is his most telling word. It signals a profound change. It states his acceptance of all that has befallen him and all that he has brought about, and it is a signal that excessive outpourings of emotion will no longer govern him. Brevity, reserve, and clarity here are counterpoints to the rush and tumble of emotion and words in earlier scenes (37:33–35; 42:36; 43:14). From this point on, in fact, this father becomes the dignified patriarch as well. In his meeting with his son, Jacob is satisfied: "Israel said to Joseph, 'Now let me die, since I have seen your face and know that you are still alive' " (46:30). It is Joseph who demonstrates in his actions deep emotion (assuming Joseph is the subject of all the verbs in this verse): "Then Joseph made ready his chariot and went up to meet Israel his father in Goshen; and he presented himself to him, and fell on his neck, and wept on his neck a good while" (46:29). From this point on, Jacob appears as a man of balance and control. He is equal to the meeting with Pharaoh, and indeed the king's equal as he blesses him. The respect Pharaoh shows for this old man is striking (47:8–10). There does seem just a hint of the earlier Jacob in his characterizing of his life as days "few and evil." He then makes appropriate arrangements for his death as the narrative takes in material dealing with the last days of this third of the patriarchs in Israelite tradition. The old man is feeble but in full control as he blesses the sons of Joseph (insisting on the reversal of the position of hands and grandsons) and pronounces a series of oracles on all his sons. His last act is to arrange for his burial in the land of promise.

The man of excessive passions laced with businesslike acumen, and the man of distinct blindness, is in his last days physically blind; but he clearly sees the weight of his position and responsibility as well as his limits. The death he feared (37:35; 42:38) is upon him, but not as a final fracture of his family. Around his death the unity of this family is revealed anew. *Rab*—"it is enough." This single word bespeaks a remarkable transformation in a man whose life more than once moved from so little to excess to loss to excess again.

The Brothers

The brothers undergo profound transformation as well. The stages seem clear, as they are signaled at all points by the narrator. In most episodes the feelings and motives of the brothers are not only signaled in their own words and deeds, but these are reinforced by narrative comments upon motives or feelings. The author takes us inside their heads and hearts, and the effect is to present them as the least complex of the major figures in the story, the least ambiguous in what stands behind their words and deeds. Alter sets out a hierarchy of narrative devices by which characters can be presented and their motives and emotions assessed.[9] On this pattern the brothers appear as a group the most transparent of the full figures in the novella, with Jacob in a middle position and Joseph the most opaque.

From the outset the brothers hate Joseph (37:4, 5, 8). Three times we are told this in the exposition to the novella, and then we are shown it: they smolder (37:11a); they recognize an opportunity (37:18–20); they seize it and act (37:22–23). A hatred provoked by their father's love for their youngest brother and his demonstration of it, further sparked by this youth's own boasting, leads them to seize an opportunity to rid themselves of him that is too good to let pass. They then cover their tracks and deceive their father. As a group they act upon the moment to remove the discomforting situation of the moment. At the outset they seem as a whole to demonstrate as little forethought as remorse. Throughout they appear hardly on top of, and often overwhelmed by, events. Their attempts to be rid of Joseph in the opening episode (37:18–20) are complicated not only by the diverse plans of Reuben and then Judah, but possibly also by the appearance of Midianite caravaners who steal the prize to sell to the Ishmaelite caravan. The stage becomes crowded by competing intentions, caravaners, comings and goings, all at cross purposes that typify life as they will live it for some time to come. Reuben's helplessness forecasts that of all. Soon they will trigger their father's grief, but they cannot comfort him (37:35).

As a group they seem simple men; the repeated notice by the narrator of their already clear and even understandable hatred of their spoiled younger brother only serves to underscore this simplicity. Need we be informed three times of what is already clear? And as a group of simple men already stumbling, they find themselves hopelessly out of their depth in the court of the grand vizier of Egypt. They would, no doubt, be outside their element in this context even in a normal situation, but this situation

is not normal. Thus when suddenly accused they blurt out not only deni-
als, but much more information than is necessary and, in fact, first inform
Joseph of the existence of Benjamin:

> And Joseph remembered the dreams which he had dreamed of them;
> and he said to them, "You are spies, you have come to see the weak-
> ness of the land." They said to him, "No, my lord, but to buy food
> have your servants come. We are all sons of one man, we are honest
> men, your servants are not spies." He said to them, "No, it is the
> weakness of the land that you have come to see." And they said, "We,
> your servants, are twelve brothers, the sons of one man in the land of
> Canaan; and behold, the youngest is this day with our father, and
> one is no more." (42:9–13)

Their words tumble out in brief phrases with no clear order, having their
impact through culmination and not through any artful sequence (cf.
Judah's speech in 44:18–34). The effect here is one of simple innocence in
contrast to the simple culpability of the earlier encounter with Joseph.
Then they saw him from afar; now he sees them and recognizes them.
They saw but did not recognize, even though they named him "master of
dreams" (37:19). Now in recognition Joseph recalls his dreams (42:8–9).

They plead innocence before the accusation of this Egyptian vizier
but confess their guilt with each other. In remembering their treatment of
their brother they now provide information about that event that was not
part of the earlier narrative: "We saw the distress of his soul, when he
besought us, and we would not listen" (42:21b). We were not allowed to
experience Joseph's plight from his perspective in the opening episode
because they themselves would not or could not experience it; now we
experience a brief taste of his terror and theirs as their fear leads to
remorse and opens them to *his* earlier fears. Affliction brings remorse—
"what did we do to deserve this?" Theirs is a common human reaction to
trouble, but in this case under the control of the moment, and it is not yet
necessarily reflective of deeper remorse. They again appear more adept at
responding than initiating, just as in the opening of this chapter—"Why
do you look at one another?" Yet changes are taking place in them, even if
once more Reuben seems out of step (42:22).

They continue in this pattern as they discover their money and then
in their confrontations with their father. In fact, when Jacob charges them
with needlessly telling the Egyptian more than necessary, they claim that
he questioned them about their family situation. This "the man" did not

do in the account in chapter 42, and this disjunction between that account and the brothers' memory of it brings an additional degree of complexity to the characterization of them. This notice subtly mutes the clarity with which they had been earlier depicted. Are we once more to view them as crass in this further deception of their father? Or are we to see them as creatively remembering what was a terrifying situation? No clues are provided this time by the narrator outside the report of their own words.

The second journey to Egypt for food is a counterpoint to the first. Again ten brothers descend to Egypt to stand before Joseph (43:16; cf. 42:3, 6b). Again the welcome throws them off stride—this time as Joseph's steward meets their protestations of innocence (43:19–22), characteristically before any charge was lodged against them—with profession of ignorance of any crime (43:23). For the guilty, even hospitality can seem ominous (43:18). Then when their fears seem calmed, the tables turn again as they are carefully set up by Joseph. In their further protests of innocence when faced with the charge that Benjamin stole Joseph's divining cup, they seem at last to speak the truth without deceiving. For once they are clearly innocent: "They said to him, 'Why does my lord speak such words as these? Far be it from your servants that they should do such a thing! Behold, the money which we found in the mouth of our sacks, we brought back to you from the land of Canaan; how then should we steal silver or gold from your lord's house? With whomever of your servants it be found, let him die, and we also will be my lord's slaves' " (44:7–9). And in these words they unconsciously set the penalty that must face their youngest brother, just as so long ago they thought they could determine their youngest brother's fate. The haste with which they prepare for the search is right in character, as is their silent grief when they return to Egypt upon discovery of the cup in Benjamin's belongings.

Balancing this depiction of the brothers as a collective unit is the presentation of the figure of Reuben, who, along with Judah, is one of two singled out for special attention. He is the eldest, but we suspect that he feels compelled to act a part for which he is not suited. He simply is not equipped for the task. A key motif in this novella is the reversal of rank, and Reuben is both a primary illustration and a victim. His scheme to save Joseph from death at their hands aborts. He bewails his misfortune as they scheme to cover their crime (37:29–30). He later blurts out an "I told you so," fruitlessly seeking to separate himself from their acknowledged guilt as he once sought to separate himself from their crime (42:22). After returning home from the first trip to Egypt, and after their father accuses them of seeking to bereave him once more by taking Benjamin from him, Reuben seeks to allay Jacob's fears: "Then Reuben said to his father, 'Slay my two sons if I do not bring him back to you; put him in my hands, and I will bring him back to you' " (42:37). As if the death, indeed the murder, of grandsons can somehow make up for the loss of another son! Jacob gives the offer short if dramatic rejection, and it is not even recalled later as the brothers attempt to convince their father to send his youngest with them on their second journey to Egypt.[10]

It is Judah's offer that replaces Reuben's, and Judah proves more effective as well as more realistic. As a second trip becomes imperative, his offer is to bear the guilt throughout his life should Benjamin be lost, guilt that he would bear in his father's eyes anyway. He then hurries his father to the business at hand; "for if we had not delayed we would now have returned twice" (43:10b). In the opening episode his attempt to alter his brothers' course of action against Joseph is both heeded and possibly more effective. His proposal is carefully calculated to financial motives: "What profit is it . . . ?" (*bezā*, "profit," carries overtones of craftiness). Through the sale of Joseph they were to rid themselves of the pest and turn a profit as well. Our understanding of the success of this venture hinges on the reading of Genesis 37:28.[11] As it stands, it is possible to read the brothers as subjects of the verbs (drawing, taking up, selling) in verse 28a. This reading is facilitated if Midianites and Ishmaelites are understood to refer to the same group of caravaners. On the other hand, if Midianites and Ishmaelites are distinct, then the Midianites become a natural subject for the same verbs in verse 28a. The brothers appear to be rid of Joseph, but the profit goes to other hands.

In any event, Judah is clearly the more effective brother, and it is in character that he should be the one finally to speak so powerfully in behalf of his youngest brother and his father's attachment to him, in words artfully constructed in terms of both sensitivity to his father's feelings and to the protocol of courtly address. Craft and sensitivity now work together to meet this last crisis, which reveals that they have changed, a change that is mirrored in Judah. They risk, and offer to risk themselves, rather than once more ridding themselves of the beloved youngest to avoid facing a situation they find discomforting. From remorse sparked by discomfort during the first journey to Egypt (42:21–22, with some discord in their ranks), they can now, through Judah's efforts, place their father's interests at the core of their concern (see 44:27–34), and there is no dissent in the ranks of the ten. Clearly they have changed. Through it all Judah carries his plea off with dignity. Guilt has caught up with them—"God has found out the guilt of your servants"—and he will accept slavery as appropriate recompense; yet he never confesses that any one of them is actually guilty of the specific crime of which they all are charged; Benjamin is simply he "in whose hand the cup has been found." Once more, as in chapter 42, the interplay between an overarching guilt that envelops the life of the brothers and innocence in the specific charges is effectively developed.

Judah is clearly the right choice later to prepare the reunion between Jacob and Joseph (46:28); he has been proven effective, and he above all the brothers must appreciate the irony of having to facilitate a union of father and son that they once sought to break for good.

Two further brief characterizations of the brothers collectively merit notice. As Joseph sends them to Canaan to bring their father and families to Egypt, he provides lavishly for them, and especially for Benjamin and his father. He then sends them off with the words: "Do not quarrel on the way" (45:24). While changed, they are what they are.

After their father's death they make one final presentation before Joseph. Just as Joseph in his above charge recognized the possibility always for disputation among them, so they suspect in him a lingering potential for revenge, especially now that their father is out of the way (50:15). They carefully stage their presentation before him, first sending messengers and then appearing themselves (as they did so long ago when coming to their father with the bloodied cloak, 37:32). Once again their recollection of the past proves to be much richer than the events narrated in the story, and the suspicion of fabrication cannot be ignored: "So they sent a message to Joseph, saying, Your father gave this command before he died, "Say to Joseph, Forgive, I pray you, the transgression of your brothers and their sin, because they did evil to you." And now, we pray you, forgive the transgression of the servants of the God of your father." Joseph wept when they spoke to him." (50:16–17)

While they are transformed from the ruthless lot at the outset, the instinct to protect themselves remains. Jacob made many arrangements before his death (47:29–49:33), and they are fully narrated in a way that alters the flow of the narrative, but this command was not reported among them. Once more, as well, they seem to propel themselves to fulfill the earlier dreams of Joseph and make a mockery of their early attempts to thwart them: "His brothers also came and fell down before him, and said, 'Behold, we are your servants.' (50:18). Compare: "They said to one another, 'Here comes this dreamer. Come now, let us kill him and throw him into one of the pits; then we shall say that a wild beast has devoured him, and we shall see what will become of his dreams' " (37:19–20). Joseph is now able to reassure them; and, as they acted in concord with him in the burial of their father, so now he places his own eventual burial in their hands and the hands of their descendants (50:25). The exposition to the novella spoke of discord. The conclusion demonstrates harmony and trust.

Joseph

Joseph is often on center stage, the center of attention of both the reader and the other characters. Yet he appears as the most ambiguous of all the full characters throughout most of the novella. There is a stark clarity in presentation of the other full characters, especially the brothers, that sets apart all the more dramatically the opacity to this figure. The narrator does not inform us in his own voice of Joseph's thoughts or motives. His words and deeds must speak to this without that added emphasis provided in the case of the brothers and to a lesser degree for Jacob. Throughout Joseph is the focus of the attention of others, and we perceive him as they experience and value him. But the narrator gives us no direct indication of his perceptions, his feelings and thoughts. And only in time will we be allowed to perceive things as he does.

We first meet him as the young and indulged son of an old man who loves him more than his other brothers. We meet him as the bearer of malicious tales and as a dreamer. We find him boasting of his dreams of grandeur, provoking the envy and hatred of the brothers and causing his parents discomfort. When he is sent by his father to check on the welfare of his brothers (who cannot speak *"šālōm"* with him), we see him in their hands as they attempt to rid themselves of this pest. We know he is loved by his father and we know that he is hated by his brothers; we are told so repeatedly by the narrator (37:3–4, 5, 8, 11). We are never informed about how he felt regarding all of this. As the novella opens, all feeling and emotion, for good and for ill, appear to flow to this lad, and little is allowed to flow from him. We are thus not allowed insight into his feelings as he is seized, stripped, and thrown into a pit by his brothers and later extracted and sold to caravaners going to Egypt. At this point he is allowed neither deed nor words. Just as all the attention of the narrative is centered on him, so all feeling, emotion, and action move toward him as well. But all he shares with others as the novella opens is his dreams.

This pattern continues in the next segment of the novella, in Joseph's adventures through his fall and rise in Egypt. His words and his deeds demonstrate here that he is discerning and skilled and that whatever he puts his hand to will prosper. He is busy managing Potiphar's estate; he interprets courtiers' dreams while in prison, and does the same for Pharaoh with added advice on dealing with the crisis revealed. By the end of this episode he is organizing Egypt to face seven years of famine. But through all this, of his internal feelings or thoughts or motives we are told nothing by the narrator. As before, all that is shown of this figure is for public consumption. Again, it is the feelings of others for him that are related. Potiphar values him for the prosperity he brings to his estate and entrusts him with all that he has. Potiphar's wife also values him (cast her eyes upon" him, as the RSV captures the Hebrew idiom "lifts her eyes to" in 39:7). Later it will be Pharaoh and his courtiers who will value him (41:37). Throughout these twists and turns of plot the interior private Joseph is a subject for the reader's speculation, but the narrator confines the basis for that speculation to his public words and deeds. He is at the center of attention, but we are kept at some narrative distance from that center. We see him from the circle of those about him; we do not see them through him.

We can divine a change in the figure of Joseph between the opening scenes of chapter 37 and as he appears in Egypt in chapters 39–41. In the former he is the spoiled youth, pampered and insensitive of the impact of his tale-bearing and his dreams. The very fact that we are not even told why he told tales or recounted his dreams to those they were most calculated to arouse reinforces this impression of insensitivity. Whether the dreams were related as an outburst of youthful self-enthusiasm or as a more calculated boast is not clear, but either motive betrays an insensitivity to others that is identical with intolerable conceit. He is a spoiled brat. It is easy to understand both the brothers' hatred and jealousy and the father's love for this only son of the beloved wife. By the time we see him again, now in Egypt, he appears more cautious in what he does and says to others, whether this is the result of enhanced sensitivity to others or a more careful calculation or both. His rather lengthy protest in self-defense (39:8–9) stands in sharp contrast to the blunt two-word command of Potiphar's wife. His position is treacherous and calls forth an ability to marshal a range of arguments, as he builds his case from what his master had done for him, to what it means in his position and relation to the master's wife, to what it means in relation to God. The effect is a heaping of arguments, but so crafted that Potiphar's wife is put at the center of the speech, bracketed by her husband and by God, to both of whom Joseph has overriding obligations (39:3–9).

There is, in fact, the same piling up of arguments at the end of his interpretation of the chief butler's dream, in his rather breathless plea that he not be forgotten when events foretold by the dream come about (40:14–15). These pleas draw us closer to the man. In the opening episode we hear no words from him after he accepts his father's charge ("Here I am") to journey to his brothers. We learn of his plea in distress only as the brothers much later recall it (42:21) when the events of their first journey have triggered their feelings of guilt.

The impassioned tone of these two pleas also stands in contrast to the measured quality of a public address that marks the remaining speeches of Joseph in chapters 39–41. He moves straight to the point in his interpretation of the dreams of the chief butler and chief baker, whether the dream is for good or ill, and offers no advice, for none is appropriate. Before Pharaoh he is more circumspect. In what may well be the conventional protocol of dream interpreters he distances himself as interpreter from the interpretation by stating that God gives both dreams and interpretations (41:15–16; cf. vv. 25, 32). Message and messenger are not to be confused. This time the crisis foretold in the dream leads Joseph into advice on how to meet it. Indeed, he states that the dream was sent as an urgent warning (41:25, 28, 32), and thereby sets a basis for advice that now follows in a seamless flow. The advice is recognized by all as sound and as an additional indication of Joseph's remarkable abilities. It launches him into the office of vizier.

Joseph in these last three chapters is shown as a youth become a man, as growing into a figure more and more in command of his words and of the situations in which he finds himself, ever more the man whose skill shapes his destiny. We watch him move from the grasp of his brothers, from which he barely escapes with his life and through no act of his own; to the grasp of Potiphar's wife, which he eludes through desperate action only to wind up in prison; to an audience before Pharaoh, a situation he seizes with complete command. But he remains throughout enigmatic, a figure now on a larger stage but still seen only in public pose. Of the inner Joseph we still know but little. With the exception of 41:51–52, where he names his sons, Joseph is silent as he is elevated to highest office and assumes full authority in the lengthy concluding segments of the episode (41:37–57). After the interpretation and the advice based on it, he falls silent and is not allowed his own speech again until he confronts his brothers. Only the naming interlude allows us, as reader, any insight into his actual feelings, revealing his perception of his situation in Egypt as one of hardship and affliction: "Joseph called the name of the first-born Manasseh, 'For,' he said, 'God has made me forget all my hardship and all my father's house.' The name of the second he called Ephraim, 'For God has made me fruitful in the land of my affliction' " (41:51–52). This first brief but striking counterpoint to the posture of the narrative with respect to Joseph up to this point sets his own feelings in marked contrast to what has occurred. Outwardly he has attained a success beyond all expectations, and his new life seems full in every way. The names acknowledge the external developments, but betray a very particular perspective on them.

By the end of the interlude in Egypt his control over the situation and himself is absolute. It is exercised as total manipulation of the context in which he and his brothers are brought together again once Jacob sends his sons to Egypt to buy provisions for the famine. Joseph is an aloof, almost godlike figure; sharp counterpoint to their confused squirmings. His pointed and blunt accusations stand in contrast to their breathless but wordy defense. However, the reader is not told why all this is taking place. Joseph recognizes his brothers and he recalls the dreams of his youth. But why this treatment of them? Is it a test of them? Is this an attempt to assess their character? Is it revenge? We have watched Joseph move from pit to pitfall to praise to power; from victim in the hands of jealous brothers to the object of his master's wife's lust; through prison, forgotten in a courtier's restoration; and finally through interpretation of Pharaoh's dreams to supreme authority as second only to the king of Egypt. Now he can manipulate his brothers as he will. But through it all we still know little of his inner emotions, thoughts, and motives. There is no aside in which he reveals his motive, and the narrator as well withholds this information. He is an enigma, and a most dangerous one from the brothers' perspective because of the total reversal in disparity of power from that of the opening scene with the family. Only as the brothers bare their souls and consciences before both the reader and unwittingly before Joseph (42:23) are we, but not the brothers, allowed a glimpse of Joseph's inner feeling. It is one narrated through words and deeds designed to hide it from their eyes: "Then he turned away from them and wept; and he returned to them and spoke to them. And he took Simeon from them and bound him before their eyes" (42:24).

The return of their money is again ambiguous: a gift and yet possibly a trap (cf. the silver cup in the second journey to Egypt) and a further goad to their conscience. The final clause of 42:25 (literally "and he did for/to them thus") must leave the reader, with the brothers, still wondering: Just what has been done to them and why?

A change begins to appear by the second visit, apparent to the perceptive reader before it is to the brothers. Genesis 43:16 is revealing: "When Joseph saw Benjamin with them, he said to the steward of his house, 'Bring the men into the house, and slaughter an animal and make ready, for the men are to dine with me at noon.'" Seeing his full brother, he prepares to dine with them. And his first actual words spoken directly to them this time are an enquiry about their welfare ($\check{s}\bar{a}l\hat{o}m$) and then about their father (43:27). And lest the reader mistake this as simply continued calculation on his part—for there is a clear dimension of manipulation in his second reception of them as well—we are next told: "Then Joseph made haste, for his heart yearned for his brother, and he sought a place to weep. And he entered his chamber and wept there. Then he washed his face and came out; and controlling himself he said, 'Let food be served'" (43:30–31). However, it is for "his brother" that he wept, the reader is informed, and not yet for his brothers.

This second private glimpse into his inner life and feelings does not vitiate his ability to manipulate the situation and the brothers. This time he balances a warm reception with the previous one that was so ominous. Soon this leads to the apparent endangering of Benjamin, taken in "theft" of Joseph's silver divining cup.[12] And this provokes the fullest evidence of a change in the brothers, with Judah taking the lead in his plea for Benjamin's life for his old father's sake. Joseph's first public show of deep private emotion is the result. "Then Joseph could not control himself before all those who stood by him; and he cried, 'Make every one go out from me.' So no one stayed with him when Joseph made himself known to his brothers. And he wept aloud, so that the Egyptians heard it, and the household of Pharaoh heard it. And Joseph said to his brothers, 'I am Joseph; is my father still alive?' But his brothers could not answer him, for they were dismayed at his presence" (45:1–3). Emotion is expressed, but there is no loss of control. His identity is revealed in words that are artfully calculated to squeeze out the last measure of suspense and dread (45:4–5). One can easily imagine the long pauses between the phrases: "I am your

brother . . . Joseph, . . . whom you sold into Egypt . . . . And now do not
be distressed . . . " This drama he has staged is nicely played out for the
reader and the brothers right to the end.

Now his control is redirected first to placing the events in a new perspective (45:5–8), through a speech that ends with a clear statement of his
power: "So it was not you who sent me here, but God; and he has made
me a father to Pharaoh, and lord of all his house and ruler over all the
land of Egypt." He then exercises his authority in bringing his family to
Egypt. In time he orchestrates their appearance before Pharaoh and settlement in Goshen.

A final important glimpse of a changed Joseph is afforded in his
response to the brothers' last appeal to him. "His brothers also came and
fell down before him, and said, 'Behold, we are your servants.' But Joseph
said to them, 'Fear not, for am I in the place of God? As for you, you meant
evil against me; but God meant it for good, to bring it about that many
people should be kept alive, as they are today. So do not fear; I will provide
for you and your little ones.' Thus he reassured them and comforted them"
(50:18–21). He has clearly changed, even if his control remains absolute on
the human stage. He now recognizes, as the brothers in their own way did
much earlier (42:21–22; 44:16), that there is another, higher perspective on
the events of the human stage that cannot be ignored, even if it is not always
clearly perceived. This is a marked transformation in one who first appears
so powerless, and then so very powerful. He does not give up this power in
the end, but his exercise of it is now clearly constructive for all and is recognized as under still greater authority.

There is a marked tendency in study of the Joseph novella to avoid
critical assessment of the character of Joseph, insensitive as he appears in
the opening episodes of chapter 37 and in his treatment of his brothers and
father in chapters 42–44. In part no doubt due to the absence of clear suggestion from the narrator about this, we are left with his generally public
and carefully staged words and deeds. The reluctance to appear critical of
this figure may also arise from the quasi-allegorical interpretation of the
text that was characteristic of Christian use of the material for so long.[13]
Joseph represented Christ, beloved of his father, sent to his brothers,
betrayed for twenty pieces of silver, symbolically dead in the pit and in
Egypt, reappearing in renewed life as lord over his brothers and all the
earth. Interpretative strategies like this would foster the inclination to find
in biblical material stark villains and unsullied heroes. The full characters
in the Joseph novella simply do not fit easily into such a bimodal schema.

A rich collection of full characters is offered in this novella, and the reader is allowed to observe their development over time in interaction with each other and with events. They are finely drawn, etched in clear but not simplistic strokes. They are not two-dimensional or stereotypes. For each the reader is allowed some sympathy; yet each must also be viewed from some distance and with a critical eye. In their feelings and their deeds they are quite understandable, even if what they do cannot be condoned. We understand the brothers' feelings at the outset even if we cannot approve their actions. We extend sympathy to the father who loves and then grieves over the one son of his beloved wife. But we are also aware of the injustice in this parental favoritism, natural as it is. We see what it does to others. We later share the brothers' confusion and dread as circumstances (masterfully shaped by Joseph) close them in, but we cannot wholly repress the feeling that they really deserve so neat a reversal. In critical ways we are least drawn to Joseph, the spoiled young man and the victim, at the outset. And yet we cannot take our eyes off him for long. Like the brothers we come to an understanding and approval of him only over time, as over time we observe his growth as well.

NOTES

1. A. Berlin, *Poetics and the Interpretation of Biblical Narrative*, 23–42.
2. Donald B. Redford, *A Study of The Biblical Story of Joseph*, 144–45.
3. W. L. Humphreys, "A Life-Style for Diaspora: A Study in the Tales of Esther and Daniel," *JBL* 92 (1973): 211-23.
4. Unlike most agents she is named, no doubt to add verisimilitude to the narrative.
5. See pp. 201–205 below.
6. See pp. 137–39 below.
7. Robert Alter, *The Art of Biblical Narrative*, 74–75.
8. Alter, *Art*, 4–5, 22.
9. Alter, *Art*, 116–17.
10. In the larger context of the novella, the book of Genesis, Reuben, Leah's firstborn, has already disqualified himself as effective heir apparent. See Gen. 35:22 and cf. 49:3–5.
11. See pp. 35–36 above.
12. The return of their money this second time (44:1c) may be an addition to the text, based on the first experience. It plays no role in the accusations that follow and is, in fact, not referred to again. See Claus Westermann, *Genesis 37–50*, 131.
13. See Westermann, *Genesis 37–50*, 18.

FIVE

THE POETICS OF THE JOSEPH NOVELLA

RHETORICAL TECHNIQUES

A number of rhetorical techniques employed by the author of the Joseph novella have already been considered in the discussion of its genre, the plotting of the work, and its depiction of characters. Attention has been directed to the pacing of the story and to its episodic qualities; to the manner by which transitions are effected over both time and space; and to the balance of narrated and narrative time. The formative role of dialogue has been stressed in several instances as particularly revealing of character and as providing the focus for concentrating not just on events but on their meaning for the central figures in the novella. In this chapter further dimensions of the author's rhetorical repertoire will be considered, with particular attention given to the use of repetition within the novella, to the layers of narrative perspective that shape the reader's experience of the story, and to the role a disparity of knowledge plays in the development of the work.

REPETITION

In chapter 4 of his basic study *The Art of Biblical Narrative*, Robert Alter brings together a number of rhetorical devices employed in Hebrew narrative under the heading "repetition." These range from the strategic reuse of key words or motifs that bind together all or part of a unit and

93

underscore basic themes, through the repeating of a key phrase or sentence by both the narrator and a figure in the story, to the verbatim or near verbatim repeating of larger units, and on to the appearance more than once in extended units of basically the same scene or motif. All of these are found in the Joseph novella, and Alter has underscored a few of them.

He indicates that key words (*Leitworter* in the phrase coined by Martin Buber and Franz Rosenzweig) such as *kōl*, "all, every," and *bêt*, "house," are binding thematic devices in the encounter between Joseph and Potiphar's wife recounted in Genesis 39. We should also take note of the use of the verbal root *NKR*, "to recognize, to identify, to disguise oneself," in its several forms in 37:32–33 and 42:7a, 7b, 8, (cf. 38:25–26). There is also the term *kesep*, "silver, money," that which the brothers lost to the Midianites as Joseph was sold into Egyptian slavery (37:28, in the reading adopted above); that which was returned to them in their provisions at the close of their first journey to Egypt (42:25, 27, 28; see also 44:lc) and which rekindled their father's grief (42:35); and that which they take with them in double measure on the second journey (43:12, 18, 21–23). Joseph's goblet is of silver as well. It is also notable that after Joseph's self-disclosure he bestows gifts on his brothers and his father, giving to Benjamin not only five garments but also to him alone "three hundred shekels of silver" (45:22). And of course throughout the novella the terms *ben*, "son," and *'ah*, "brother," are used with telling and sometimes ironic effect, for example in the brothers' protests before their brother Joseph when accused of being spies: "'We are all sons of one man, we are honest men, your servants are not spies." He said to them, "No, it is the weakness of the land that you have come to see." And they said, "We, your servants, are twelve brothers, the sons of one man in the land of Canaan; and behold the youngest is this day with our father, and one is no more.'" (42:11–13). Clearly they say more than they intend in more than one way here.

Indicative of a quiet countermelody running throughout the composition is the use of the word *šālôm*, "harmony, peace, well-being." We are told in the last clause of the opening exposition that sets the stage for the novella that Joseph's brothers hated him and "could not speak peaceably (*lᵉšālôm*) to him" (37:4b). After the opening episode in which the dreams of the young Joseph are recounted and elicit characteristic reactions from his brothers and father, we find that Jacob sends Joseph to his brothers and instructs him: "Go now, see if it is well with (*rᵉʾēh ʾet šālôm*) your brothers, and well with (*'et-šālôm*) the flock." Translations, like the RSV here cited, often omit all indication of the second *šālôm* before flock and use different words to capture distinct nuances of *šālôm* in 37:5 and 37:14. While offering more natural English, they deny the reader the pleasure of recognized irony: Jacob, earlier blind to or unconcerned with the wider impact of his token of special favor bestowed on his youngest, now sends the favored one to look into the *šālôm* of just those with whom this emissary has absolutely no relationship of *šālôm*, as the narrator told us at the outset. What will take place is, of course, the antithesis of *šālôm*. In Egypt, just after he is summoned from prison to an audience before Pharaoh, Joseph responds to the ruler's request for an interpretation of his dreams with "It is not in me; God will give Pharaoh a favorable answer (*ya'ªneh 'et šālôm par'ōh*)" (41:16). However, the interpretation of the royal dreams do not anticipate *šālôm*, and it is Joseph's advice and his ability to execute it that will preserve *šālôm* in Pharaoh's Egypt. Later, as Joseph and his brothers meet face to face again on the second journey to Egypt for provisions, the conversation between these sons of Jacob who earlier could not speak to each other in *šālôm* opens with a veritable burst of *šālôm*s: He inquired of their welfare (*l'šālôm*), and said, "Is your father well (*hªšālôm 'ªbîkem*), the old man of whom you spoke? Is he still alive?" They answered, "Your servant our father is well (*šālôm*), he is still alive" (43:27-28). Finally, in a setting characterized by anything but *šālôm* for the brothers, Joseph addresses them with pretended fairness: "Only the man in whose hand the cup was found shall be my slave; but as for you, go up in peace (*l'šālôm*) to your father" (44:17). The quite conscious twist given to the term in this last use by Joseph simply underscores its use throughout as a counterpoint to the actual situation of this family throughout the novella. The term is used no more, for following Judah's extended plea and the climactic self-revelation by Joseph, *šālôm* is truly restored to the family and the counterpoint no longer serves a purpose. It is a nice touch that when *šālôm* is restored, the term is absent.

Repetition of apparent incidental bits of information, in literature in which incidental information is rare indeed, serves also to emphasize. For example, the opening line of the second episode in chapter 37 states that "his brothers went to pasture their father's flock near Shechem", (v. 12). His father's first words to Joseph in the next verse are, "Are not your brothers pasturing the flock at Shechem?" The repetition of the narrator's words by Jacob is not verbatim, but the double *bišekem*, ("in Shechem"), at first glance superfluous, serves to stress the great distance that separates the brothers to whom Joseph is being sent and the father who is sending him. Jacob is sending him to those who cannot speak to him in *šālôm*, who hate him, and who will be far from any restraining influence their father's presence might exert. This is followed by the chance encounter with the unnamed man in the fields of Shechem, which serves to remove the encounter still farther to the isolation of Dothan. Jacob's own words, which echo the narrator's, underscore his blindness to the wider impact or consequences of his own actions in sending his son on this mission. He could not set up his beloved son for trouble more effectively had he designed the situation for just this end, and the mode of narration nicely reinforces this.

Another small partial repetition reaches across a wide expanse of the narrative and once more seems at first glance to be gratuitous. The Ishmaelite caravan on its way to Egypt carries "gum, balm, and myrrh" (37:25), and will also carry Joseph, the youngest of the brothers. As Jacob supplies his sons for their second journey to Egypt, he instructs them to take not only "a little balm, gum, myrrh," but also some of the "choice fruits of the land, . . . a little honey, . . . pistachio nuts, and almonds." And of course they must also take their youngest brother, Joseph's surrogate, Benjamin. In their extreme uncertainty based on their experiences earlier in Egypt, they become a traveling scent and sweet shop. The repeated and augmented list, which may be simply a standard summary of goods in the caravan trade of the region, in this narrative becomes a quiet but apt comment on the state of mind of Jacob and of his sons as they prepare to return to Egypt.

Another motif that appears at several strategic points in the narrative involves clothing. There is, of course, the cloak (*kᵉtōnet passîm*) that is the token of Jacob's special love for his Joseph and the spur to the brother's hatred. The same cloak also is the instrument of the deceit (37:31–33) that Jacob is so ready to interpret in the most tragic manner. Again, Joseph's outer garment becomes evidence against him when abandoned in the hands of Potiphar's wife (39:12, 15–16, 18). (Items worn or carried by their owner also stand as tokens of identity in 38:18, 25). Joseph's sudden rise from cell to court is marked by a change of clothing (41:14). "Festal garments" are given by Joseph to his brothers—five for Benjamin—as he sends them home, knowing who he is, to return with their father and families (45:22). The specific terms are different (*kᵉtōnet passîm* in Gen. 37, *beged* in Gen. 39, *śimlāh*, with the verb *ḥalāp* in Gen. 41 and 45), but each use of apparel marks a key transition in the novella.

We have already noted the remarkable effect of the altered repetition of her contrived story on the characterization of Potiphar's wife.[1] We have also seen the subtle but telling additions by Pharaoh, as he related his dreams to Joseph, to the version already provided by the narrator.[2] In each of these cases we have the virtual repetition of a few clauses or a limited number of sentences in which minimal alteration provides telling touches of very effective characterization. The entire pattern of paired dreams is an additional example of a repeated motif in this material. It traces a path from the brief and transparent, in need of no interpreter (Joseph's in 37:5–11), to those of the chief butler and chief baker, which are fuller and which as interpreted seem clear enough (40:8–18), on to the complex dreams of Pharaoh, themselves repeated, which demand both interpretation and advice on how to meet the crisis foretold in the interpretation (41:1–36).

The largest example of repetition in the Joseph novella is found in chapters 42–44 in the paired journeys to Egypt undertaken by the brothers. Table 1 sets out points of connection which also serve as counterpoints that transpose each journey into a commentary on the other.

TABLE 1

STRUCTURE OF THE JOURNEYS TO EGYPT BY JOSEPH'S BROTHERS

Points	Gen. 42	Gen. 43–44
Initiation:		
Sent by Jacob	42:1–2	43:1–2, 11–12
Benjamin excepted/sent	42:4	43:3–10, 13–14
Journey by ten brothers	42:3, 5	43:15
First Audience with Joseph	42:6–16	43:15c–16a
Interlude: Prison/welcome	42:17	43:16b–25
Second Audience with Joseph	42:18–22	43:26–34
Joseph's private reaction	42:23–24	43:30–31
Interlude: Homecoming	42:25–28	44:1–13 (aborted)
Third Audience with Joseph	42:29–34 (anticipated)	44:14–34

97

The same fundamental structure clearly shapes the account of each journey, even as the specific elements of this structure serve often as contrasts to counterparts in the other account. Accounts that are structurally mirror images of each other tell of journeys that are in impact and in import very different in many ways. Each is initiated by the father, the first briefly and brusquely, the second with elaborate preparations that overcome the father's reluctance only with difficulty. In each Benjamin is noted as he is first excepted and then included. In the first it is stated that ten brothers went; in the second it is all too poignantly clear to the reader and the family that ten brothers set out for Egypt.

There are three audiences between the brothers and Joseph, either related or anticipated. The first, harsh and threatening in chapter 42, is summarily narrated in 43: 15c–16a. The interludes offer the contrast of imprisonment with the welcome into Joseph's establishment by his steward. In chapter 42 the second audience provides small relief for the brothers, as they are sent home without Simeon. The account of the second audience in chapter 43 continues the tone of the interlude, opening as it does with its burst of *šalôms*. The second audience is punctuated in each instance by a notice of Joseph's personal and private reaction to the words of his brothers. In both accounts the second audience ends with the return of the brothers' silver,[3] and on the second occasion the addition of a special gift for Benjamin (44:1–2). The interlude between the second and third audiences relates in chapter 42 a homecoming that is accomplished if troubled and in chapter 44 a homecoming that is aborted. The third audience is only anticipated in chapter 42 as the brothers tell their father of the reception they experienced and the conditions "the man" set for any future journey to Egypt. One knows that even in their anticipatory account of what befell them they hope never to make that trip again. As readers we know with Joseph that the famine will be of extended duration and trust that the supplies provided by Joseph were so measured out as not to last. They must seek the third audience in their second journey, for the homecoming is aborted; this leads to the further heightening of tensions just prior to the climax. Even on the level of word selection is this development across these journeys carefully revealed. In each case the brothers fulfill unintentionally Joseph's dreams of chapter 37 as they prostrate themselves before him. In 42:6 and 43:26, they "do obeisance to him" (*wayyištaḥªwû-lô*; RSV "bow themselves before him"/"bowed downed to him"). After the aborted return on the second journey, Judah and the others starkly "fall before him" (*wayyippelû lᵉpānāw*; see also

50:18). Homage gives way to fear; and with the niceties of formal respect stripped from them, the stage is set for the resolution.

The first journey, begun so ominously, promised total disaster for a time, but came to a conclusion in which provisions were obtained, their money returned, and only one brother held in "temporary" custody. The second journey began auspiciously, in spite of the brothers' fears, and then degenerated into disaster. The first journey clearly anticipates a second, and the second is experienced by reader and the family of Jacob in the light of the first. At this macroscopic level of repetition as well as at the more microscopic level of key words and repeated occasional phrases or sentences, we find a rich tonality provided through a technique that may seem at times inelegant to modern ears and too often therefore lost in translations. But it is through this rhetorical technique in its many forms that the author highlights, nuances, and shapes the narrative so that it provides commentary on itself.

NARRATIVE PERSPECTIVE

A story is always told from some perspective; sometimes more than one perspective is presented in the course of the telling. The perspective from which a story is told or written fundamentally shapes the reader's or hearer's experience of it. We have all encountered, for example, stories told from a third-person perspective and other stories told from a first-person perspective. In the one the narrator stands outside the viewpoint of any one of the characters and is able to tell us things they may not know, even things that none of them could know. At the outset of the book of Job, for example, the narrator is able to inform the reader not only about disasters that strike Job, but about the cause of them in a heavenly wager of a sort between Yahweh and that member of his divine council called the "Adversary" (Job 1–2). Not only events set on earth, but those in the heavens can be reported by this narrator. No point of view is impossible or hidden from the one who tells this tale. As readers we know from the outset information that Job and the others in the story (Yahweh excepted) will never know: Job is innocent, blameless, upright, fearing God and turning from evil. In a similar way the reader is told at the outset of the brief but poignant story of the near sacrifice of Isaac (Genesis 22) that God's motive behind his awful request is to test Abraham (22:1). Abraham and Isaac

99

do not share this knowledge with the reader, and the brief notice in the exposition clearly shapes in formative ways our experience of their story. The perspective of this type of narrator is rightly characterized as "omniscient."

Other stories are told from the point of view of one of their characters. "Call me Ishmael." So begins Herman Melville's novel *Moby-Dick*. The story, and all the other information given in the course of the novel, is related by this Ishmael, who is a member of the crew of the ill-fated whaler, the only one to survive its last voyage. In the novel itself he is a relatively minor figure, but it is essentially from his perspective that we encounter the events and other characters in Melville's classic. In the narrative material in the Hebrew Bible the only instance of first-person perspective is found in the memoirs of Nehemiah. Note the concluding plea: "Remember me, O my God, for good" (Neh. 13:31b). This work is sometimes called an "apologia," a defense of his life and actions on Jerusalem's behalf by one whose significant place in his people's history was also the source of some controversy.[4]

This distinction between a third- and a first-person point of view in narrative perspective presents the matter in its simplist form. Perspective is much more complex. In the case of the Joseph novella, even within what is overall the perspective of an objective omniscient narrator, it is quite possible for the material to be so shaped that we experience it through first one point of view and then another. While Joseph is clearly the center of attention in Genesis 37, we encounter him and the events that take place through the perspectives of the brothers, his father, even that unnamed man in the fields outside Shechem, but not from the point of view of Joseph. It is the schemings and the fears of the ten brothers that determine our perspective throughout their attack on their youngest brother. The narrative in no way invites us to experience the terror of the young man attacked by his older brothers, thrown into a pit and apparently left there, and then taken by others and sold into slavery.

A skilled author will draw on a range of rhetorical devices for shaping the reader's perception of the material related. The analogy of film is useful in discussions of this. Sometimes the camera may present a panorama that will take in much more than any figure within the filmed events could perceive. At other points the camera will zoom in on one figure for a close-up. At still others it will present events and other figures from the perspective of a particular individual within the story being filmed, the camera becoming his or her eyes, in effect. Thus we observe Joseph's approaching his brothers and danger from the perspective of these brothers as they first espy him from afar and immediately begin to hatch their plot against him. It is as if the camera is located amid the brothers and is trained on him in the distance as he slowly approaches. We do not see them but with them as they apparently are watching Joseph while their dialogue overlaps this shot, shaping the reader's perspectives in an effective manner. It is thus an especially telling touch that we are not permitted to experience the terrors of the young Joseph, for in a sense it is not his story yet. His attackers indeed could not permit even themselves that experience; it is only much later that they can even recall his pleas to them (Gen. 42:21). Our perspective as readers is governed and limited by the necessary hardening of the sensitivities of Joseph's brothers, as they in their efforts to put distance between themselves and their brothers must initially distance themselves psychologically. While he is in the pit, we are with them as they sit down to eat (37:25).

Extensive analysis of literary point of view has distinguished different kinds or levels of perspective.[5] There is, for example, what we have been concerned with in our example to this point: the point of view from which events are perceived. There is also what has been called the "conceptual" point of view—the attitudes, concepts, and general world view that shapes a reader's or hearer's perceptions of the figures and events in a narrative. Tension and very often irony are heightened in a story as the audience becomes aware of more than one conceptual point of view. For example, the recounting of the dreams of the young Joseph in the opening episode presents a potential perspective that is defined by a world view in which dreams are often significant, if sometimes cryptic, indicators of the future, a future shaped in part by forces above and beyond normal human control. In fact, these particular dreams are not all that cryptic. They suggest that the readers keep in mind that in this world the fate of individuals and families, and even of nations, is often the result of more complex interactions between human design and divine intent than is first apparent.[6] It is, of course, also possible to perceive these dreams with the brothers as but one more especially annoying example of a spoiled youth's conceited boasts and to dismiss them as such or allow them further to fuel the fires of hatred and jealousy. The tensions between these perspectives on Joseph's dreams will provide delightful irony later as the brothers unknowingly appear before Joseph in a posture that both recalls and fulfills the dreams (42:6, 9a; 43:26; 44:14; 50:18).

Another example of the shaping of a conceptional point of view that transcends the immediate narrative point of view is provided by the setting of the Joseph narrative within the book of Genesis, and even more broadly within the stock of Israelite literary motifs. The theme of a younger brother surpassing the elder is found not only in the families of both Abraham and Isaac, but also in the case of Gideon (Judg. 6:15), and David (1 Sam. 16:1–13). The introduction of a family torn by strife between brothers would recall this motif, which will become more and more apparent in the course of the narrative.

A third type or level of perspective can be designated the "interest" point of view. This defines perspective in terms of some character's benefit or disadvantage. For example, while the dreams of Joseph as related by him in the opening scene bring a broader conceptional point of view to the narrative as a whole, they also allow us to savor the marked disparity of interests among the central figures. For the brothers the dreams serve only as further goads for their jealousy and hatred. Jacob's interests are perceived as more complex in that he both rebukes Joseph (for relating the dreams?) and yet also "kept the saying in mind" (37:11). Joseph's interest is served as well in a boastful, if insensitive, self-inflation. It is, of course, the marked clash of interests revealed here that leads to the attack and deception in the latter part of the chapter, and even to the brother's impotence as they seek to comfort their grieving father (37:35). If, as has been suggested,[7] the first direct speeches of characters in a narrative can sometimes be especially revealing, we can further appreciate the opening episode of this novella as Joseph relates his dreams and his brothers and then his father respond. Joseph's first words are an account of dreams of greatness, and his first word is a command in the imperative, "Hear!" and this is hardly softened by the particle ná: "Hear this dream which I have dreamed." Command them he will, time and again. Their first words form a question: "Are you indeed to reign over us?" It is a question that has within it a statement of just what will come. It is offered rhetorically here; they expect no answer, and certainly not the one that will come. Yet their first words are a question, and in time they will face puzzlement that leads to fear. Jacob's first words are a question as well and they follow a narrated but not reported rebuke. His question seems less rhetorical, less scornful of the claim of the dreams, more open to wonder. His is a more complex position, and his first actual words reflect this. Perspectives in tension that reveal character are manifest in the opening speech of each figure.

It is not always possible or desirable to keep these three levels distinct. We have seen how they can interact in the account of Joseph's dreams. Yet an awareness of these three levels enriches our appreciation of the narrative and also allows us to trace on the plane of perspective its development. Broadly, the trajectory of this narrative from discord to harmony, from alienation to reconciliation, and from death to life, traces a gradual confluence within each level. We can now develop in more detail:

1) How the narrative moves from distinct perspectives on the figure of Joseph, shaped and controlled by others (his brothers, father, Potiphar and his wife, Pharaoh's courtiers, and Pharaoh), to a perspective defined by Joseph's perceptions of figures and events, and then to a more panoramic perspective that takes in the entire family as a unit that is whole and reconciled.

2) How the interests of these several family members, so set at odds at the outset as to spark nothing but discord, deceit, and potential death, slowly converge in a manner that fosters harmony, reconciliation, and life.

3) How the conceptional point of view first hinted at as Joseph recounts his dreams at the outset gradually becomes that shared by the several major figures in the narrative; that is, how a conceptional point of view, suggested to the reader to shape his or her perceptions of the story, becomes more and more that of the figures in this story as well. These developments in all three levels of perspective dovetail nicely with the trajectory of plot development and the unfolding of the central full characters within the novella.

We have already seen that from the opening episode Joseph is the center of attention, and that we first take in this focal figure from the perspective of the other figures in the story. His recounting of his dreams is bracketed by a summary of the brothers' reaction (37:5), by the actual responses of both brothers and his father (37:8, 10), and finally by an additional summary of the reactions of both (37:11). They are Joseph's dreams, but we receive them through others. We next watch him leave his father (37:14b) and approach his brothers through lenses that reflect the eyes first of the doting older man and then of the hate-filled older brothers. A very effective transition in this movement of Joseph from father to brothers, from love to hatred, is found in his brief encounter with the unnamed man in the fields outside of Shechem. Joseph is suspended for a moment, alone between father and brothers; but not quite alone, since we encounter him in a sort of swing of the camera angle through his meeting this man and being directed to his brothers near Dothan (37:15–17).

Joseph is at the center of our attention, but we are nevertheless not allowed to take in events from his perspective or to dwell on his feelings. We are not invited to empathize with Joseph by sharing his sense of isolation or fear as he approaches his brothers. As we have seen, his brothers' feelings are expressed time and again, both through their own words and actions and in the information contributed by the narrator. While Jacob's perceptions are less clear-cut and more varied, they too are signaled by his own words and deeds as well as by the narrator.

The same pattern holds as we move with Joseph to Egypt. It is from the perspective of the contented but unattentive Potiphar and then his attentive wife and finally the outraged Potiphar that we move through chapter 39. Joseph's position over the household of his master, his physical appeal (introduced at this point for the first time as he is observed by Potiphar's wife), and his comings and goings as he is about his tasks are all presented from the perspective of his lord's wife. The fact that she is not named and is identified always as "his lord's wife" also defines our perspective on her and her actions.

Joseph's descent from Potiphar's household to prison as an attendant to the courtiers held in detention, and then his remarkable rise to the position of vizier in Egypt, are recounted in a manner that keeps Joseph at the center of attention; at the same time the reader's attention continues to be defined by the point of view of someone else. Joseph's abilities are first introduced as they are perceived by the captain of the guard and prison keeper, and then by the chief butler and chief baker as he interprets their dreams. Thereafter he drops from narrative view, just as he is forgotten by the chief butler (40:23), only to reappear as he is recalled by this official when there is a need for a skilled interpreter of dreams (41:9–13). We are then allowed to view him in action as both interpreter and adviser only as Pharaoh and his court come to see and appreciate his abilities (41:37–38). We see him as Pharaoh values, elevates, and heaps honors on him (41:39–44). He becomes an Egyptian, the creation of the king. As he moves out over the land, the narrator takes a more panoramic view of the years of plenty and the years of famine, placing the actions of Joseph in this context (41:46–57).

In the midst of this we are given our first brief experience of Joseph's own point of view in 41:50–52, which tells of the birth of his sons. In his naming them we are allowed a brief glimpse of his perception of all that has happened. "Joseph called the name of the first-born Manasseh, "For," he said, "God has made me forget all my hardship and all my father's house." The name of the second he called Ephraim, "For God has made me fruitful in the land of my affliction'" (41:51–52). This first taste of Joseph's perspective is important in that it is jarring in context. All that has happened to Joseph, in chapter 41 at least, appears to have been positive: he moves in one day from prison to power and position. Now we recognize that there is another perspective, one not shaped by the conceptual world of Egypt and its royal court or even the interests of Joseph as an Eyptian official. This other perspective is shaped by the family in Canaan and by Joseph's absence, by his "father's house" and his "hardships" which make the land of his remarkable success also from this point of view the "land of my affliction." This becomes a brief foretaste of very basic changes in perspective that we will soon experience. We will take up the family's story once more, and we will take it up from a perspective shaped by the vantage point of Joseph, who is both brother and son as well as a powerful Egyptian, an official of Pharaoh. This first experience of the distinct perspective defined by the figure who to this point has been the center of attention will soon be repeated and enlarged.

The panoramic view of plenty followed by famine and of Egypt's readiness provides the transition from the extended account of Joseph's rise in the Egyptian court back to the story of the family of Jacob. In the opening episode Joseph was the center of attention; first of his father and then of his brothers as he was sent to report on them only to fall into and then out of their hands; now the brothers are the center of attention as they are sent by their father to Egypt and into the hands of Joseph. We watch them leave Canaan at their father's urging and come to Egypt and Joseph. Our perspective is markedly shaped by the fact that we as readers now share knowledge with Joseph that the others do not have. This determines how we must view all that transpires. As we once saw him through their eyes, we now see them through his. Indeed we are allowed to step aside with Joseph on several occasions to share privately in his point of view (42:8–9a; 42:23–24a; 43:30–31). We share Joseph's perspective because we know the identity of this ominous and powerful official they encounter. This is the case in spite of the fact that we do not fully understand or share his motives; that is, we cannot share wholly in his interests. Narrative and interest perspective diverge at this point, and with regard to the latter we are in important ways more in the position of the puzzled brothers. This gives more complexity and a richer texture to chapters 42–45 than is apparent in what has come before.

There are, of course, points in the narrative now when attention centers on the brothers or on them and their father and Joseph is physically absent. But as "the man" he is always present as a conscience-goading memory, and as the "dead" son as a grief-provoking memory. We continue to share at times the perspectives of both father and brothers as we had earlier. But in Egypt it is Joseph's perspective that defines the narrative for the reader right up to its resolution in 45:1–15. Indeed, our knowledge of who "the man, the lord of the land" (42:30, 33) and "the man" (43:3, 6, 14) is shapes our perspective in the dialogue between Jacob and his sons in Canaan between journeys to Egypt.

At the resolution, as knowledge withheld is now shared, the perspective becomes more panoramic, and we take in Joseph from the brothers' point of view even as we continue to take them in with him. In the lengthy speech of Judah that leads up to the resolution the perspective widens. We perceive these sons of Jacob as changed when we are allowed in Judah's words to share their new perception of their father and his attachment to his youngest son. As the family becomes reunited in reconciliation, we can step back to take them all in as a unit. No longer are they divided by hatred, deceit, or disparity of knowledge.

As the brothers and then Joseph and Jacob are reunited in Egypt, the narrative broadens to encompass them all and to take in all that happens from their distinct but no longer discordant points of view. Through genealogy, in blessing, and in further narrative we now perceive the whole family and the family as a whole. The development of this trajectory in the narrative point of view first places Joseph at the center of attention only as others perceive him; then events and others from Joseph's point of view; finally moving to a more panoramic perspective. All this parallels exactly the trajectory of the novella's plot.

This pattern in narrative perspective and the parallel plot trajectory is mirrored in the development of interest points of view in the novella as well. At the outset the interests of the major figures are wholly at odds, in that actions or events which serve one counter those of others. Jacob's demonstrations of love for Joseph spark the hatred of his other sons for their youngest brother; Joseph's recital of his self-serving dreams provokes enhanced jealousy and hatred in his brothers and troubles his father enough to make him rebuke his favorite. The brothers' attempt to rid themselves of Joseph clearly cuts to their father's heart. A family torn by discord at the outset of the novella is further rent by deceit at the end of the opening episodes, as actions and events that serve one interest undercut others.

In the interlude in Egypt, with the rise of Joseph, new interests emerge; again several are served, sometimes in harmony, sometimes in discord. Thus both Joseph's interests (in part) and those of Pharaoh and Egypt are served in his elevation and success in Egypt (see especially 47:13–26). Joseph's interest is furthered in time, as is that of the chief butler, through his interpretation of the latter's dream. On the other hand, the interests of Potiphar's wife and Joseph are clearly counter, and Joseph's success in interpreting the baker's dream serves to reinforce the impression held of his skill, but not the interests of the dreamer. Joseph's own interests, in fact, are not as clear now (see 41:50–52), but his power is greatly enhanced. This is the critical new factor present as we take up the family's story once more, and is effectively presented as the brothers come under his control, whereas before he was thrust into their power.

The famine provides a second new factor. The interests of the brothers and of their father are now complicated by their need to ensure the family's survival. This is clearest in the scenes involving the brothers and their father between the trips to Egypt. The underlying interests and tensions are vastly complicated by the need for food. The father cannot have that need met and retain his new youngest son. Judah makes this clear when he indicates that others, including young children, face starvation: "Send the lad with me, and we will arise and go, that we may live and not die, both we and you and also our little ones" (43:8). The nexus of attachments and claims of "little ones" is a web that entangles Jacob and the brothers whichever way they turn. The brothers can obtain needed supplies only by taking into their control another son and brother favored by their father. The uncertainty about the motives of the strange but powerful Egyptian, "the man, the lord of the land," who has shown such an unusual and ominous interest in the affairs of this family provides additional lines of tension in this complex of competing interests. It is this matrix of tensions that underlies the finely wrought surface of Judah's long speech on behalf of Benjamin, his father, and the family in 44:18–34. Here the tension reaches its apex, either to be resolved or to break their lives and the family itself finally apart.

The result is, of course, resolution. The interests of the brothers and of Joseph have changed, even if their perception of this is slow in coming (see 50:15–18). The family members can work together to bring their father and wives and children to Egypt, to secure a place of settlement of

Goshen, and brothers can act together as they bury their father in the homeland upon his death. In Joseph's final words it is the larger fate of the family that is in view, and his own personal destiny beyond death is linked to theirs in a charge to them that is also a statement of trust: "And Joseph said to his brothers, 'I am about to die; but God will visit you, and bring you up out of this land to the land which he swore to Abraham, to Isaac, and to Jacob.' Then Joseph took an oath of the sons of Israel, saying, 'God will visit you, and you shall carry up my bones from here' " (50:24–25). The convergence of interests models once more the trajectory of the plot and mirrors the developmental shifts of narrative perspective.

All of this is informed by developments in the conceptional point of view. Considering the words, deeds, and events of the novella from the perspective of whose interest is served or countered is perhaps the narrowest point of view that can be assumed. Narrative perspective serves at times to widen the circle, especially as we move from the perspective defined by one of the figures in the story to a more panoramic perspective. From the opening episode there are hints of a wider interest or point of view within which the words, deeds, and events of this story can be perceived. It is in the gradual unfolding of this into a shared clarity (shared by Joseph and his brothers; shared by Joseph and the reader) that we can understand how the first dreams of Joseph and then of others and then the gropings toward understanding shape the largest conceptional world within which the novella is experienced. The path from Joseph's first dreams, which could be nothing more than the boasts of a spoiled youth, through later dreams, on to recollection of the first, the guilty reflections of the brothers, and finally to Joseph's remarks on God's purpose underlying their own story, is very long indeed. In its development, which once more parallels the trajectory of plot, and in other types of point of view, we discover theological dimensions in a narrative that on first reading seems remarkably laconic in its reference to the deity.

DISPARITY OF KNOWLEDGE

Fundamental in the unfolding of the Joseph novella is a disparity of knowledge and the power that knowledge brings. Joseph appears from the outset as trading in knowledge, bringing to his father malicious tales concerning his brothers and boasting of dreams he has received that clearly magnify him. In the Near East, before the Common Era, dreams bore a potential significance that was immediately recognizable. Not only did they give some insight into the dynamics of a human character (which they are still perceived as doing), but they gave insight, sometimes cryptic and in need of interpretation, into the future. Dreams and knowledge went hand in hand; and when in need of interpretation dreams went hand in hand with power and its use by the interpreter as well. It is when faced by the future that human knowledge so often finds most markedly its limits, and it is the future that so often thwarts the exercise of human power. To tap into the future is to extend one's power and control of others. Thus Joseph's tale-bearing and his boastful reporting of his dreams tell us something important about him, and also develop in the reader and those in the narrative a disposition to hear hints of the future. There is an imbalance in the scene depicted at the outset of the narrative: the boastful, self-centered, and spoiled youth is also the one to whom significant dreams come, and to whom in time will come the ability to interpret dreams of others as well as the cunning to use that ability to good effect.

Joseph's dreams seem boastful as he relates them; and they reinforce both his brothers' hatred, fed by envy, and an ambivalence in his father. The second dream elicits Jacob's rebuke and incredulous question: "What is this dream that you have dreamed? Shall I and your mother and your brothers indeed come to bow ourselves to the ground before you?" (37:10). But we are also told in the summary contrast (37:11) that whereas Joseph's brothers hated and were jealous of him—no surprise there—Jacob "kept the saying." The import of his father's response is not as clear; on the one hand this doting father would no doubt keep any and every memory of this precocious favorite of his; on the other he could have found in these dreams, however disquieting and upsetting of domestic harmony they might have been, some important hints as to what the future had in store. Certainly this notice reinforces for the reader the suspicion that we have more here than simply reflections of a boy spoiled by special attention that feeds grandiose visions. This is more than telling tales on siblings.

The predictability of the brothers' response in the summation also underscores for us that the impact of knowledge in a narrative is shaped by the disposition of the characters toward each other and events. Three times we have been told they hated him, and once that they could not say a civil word to him. Their malice is no surprise, and it prepares us both for the course of action they will later undertake and for their sarcastic reference to their brother when he falls into their power as "master" or "lord of dreams" (*ba ʿal haḥᵃlōmôt*; "this dreamer" of the RSV captures the sarcasm nicely, but not the irony in their use of *ba ʿal*). Joseph will in time truly demonstrate his mastery of dreams and, through them, of so much more. Sarcasm leads to action, to attempts to fix the future by ridding themselves of this thorn in their flesh. They will, they believe, shape the future for themselves—dreams or no dreams—as they jettison Joseph: "And we shall see what shall become of his dreams" (37:20). Confidence shades over into a certain desperation as they must begin to scramble; Reuben to deliver him from the others; Judah to avoid bloodshed and turn a profit; all finally to deceive their father. Shaping the future proves not to be such an easy task.

Joseph's attitude toward the dreams of which he boasts is not wholly clear either. Indeed, as we have seen, throughout the opening episodes we have no narrative report of his thoughts and feelings, and this is in marked contrast to both his brothers and father. How much weight, for example, Joseph placed on his dreams is not clear. His brothers dismiss them and attempt to dismiss him; his father "keeps" them. Of Joseph's stance we know nothing, and are not even told that he remembered them until much later (42:9).

A disparity in what is known, which is rooted in different emotional attitudes toward what all see and hear, is now deepened through deceit. Joseph's brothers fabricate a scene that will allow—without their ever actually saying so—Jacob to presume Joseph torn apart by a wild beast. Just as they were primed through envy and hatred to dismiss Joseph's dreams, so Jacob is primed by excessive love quickly to fear the worst and then to an excessive expression of his grief. The brothers know Joseph was not torn apart by a wild animal. Having lost him to others, they seem rid of him, and now have knowledge which Jacob lacks. They, of course, know no more of Joseph's actual fate; but they are at least rid of him. We might note in Genesis 38 counterpoints to these themes in the Joseph story. Judah seeks to rid himself of a difficult situation, only to find himself deceived when he acts as if he knew more than he indeed knows. As a deceiver he is deceived; deceit always involves this disparity in knowledge.

Dreams stand at the center of Joseph's timely rise to power in Egypt. The knowledge they provide of the future and the ability to use this knowledge shrewdly bring Joseph to the most powerful post in the land of his imprisonment. The route is not smooth, for there is a false start and a pause. His success in interpreting the dreams of the chief butler and chief baker is demonstrated soon enough by events, but in spite of his plea to be remembered, he is forgotten (40:23). Only when Pharaoh has dreams of his own will Joseph be remembered and recalled from prison. This time his interpretive skills serve him well, for upon the interpretation and the important piece of intelligence about the future the dreams reveal, he is able to build a careful plan of action. His shrewdness so impresses Pharaoh and his court that Joseph is immediately authorized to execute his plan and is given the power and position from which he does so. Joseph here uses knowledge and the potential power it holds to good effect, shaping his own life and benefiting Egypt and its ruler.

We have encountered three sets of paired dreams in this material. The first, his own, are the simplest and in no need of interpretation. His brothers readily perceive their import and take action to counter what they imply as soon as the opportunity arises, and the result sends Joseph to Egypt and servitude. The second pair is more complex, but still clear enough. Joseph provides interpretation but no advice, for none is called for. The third are the most complex—indeed almost baroque—and both demand interpretation and also provide the occasion for advice based on it. The movement from short to long, from simple to complex, and from self-evident to needing interpretation, follows a path into greater depth and disparity in knowledge and power. The reversal of the situation set out in chapter 37 is complete by the end of chapter 41. Now Joseph has the knowledge and great power the brothers lack, and they come unwittingly into his hands.

As his brothers reappear, the deceivers are of course deceived; the future proves more elusive to human manipulation than they supposed. Driven by famine to find sustenance in Egypt, they stand in the presence of the one whose famine relief program gives him absolute power. The disparity of power—petitioners from the outlands stand before the most powerful official in the most powerful land on earth—is accented by the disparity of knowledge:

> Now Joseph was governor over the land; he it was who sold to all the people of the land. And Joseph's brothers came, and bowed themselves before him with their faces to the ground. Joseph saw his brothers, and knew them, but he treated them like strangers and spoke roughly to them. "Where do you come from?" he said. They said, "From the land of Canaan, to buy food." Thus Joseph knew his brothers, but they did not know him. And Joseph remembered the

dreams which he had dreamed of them; and he said to them, "You
are spies, you have come to see the weakness of the land." (42:6–9)

The brothers find themselves in fact in a Kafkaesque situation. Joseph's
recollection of his dreams leads immediately to his accusation that they
are spies. The logic of 42:9 is psychological; its formal disjunction underscores their shock at the charge leveled against them by this very powerful
man. Protests of innocence include more information than is called for.
Charges without apparent foundation are arbitrarily repeated (42:14),
and then the brothers are imprisoned. An arbitrary accusation is followed
by a defense and then renewed accusation, and prison is followed by
release and a test. The logic of all this is not clear on a formal level;[8] it is
the psychological logic of guilt that binds it together. That and the
reader's experience of knowing what Joseph knows and what the brothers
do not know shape the unit as a whole. Having many years before set
Joseph, their brother, in mortal danger, the brothers now find themselves
inexplicably placed in just such a situation. The entire scene is infused
with their disorientation as they move from Canaan to Egypt, from this
imposing official's establishment to prison, from prison to official audience
again, from Egypt to the discovery in the encampment en route to home,
and then home to their still grieving father.

In a second audience Joseph trades on the one piece of information
he gained from them in the first encounter. Jacob is not only alive, but
Joseph has a younger brother. Earlier their announcement of this had
been arresting: "We, your servants, are twelve brothers" (42:13). We as
readers, learn of this before Joseph, for in the preparation for the journey
Benjamin is mentioned as exempted from the dangerous trip (42:4). They
were eleven when Joseph last was with them, and he might well expect
them to reduce that number by one and not increase it. He demands the
presence of the "twelfth" as the condition for any future return to Egypt:
"Bring your youngest brother to me; so your words will be verified, and
you shall not die" (42:20). The brief "and they did so" is ironically anticipatory. Indeed they will do so, but clearly it is not their present intent to
do so. To be free of Egypt, even if they must jettison another brother,
seems all they can now hope for. We must remember that they, unlike
Joseph, do not know the duration of the famine. Joseph knows that it will
last seven years and can assure that the provisions they receive will be
depleted before the famine has run its course. Knowledge is power, power
to shape the future lives of others if used shrewdly.

Before the ten leave Egypt the first time, we are allowed to eavesdrop with Joseph on their private musings. In fact, we hear them speak of something omitted in the narrative report of the earlier scene in which they sought to rid themselves of their youngest brother. They now remember that he cried out in distress to them, but they would not heed him. In chapter 37 the center of attention was on them, and the victim remained silent. Now in their recollection of the event Joseph comes to dominate with his pleas, just as he now so effectively dominates them through his knowledge and shrewd manipulation of them, knowledge that they seem unable to do anything but augment: "They did not know that Joseph understood them, for there was an interpreter between them" (42:23). As earlier, when the narrator underscored the fact that Joseph recognized them but they did not recognize him (42:7–8 with the *Leitwort NKR* in several forms), now the difference between his position and theirs is again underscored through the incidental mention of the translator between them. All along they have spoken indirectly through this intermediary.

In a world of dislocations and disjunctions, in this Kafkaesque context designed by Joseph, even apparent good fortune is not to be trusted. "What is this that God has done to us?" they ask each other as they discover their payment for supplies in their sacks at a lodging on the journey home (42:26–28). It is a question filled with potential whose dimensions will unfold only in time. They seem to recognize that they move in a matrix of forces that are beyond their ken or control. Already they recognize this in language that is not yet explicitly theological, as they acknowledge their guilt with regard to their brother, a point which Reuben effectively, if with characteristic lack of refinement, drives home: "And Reuben answered them, 'Did I not tell you not to sin against the lad? But you would not listen. So now there comes a reckoning for his blood' " (42:22). On the journey home the language becomes overtly theological: "What is this that God has done to us?" Only in time will the fuller meaning of the action of God become clear, and it will include a world that is considerably larger than their "us."

As they return home and relate in their own way the substance if not the whole tenor of their strange encounter with "the man, the lord of the land", the reader is reminded of the levels of knowledge that shape this narrative and his or her experience of it. Jacob seems to know least. His ten sons know they have deceived him, and they can assume that Joseph is gone, even if his exact fate is not known. They do not know that Joseph has staged all that befell them in Egypt and on the return. Joseph, of course, knows all they know and much more. We share most of this with him as readers. But we do not know yet just what his motives are in the game he plays with them. Where does he stand in his use of power over others, and in relation to the "God" he spoke of so easily in chapter 41 and of whom the brothers spoke on their way home? Are his godlike powers over them to be set in a still larger realm of power, intent, and knowledge?

The brothers could well assume they will not have to return to Egypt, especially as Jacob now declares Simeon lost like Joseph. Joseph knows that they will, and he is ready. Return they do, to further dislocation and disjunction. We have seen that the two journeys stand as counterpoints to each other. Harshly accused at the outset of the first visit, they are now warmly received. Once secure in hope of gaining food, they are now afraid. Jolted out of security before, they are now lulled into trust. Formerly seeming to know so little, they now find they face puzzles again. They deny knowledge of how their payment was returned to their sacks, and Joseph's steward denies all knowledge of the business, saying he received their payment. And he does so in words that retain the theological tones of their earlier words: "He replied, 'Rest assured, do not be afraid; your God and the God of your father must have put treasure in your sacks for you; I received your money.' Then he brought Simeon out to them," (43:23). The circles of knowledge seem to widen to take in another, still undefined. They dine with Joseph, who shows not only a quite different attitude toward them, but further knowledge as he seats them according to the protocol demanded of age, but then honores the youngest (his full brother) with the largest portion (43:33–34; cf. 1 Sam. 9:22–24). Their amazement is quite understandable, but their merry-making is not to last. The return of their money and placement of the silver cup, the pursuit by Joseph's steward, the accusation and protestations of innocence, the search and discovery, and their return to Egypt—all thrust them back in the Kafkaesque world of the first visit.

The tension reaches resolution as Joseph discloses his identity and then assures them of his good intentions toward them. We have already seen how this is drawn out. At first, even as they know who he is, they still do not know how he is disposed to them, and they have every reason to fear his vengeance. The reader is not much better off in this regard, having only hints of a changed disposition in Joseph's rare demonstrations of emotion, so carefully kept private (42:24; 43:30). Throughout we have viewed these journeys from the perspective of, and with the knowledge of, Joseph. We share his knowledge in all but this critical factor of his motive—how finally will he treat them? Thus the reader can both squirm, as the brothers do in their profound discomfort when faced with these latest dislocations, and also appreciate the irony in their protests of innocence and plea for the release of the "guilty" Benjamin. And we must appreciate that once again they find themselves discomforted by a youngest brother and faced with the temptation and opportunity to rid themselves of him.

In time they come to know all that Joseph knows, as will Jacob soon after. And we come to know Joseph's intentions as well. But as Joseph informs them of all in a speech of reassurance, he also defines a level of meaning that transcends any shaped by the intentions and actions of the human actors in this novella. An overarching providence whose designs are the preservation of life, and especially that of his family, is now uncovered behind all human actions:

> And now do not be distressed, or angry with yourselves, because you sold me here; for God sent me before you to preserve life. For the famine has been in the land these two years; and there are yet five years in which there will be neither plowing nor harvest. And God sent me before you to preserve for you a remnant on earth, and to keep alive for you many survivors. So it was not you who sent me here, but God; and he has made me a father to Pharaoh, and lord of all his house and ruler over all the land of Egypt. Make haste and go up to my father and say to him, "Thus says your son Joseph, God has made me lord of all Egypt; come down to me, do not tarry." (45:5–9)

In this striking speech not only is Joseph linked firmly and consistently with the action of the God who sent him to and empowered him in Egypt, but with verse 10 Joseph describes himself as the architect of his family's fortunes in a transition from God to himself so smooth that it reinforces this bond:

> You shall dwell in the land of Goshen, and you shall be near me, you and your children and your children's children, and your flocks, your herds, and all that you have; and there I will provide for you, for there are yet five years of famine to come; lest you and your household, and all that you have, come to poverty. And now your eyes see, and the eyes of my brother Benjamin see, that it is my mouth that speaks to you. You must tell my father of all my splendor in Egypt, and of all that you have seen. Make haste and bring my father down here. (45:10–13)

From God to Joseph, from an overarching providence to Joseph's splendor and position as "father to Pharaoh": whatever Egyptian titular may stand behind this title, it is important that Joseph's position as father to the god-king of Egypt stand at the center of this speech. Joseph's earlier power to see into the future, as a master of dreams and then as a diviner (44:5, 15), has already set him in a sphere of knowledge and power beyond that of most mortals, including all the established authorities of Egypt. Joseph's declarations on providence serve to underscore the more subtle undertones of the earlier references to retribution and to the deity found in the words of the brothers and of Joseph's steward. He now clearly defines an even higher sphere of knowledge and power that can take up human actors and deeds. But what of Joseph's relation to that sphere?

It is not until the denouement that this is resolved, once more in the words of Joseph himself. After Jacob's death and burial, as the brothers approach him in their lingering suspicions, he responds to their entreaty with these words: "Fear not, for am I in the place of God? As for you, you meant evil against me; but God meant it for good, to bring it about that many people should be kept alive, as they are today. So do not fear; I will provide for you and your little ones" (50:19–21). These words are not only significant as a type of motto for the novella stressing a hidden but pervading providence that directs all things for human good; they also show Joseph's own recognition that he is not in God's place—in spite of his godlike splendor, his manipulation of his brothers and father, and his authority now to preserve the family. He is not God or in God's place. There is a sphere of knowledge and power that can envelop even him. At the end disparity in knowledge and its attendant power is resolved, and with it the family is united. The novella has developed about a carefully structured disparity in knowledge defined in several layers: that of Jacob, that of the brothers, that of the reader, that of Joseph, and that first just hinted at which will come to be seen encompassing them all. It is as these layers come finally together in shared knowledge and understanding that the novella's complications and tensions find resolution. The widest layer of knowledge is profoundly theological; thus it is to the theological dimensions of the novella that we must next turn.

NOTES

1. See above, pp. 71–72.

2. See pp. 74–75 above.

3. Possibly a later addition in Gen. 44:1; see ch. 4 n. 12, above.

4. Some first-person narration is found in prophetic material as well; e.g., the call of Isaiah (Isa. 6), and Hosea's account of his (re?)marriage (Hos. 3).

5. See A. Berlin, "Point of View in Biblical Narrative," in *A Sense of Text: The Art of Language in the Study of Biblical Literature*, 71–113.

6. See ch. 6 below on the theology of the novella. It should be observed that at no point does the narrator directly tell us something that radically alters our perspective on this level. Cf. such narrator intrusion as found in the Succession Narrative in 2 Sam. 11:27b; 12:24b; 17:14b.

7. See Robert Alter, *The Art of Biblical Narrative*, ch. 4, on the use of speech in Hebraic narrative.

8. See above, pp. 43–44.

SIX

THE THEOLOGICAL VISION OF
THE JOSEPH NOVELLA

Set in its context in the Torah as a bridge between the patriarchal stories in the book of Genesis and the account of Israel's deliverance from bondage in the opening segments of the book of Exodus, the Joseph novella seems remarkably sparing in overt references to the deity, either by the name Yahweh, the generic "God" (ʾelōhîm), or other titles or allusions. This lack of indirect reference to the deity and the deity's apparent absence from center stage in the novella set this work apart from material that surrounds it. For throughout much of the rest of Genesis and Exodus reference to the deity is boldly direct in almost every segment or episode: God is the prime mover and shaker within this cosmos he created. There is no doubt as to who delivers Israel from Egypt with dramatic signs and wonders, and the brief summary of this event at the core of Deuteronomy 26:5–9 is an accurate reflection of the larger tradition: "Then we cried to the Lord the God of our fathers, and the Lord heard our voice, and saw our affliction, our toil, and our oppression; and the Lord brought us out of Egypt with a mighty hand and an outstretched arm, with great terror, with signs and wonders; and he brought us into this place and gave us this land, a land flowing with milk and honey" (Deut. 26:7–9).

Both Abraham and Jacob have very direct encounters with the deity, who is recognized in the stories about them as the formative force shaping their lives. And, in the prehistory found in the first eleven chapters of Genesis, God's presence in creation or in life-sustaining blessing or in curse is undeniable at every stage.

Whole episodes within the Joseph novella, however, pass without mention of the deity or with just the most formulaic reference on the lips of one character or another. With the exception of chapter 39—which seems to stand apart from the remainder of the material for just this reason—and the notice of the night vision that inaugurated Jacob's descent into Egypt and reunion with his son Joseph (46:1–4), the narrator makes no direct mention of the deity. The few references to God are all spoken by some figure in the novella. In spite of this, a remarkably sophisticated theological vision pervades the Joseph novella, one that develops a final nuanced understanding of events in the human sphere and their interaction with the divine. Indeed it is the very nature of those references to the deity, almost exclusively on the lips of central characters, that shape this theological vision. It does not emerge from direct observations by the narrator.

The theological characteristics of the Joseph novella are distinctive in the interplay between this work and the context within which it is set. For the infrequency and particular quality of reference to the deity in this material becomes most apparent within criteria defined by the context that provides its present setting in the Torah. It is only as it is set in the midst of material in which God is ever present—and usually front and center—often in the most dramatic and earth-shaking manner, that the distinctive features of this novella emerge. This context shapes the way in which we appreciate the novella and its theological dimensions. In a context shaped by material steeped in a vision of ever-present and effective divine intervention in human events, in one conditioned to see the hand of God in all that is fortuitous or untoward, the remarkable series of ups and downs, of reversals and counterreversals, that form the plot of the Joseph novella must also be read as indications of the guiding presence of the deity, even if overt attention is not always called to this. The God who preserved Abraham in his initial blundering into Egypt in the face of famine; the God who secured Jacob in his long sojourn with kinfolk outside the land of promise, in spite of his deeds or misdeeds, surely could and would preserve this family in their self-inflicted trials. Readers and hearers of the book of Esther who are steeped in the traditions that shape the celebration of Passover have not failed to attribute to God the deliverance of the Jews from Haman's pogrom simply because the deity is not directly mentioned in that book (see Esth. 4:14). So those steeped in the Israelite traditions would be primed to see God's providential care reaching across the pages of the Joseph novella. The Israelite reader of the Joseph novella would not need to be convinced of God's active shaping of the story of this family. The issue would be the particular perspective on this that the novella permits, the special dimensions of Israel's theological self-understanding developed therein.

But why then is not a divine presence more clearly and directly depicted? Why no oracles, divine promises, epiphanies, miracles? Or why is it only in the account of Joseph's rather brief interlude in the house of Potiphar that we are told—seven times no less—that "Yahweh was with Joseph, and Yahweh caused all that he did to prosper in his hands"? Even here we should note that these references are confined to the exposition before the central event and dialogues of Genesis 39 are narrated, and to the material following its denouement that links it with the next episode (39:21-23). From the moment we, with his master's wife, lay eyes on Joseph and take note of his physical appeal (39:6b), through his confinement in prison (39:20)—that is, throughout the central events of the episode—the only mention of the deity is on the lips of Joseph. It concludes his rather extended rejection of the blunt invitation by Potiphar's wife: "How then can I do this great wickedness, and sin against God?" (39:9).

In important ways this reference by Joseph to God is characteristic of others in the narrative. We can compare Joseph's words to his brothers on their first journey to Egypt, after he had all ten of them confined in prison for three days: "Do this and you will live, for I fear God" (42:18; thinking him Egyptian, they might have wondered what god this was, but they already faced enough confusion). On one level this can be taken as little more than a general recognition that some sort of all-pervading justice shapes the cosmos and that the deeds of men and women must be in harmony with it if they are to prosper—an idea akin to contemporary allusions to fate. To act in certain ways is to go counter to the will of the divine sustainer of cosmic order. These words are not necessarily reference to a particular deity or to the deity as understood within a specific tradition. They sound no more strange on the lips of a Hebrew slave (39:9) than they do coming from the vizier, the most powerful official in Egypt next to Pharaoh, or later from that vizier's steward (43:23). In fact, we will find Pharaoh himself using such words as he takes note of Joseph's particular skill as a dream interpreter and as a counselor: "And Pharaoh said to his servants, "Can we find such a man as this, in whom is the Spirit of God?" So Pharaoh said to Joseph, "Since God has shown you all this, there is none so discreet and wise as you are; you shall be over my house, and all my people shall order themselves as you command; only as regards the throne will I be greater than you," (41:38–40). There is an especially nice touch here in that the reference to the "Spirit of God" (*rûaḥ ʾelōhîm*), like the mention of "the God of your father" by Joseph's steward (43:23), is put on the lips of Egyptians, for all their more Israelite of Hebraic ring, while the more general references to God are placed on the lips of Israelites from Palestine.[1] Egyptians, in this material at least, seem particularly sensitive to the religious niceties of their visitors.

We must take particular note of the several comments by Joseph describing the relation of dreams and their interpretation to the deity. In prison Joseph opens his offer to interpret the dreams of the detained and quite troubled royal officials with, "Do not interpretations belong to God?" (40:8b). More expansively in his initial encounter with Pharaoh, Joseph links both dreams and their interpretation with the deity. Dreams come from the deity as indication of what is to come, and the interpretation of them is also under the authority of the deity.

> And Pharaoh said to Joseph, "I have had a dream, and there is no one who can interpret it; and I have heard it said of you that when you hear a dream you can interpret it." Joseph answered Pharaoh, "It is not in me; God will give Pharaoh a favorable answer." . . .
> Then Joseph said to Pharaoh, "The dream of Pharaoh is one; God has revealed to Pharaoh what he is about to do." . . . "And the doubling of Pharaoh's dream means that the thing is fixed by God, and God will shortly bring it to pass." (Gen. 41:15–16, 25, 32)

On one level, as suggested above,[2] these statements might be little more than elements in the protocol of ancient Near Eastern dream interpretation, especially serving as formulaic language that sets the dream and its meaning apart from the interpreter. This would be particularly to the point when the dream and its interpretation signaled ill tidings, for in the face of bad news powerful people can mistake messenger and message and react as if the one were responsible for the other. This formulaic invitation to relate the dream and then prefacing its interpretation with notice of the divine source for both helps keep this distinction clear to all concerned.

Set within the entire novella, however, these bits of protocol cannot remain simply on this level. As we have seen, from the first dreams of Joseph himself as a youth, there are hints that the events in the lives of this family are to be comprehended within ever larger circles of knowledge and assessed from perspectives that appear ever to widen out to take in all of them and much more. In these brief and apparently confined references to God by Joseph and others, suggestions of these larger spheres of significance accumulate and grow in importance. By chapter 42, when the brothers (save their now youngest sibling) are reunited in circumstances so ironically the reversal of those of their last time together, we view them from not simply the perspective of what they know but also from that wider perspective of what they know not. It is just at this point that Joseph, who has by now shown mastery of the dreams of others, recalls his own dreams of so many years ago (42:9). By now we also are coming to realize that all dreamers are themselves caught up in a context shaped by the deity and that the comprehension of that context may come only with time, for "interpretations belong to God." This can lead to the growing recognition and appreciation of remarkable reversals and dramatic changes in fortune as under divine sway. Joseph suggests this regarding his fortunes as he names his sons: "Joseph called the name of the first-born Manasseh, "For," he said, "God has made me forget all my hardship and all my father's house." The name of the second he called Ephraim, "For God has made me fruitful in the land of my affliction," (41:51-52). It is not immediately clear, however, that the full import of this recognition strikes home in him as he soon (in narrated time) sets out to extend the "hardship" and "affliction" of his brothers and father over a number of years.

As the novella develops, it becomes clear to each of the major figures that their lives are shaped by more than their own intentions and deeds. For the brothers the recognition comes slowly that family relationships are much more complex and interlocked in a web of binding ties than they first suspected when they believed they could simply take action and rid themselves of the thorn in their flesh they found their youngest brother to be. Not only do their initial attempts to be rid of him become immediately more complex because of efforts by Reuben and Judah to modify their plan and then by the need (unanticipated, it appears) to deceive their father, but at the heart of the turmoil of their first reencounter with Joseph they recognize a larger matrix of forces at work in their lives: "Then they said to one another, 'In truth we are guilty concerning our brother, in that we saw the distress of his soul, when he besought us and we would not listen; therefore is this distress come upon us.' And Reuben answered them, 'Did I not tell you not to sin against the lad? But you would not listen. So now there comes a reckoning for his blood'" (42:21-22). And yet they are finally not allowed to conclude that the twists and turns in their fortunes are to be explained by a simple application of some mechanical principle of retribution. For in their uncertainty and even dread in their second meeting with Joseph, their fear of retribution is countered by the reassurance of Joseph's steward: "'Rest assured, do not be afraid; your God and the God of your father must have put treasure in your sacks for you; I received your money.' Then he brought Simeon out to them" (43:23).

What could have appeared more arbitrary from their perspective than this? But by now we as readers have been able to watch them for some time in a contrived context where their motives, deeds, and expectations seem to be met time and again with the most unexpected consequences. Throughout the first part of this second journey to Egypt, events do not correspond to their pervading sense of guilt. It is only when the guilt seems lulled once more—"So they drank and were merry with him" (43:34b)—that the twist of events once again triggers it and they acknowledge through Judah: "What shall we say to my lord? What shall we speak? Or how can we clear ourselves? God has found out the guilt of your servants; behold, we are my lord's slaves, both we and he also in whose hand the cup has been found" (44:16).

But theirs is the lowest level of comprehension, and their father's is not much higher. Early on, for whatever reason, he does not simply dismiss Joseph's dreams (37:11). Yet, unlike Joseph, he does not recall them. On one level he seems more willing to leave affairs in the hands of larger forces, at least when driven to it by dire need. When he has no real choice, as his son Judah makes clear, but to send Benjamin with the other nine to Egypt a second time for food, he states with rather dramatic resignation:

> If it must be so, then do this: take some of the choice fruits of the land in your bags, and carry down to the man a present, a little balm and a little honey, gum, myrrh, pistachio nuts, and almonds. Take double the money with you; carry back with you the money that was returned in the mouth of your sacks; perhaps it was an oversight. Take also your brother, and arise, go again to the man; may God Almighty grant you mercy before the man, that he may send back your brother and Benjamin. If I am bereaved of my children, I am bereaved. (43:11–14)

We have here an interlacing of resignation and practical measures taken to do all possible to ensure success. Yet by now he must recognize that all that is humanly possible may still not be enough.

123

Circles wheel within larger circles as we come with the members of this family slowly to see that human intentions and deeds are caught up in ever larger contexts of will and design. Of the largest we have had only hints to this point. But in these hints there has been movement, and that movement is designed to follow the rhythm of the plot of the Joseph novella, along with changes in narrative perspective, shared knowledge, and the trajectory of character development. It can be traced from the initial complication (Joseph's dream), through the interlude that follows the career of Joseph from prison to power in Egypt (dreams and interpretation come from God), to further complications as ten brothers of one father journey twice to Egypt to buy relief from the famine (the brothers' confessions, the steward's statement, and Judah's plea), and finally to the resolution at the climax of the second journey. In Joseph's words of self-disclosure much more is disclosed as well.

> And now do not be distressed, or angry with yourselves, because you sold me here; for God sent me before you to preserve life. For the famine has been in the land these two years; and there are yet five years in which there will be neither plowing nor harvest. And God sent me before you to preserve for you a remnant on earth, and to keep alive for you many survivors. So it was not you who sent me here, but God; and he has made me a father to Pharaoh, and lord of all his house and ruler over all the land of Egypt. Make haste and go up to my father and say to him, "Thus says your son Joseph, God has made me lord of all Egypt; come down to me, do not tarry." (45:5–9)

These words about God's purpose in all that has happened are bracketed by Joseph with words about himself, about his identity (45:3–4), and about what he proposes now to do for his father and brothers (45:10–12) and his power to do it (45:13).

It is important to note once more that the words are uttered by Joseph; they are not a statement addressed directly to us by the narrator. We have no comment on any larger theological dimensions in this family's story presented as narrative asides to the reader. It is instructive to compare the Joseph novella with a unit such as the Succession Narrative in this regard, for the latter is also sparing in its direct references to the deity, and most of those that do occur are in the direct speech of one or another of its characters. Yet the importance of at least three direct statements by the author about divine intent or evaluation have been noted (2 Sam. 11:27: "But the thing that David had done displeased Yahweh";

12:25: "So he called his [Solomon's] name Jedidiah, because of Yahweh"; 17:14: "For Yahweh had ordained to defeat the good counsel of Ahithophel, so that Yahweh might bring evil upon Absalom"). Here the most omniscient of narrators provides in an aside to the reader direct information about the perspective of Yahweh and his intentions. The author in a brief but effective way sets all that takes place in a theological context. In the Joseph novella, with the exceptions to be noted, there is no comparable statement by the author. What is said of God is in the reported speeches of the characters, not in the narrated report of the author. As Joseph and his brothers came to acknowledge a divine providential design behind and through their intentions and actions only at the end of a long history of hatred, blindness, deceit, and discord, so we can recognize it only in their acknowledgment. This is not priviledged information for the reader alone.

A congruence of knowledge is reached at this point, even if it will take restating and some time for its full implications to be clear to all. But finally the brothers come to know what Joseph and the reader know, and all come to know through Joseph's recognition that the tug and pull of this family's story must be comprehended within a larger divine design, and the design is one that seeks to preserve life. Following this vision of a larger context within which these figures have lived their story, there is now the bustle of the resolution: the brothers return home, report to their father, and journey with him and their families to Egypt; the reunion of father and son; preparations for and an audience held with Pharaoh; and the family settled in Goshen. In the midst of this is an accounting of the members of the family and the account of Joseph's acquisition of Egypt and the Egyptians for Pharaoh. Finally there is the death of Jacob, the old patriarch, and the formal deathbed scenes of blessing and the passing on of family authority. Following the burial of Jacob in Palestine, we return to the theological emphasis, and the fullest implication of what was stated by Joseph in the resolution is realized. Fearful that with their father gone Joseph might now seek to repay them for what they did to him so many years ago, the brothers approach him with a version of what they (and we) can hope their father would have said before he died:

> When Joseph's brothers saw that their father was dead, they said, "It may be that Joseph will hate us and pay us back for all the evil which we did to him." So they sent a message to Joseph, saying, "Your father gave this command before he died, "Say to Joseph, Forgive, I

pray you, the transgression of your brothers and their sin, because they did evil to you." And now, we pray you, forgive the transgression of the servants of the God of your father." Joseph wept when they spoke to him. His brothers also came and fell down before him, and said, "Behold, we are your servants." But Joseph said to them "Fear not, for am I in the place of God? As for you, you meant evil against me; but God meant it for good, to bring it about that many people should be kept alive, as they are today. So do not fear; I will provide for you and your little ones." Thus he reassured them and comforted them. (50:15–21)

Certainly we can hope that Jacob would have granted this much attention to his sons by wives other than Rachel, and we might detect behind this feigned speech recognition of his role in the earlier events and his own provocation of the brothers. It is of course all very indirect, and perhaps more a reflection of our desire for this full realization by all the characters in the novella that leads to this reading. For as we have seen, there is no indication in the novella itself that this is any more than a ploy by the still uneasy brothers to ensure their safety as aliens in the land that Joseph rules with such authority. It is significant for the tone of this meeting that before this encounter we had the account of Joseph's taking advantage of the seven-year famine to bring both the land and people of Egypt fully into Pharaoh's power. Now the material dealing with the death of Jacob (chs. 48–49) stands between this demonstration of Joseph's powerful position in Egypt and Jacob's death, followed by the brothers' final approach to him. In the development of the narrative, many record the material in chapters 48–49 to be secondary, brought in as the novella entered the larger traditions of Israel's history found in Geneis and Exodus as a bridge between the two units. In the expanded context the father of this family, named Jacob/Israel becomes the patriarch Jacob/Israel. If chapters 48 and 49 are omitted, the demonstration of Joseph's power in Egypt and the brothers' plea would be set in conjuction, and the former would set a distinct context for appreciation of the latter.

Whatever we may glean of Jacob's changed perspective behind the brothers' words, we do learn more of Joseph's perspective, and we learn of it along with the brothers. It would not be at all off the mark to state that from their first appearance in Egypt even until now, Joseph has played God with their lives—at first a God whose power seemed absolute, but who appeared arbitrary in his execution of it. And only since the resolution has that power been exercised in a manner less arbitrary or crass if no less absolute. In important ways what was said in 50:19–21 is more than just a repetition of what was said in 45:4–13. In 45:4–13 Joseph begins with words about himself, and then moves to words about what God has done for him, and then on to what he in this position will now do for his family. God has larger designs that were accomplished in Joseph's rise to and exercise of power in Egypt, and Joseph in these words fits himself into the overarching divine purpose. But were all the years of turmoil and anxiety and extended grief and possible testing he staged necessary to "preserve life?" Whatever the response to that, it is clear that in 45:4–13 Joseph, in the design of his words, sets God at the heart of his own position and authority: Who and what he is and does is enjoined fully with God and his providential care. Now in 50:19 Joseph sets himself in contrast to God, and this is very important. Divine intent remains the same—"to bring it about that many people should be kept alive, as they are today"—as does Joseph's intent as well—"I will provide for you and your little ones." Joseph, however, is not God: "Fear not, for am I in the place of God?" "Thus he reassured them and comforted them." No overt judgment is sounded concerning Joseph and his role in all that happened. Yet in this statement it is recognized that he too stands under the judgment of God.

This is as far as the reassurance and comfort are allowed to go. There is still no direct mention of his manipulation of their lives throughout the time encompassed by chapters 42–45, from their first journey through the second. No reason is given for his words and deeds, no motive is supplied. And while we see that Joseph too has grown in these final words, there is still something about him that cannot be determined, something at the heart of him that remain less than clear. The more encompassing vision that shaped his words to his brothers at the resolution and again at the end of their story does not bring everything into clearer focus. At points the picture of Joseph remains blurred—indeed it was always less clear than that of his father or brothers—and it is just these points that provide a continued degree of complexity and finely hued subtlety to the character of Joseph through all his growth and development.

Throughout the novella occasions have been provided for reflection on human power and the exercise of it. Power can come from position or from simple strength of numbers. And it can be abused, as the brothers do in their attack upon Joseph; as their father does in his blindness to the effects of his love on others and in sending Joseph into their hands; as Potiphar does in his failure to see or inquire; and as his wife does in her grasping. Power can also be used wisely to preserve life. Pharaoh exercises his power to appoint Joseph to office, and Joseph exercises the office to per-serve alive many people (as well as bind Egypt to Pharaoh's rule). Misuse of power by the brothers and by Potiphar's wife stands under judgment. What remains is the use of power by Joseph in the lives of his brothers and father. The end is a family preserved alive, but the course was in signifi-cant respects brutal. Yet it is left to the reader to assess the merit and rela-tionship of means and ends here.[3]

Robert Alter suggests that the ancient Israelites selected the medium of narrative fiction as the vessel for theological reflection because it allowed and even demanded the "perception of two, approximately par-allel, dialectical tensions":

> One is a tension between the divine plan and the disorderly character of actual historical events, or, to translate this opposition into specifi-cally biblical terms, between the divine promise and its ostensible failure to be fulfilled; the other is a tension between God's will, His providential guidance, and human freedom, the refractory nature of man.

The Joseph novella stands finely balanced within the field of tensions defined by these poles of "design and disorder, providence and freedom."[4] Seen from enough distance to blur or make details invisible (as in apoca-lyptic), the history of a nation, an individual, or a family can seem to fit nicely into a clear design. Seen from too close it can appear as nothing more than a random set of finely focused but unconnected and unrelated events (possibly the "Chronicles of the Kings and Israel and of Judah"?).

Most narratives will function within the field of tension set by these poles. Thus it is only at the end of the novella, in hindsight, that Joseph can detect the benevolent hand of providence in his family's story and appreciate this divine plan as one finally promoting good, keeping many people alive—Egyptians as well as one's own family. And that vision is held in balance with human freedom, especially the freedom not simply to intend but to bring about evil in ways not always fully intended, what Alter calls the "refractory nature of man." Just as everything does not snap into clear focus with Joseph's final assurance to his brothers, so claims of God's providential design working around and through the tug and pull of the life of this family are not allowed to blunt human freedom and responsibility for the exercise of that freedom in this novella. We do not suddenly discover at the end that we have been an audience in some grand puppet show staged by a divine puppeteer. Jacob, Joseph, and the brothers confronted and made real choices, and were faced with and responsible for the outcome of those choices they made, even if very often that outcome was more complex and revealed ramifications not conceived of even in their dreams. Jacob did not have to favor Joseph with such overt tokens as the cloak, and his blindness to his other sons' reaction seems almost willful, especially when he sends the favored alone into their hands. Joseph need not have carried tales, boasted of his dreams, let alone toyed with his brothers later when they in turn fall into his hands. Nor need the brothers have acted as they did. All act upon choices freely made.

We have also seen that all suffer in one way or another for what they intend and do. Jacob loves to excess and unwisely demonstrates it, and is forced to live for years in excess of grief. Joseph's brothers move in one stroke to remove the object of their father's love and the thorn in their own flesh, only to find themselves victims of a whole series of apparently arbitrary blows of misfortune. And Joseph, who seems to revel in the elevated position his father sets for him, must pass through prison and years of separation from his homeland and doting father. All have freedom to act with intent or through willful blindness to consequences, and all suffer for their action in ways they did not intend. There is a rough balance here: "He who digs a pit will fall into it." But the balance is rough; there is not the full tidiness of some stories that seem in danger of falling to the side of divine design in the tension defined by Alter. We do not have here the neatness of the book of Esther, for example, in which Haman is hanged on the very gallows he erected to hang Mordecai, and Mordecai given the office and estate of Haman. Yet the one who loves must lament the loss of the beloved; those who seek to shape in one bold stroke their lives find themselves both immediately and in the longer course out of control and their lives shaped by another. Even he who struts must be debased before he can strut again and then walk with his brothers as one.[5]

This finally is not a story of villains and heroes. The central figures are too finely and complexly drawn for that. Joseph's tale-bearing and boasting of his dreams as well as the token of special favor given him by his father make the brothers' feelings understandable, even if we cannot condone their deeds based on these feelings. The same is true of the actions of Joseph and of Jacob. Even the interlude that treats Joseph's rise in Egypt does not pit him against the native courtiers (cf. the stories of Esther and Mordecai and of Daniel and his companions), and Egypt is a supportive context for this family. Pharaoh not only welcomes them (and is blessed by Jacob) but, in fact, offers more generous terms for their settlement (47:5–6) than they request (47:1–4). The only villain is Potiphar's wife, and even she is not punished for her crime. This is not the story of good set against bad people, of heroes and villains, but of the complex interplay of good and evil, of selfish and selfless motive in men who live within the context of the complex bonds that define a family in situations that are shaped by an uneven allocation of power and knowledge.

In the light of all this, and especially of Joseph's words in 45:5–9 and then in 50:20, the earlier reference to God's design and the revelation of that design in dreams cannot remain within the restricted context of simple protocol for the interpretation of dreams. The dreams of a spoiled youth become more than simply the subject of his boast and the object of his brothers' scorn. The God who could reveal particulars of the future to two courtiers held in detention and then to their king is now understood by Joseph and his family, and by the reader, to have set a stage and a larger backdrop on and against which, with at least limited but important freedom and responsibility, these figures must live their story. If the central figures acted with a willful blindness to consequences at the outset, they and the reader now perceive this larger stage more clearly. They acted in a context shaped by God, which would mean their deeds would have consequences for ill and for good that go beyond what they could expect. "You [and Joseph might well have said "we"] meant it for evil, but God meant it for good," and for a good that takes in more of the earth than occupied by this one family. Intended evil is neither excused nor avoided, but is caught up into a larger design that is shaped by divine will for good and life. This is indeed a remarkable balance for any narrative to maintain.

In concluding this consideration of the theological dimensions of the Joseph novella we must turn to two exceptions to what has been said, to two episodes that stand between the initial complication in the plot and the interlude that deals with Joseph's adventures in Egypt. Chapter 38, dealing with Judah and his daughter-in-law Tamar, has been discussed[6] both in terms of its apparent interruption of the flow of the plot and in terms of devices by which it is linked to the Joseph novella. Alter, in a sensitive treatment of this unit, has suggested that it is not uncharacteristic for biblical narrative to set two units in juxtaposition to serve as commentary on each other.[7] In this case not only are there certain verbal links between chapter 38 and the Joseph novella, as well as dimensions that develop the characterization of key figures in each, but the neatly developed pattern of reversal depicted in this first interlude stands as a foretaste for the sensitive reader of the reversals that will later shape the Joseph narrative, even if in the latter those in the right and those in the wrong are not as clearly defined. Genesis 38 does depict a world in which "good will win out" in spite of apparent insurmountable obstacles. It is also worthy of note that in itself chapter 38 is a wholly secular story; God is not mentioned after the opening verses.

Less subtle is the sevenfold set of theological notices that take us into and out of the episode related in Genesis 39. Only here is the deity given the name Yahweh in the Joseph novella, and only here is it explicitly stated by the narrator that Yahweh shaped for success the actions of this key figure in the story. Surrounding this common motif of the spurned woman who becomes the accuser is the declaration that Yahweh made to prosper all that Joseph did, both in the house of Potiphar and in the house of confinement to which Potiphar sends him. As Joseph is confronted by the wiles of a lustful woman and then by prison, at what must appear the nadir of his fortunes, the narrator at just this point tells us several times that Joseph stood within divine protective care that would ensure success. The remainder of the novella, with its references to the deity only through the words of the characters themselves, makes less clear just what these striking notices imply. Yes, we can agree at the end, Yahweh seems with Joseph, and God brings this apparently self-destructive family to life and reconciliation; but the relation of this to human freedom and perversity, and to the complexity of human motivation and action, is not as simple as this sevenfold statement might initially imply. In the face of this remarkably complex and realistic family history the neatness of such theological assertions is blurred, even if not denied.

NOTES

1. An exception is the reference to the specifically Hebrew *ēl šāday* ("God Almighty" in the RSV) by Jacob as he sends his ten sons on their second journey to Egypt (43:14).

2. See above, p. 74.

3. See Claus Westermann, *Genesis 37–50*, 44–45, for larger political issues in relation to the Joseph novella.

4. Robert Alter, *The Art of Biblical Narrative*, 33.

5. Cf. the legends in Dan. 1–6, especially ch. 3 and 6, in which the fate of the villains is just what they sought for the heroes, while the latter take over the positions and possessions of the former.

6. See above, pp. 37–38.

7. Alter, *Art*, 3–11.

PART II

THE DEVELOPMENT OF THE JOSEPH NOVELLA

SEVEN

JOSEPH THE EGYPTIAN COURTIER

To this point the approach to the Joseph novella has been to take it generally as a whole, to consider Genesis 37–50 as a unit. This perspective is often called by scholars "synchronic." Even in this approach we were able to note certain units or blocks of material that appeared, if not intrusive, at least fundamentally to change the emphasis of the story line or the perspective from which we viewed the characters and events. Genesis 38, for all its thematic and linguistic links with the Joseph novella, does radically change our focus from the family of Jacob to that of one of his sons and his relation with his daughter-in-law. In chapters 48 and 49 the emphasis is on the family, on Jacob and his sons and grandsons; but it is less the doting and sometimes blind father and more the revered third patriarch of Israel, who came to bear the very name Israel, who is before us as he blesses the generations to come and pronounces on the destiny of his sons, who now seem, moreover, to represent tribal units rather than individuals within the family. Genesis 39 stands in marked contrast to the rest of the novella in the repeated emphasis in its exposition and conclusion that Yahweh was with Joseph and was the source of his success, as the plot of this episode has him move from the clutches of Potiphar's wife to prison and servitude. We have already seen that the larger novella is strikingly reticent in speaking of the deity and generally mentions God only through the speeches of one of the characters.

It is, of course, possible for an author to make marked and sudden shifts in a plot's trajectory or in the perspective within a narrative. It is also possible that material of this sort reflects the efforts of later hands as well as later uses of the novella in larger contexts, especially its present setting within the Torah. The units noted above will be further discussed in chapter 9. At this point we must turn to still another distinct unit within the Joseph novella, one that shifts the focus of the narrative and alters our perspective; that appears as complete within itself and yet also stands as a kernel incorporated into the heart of the larger family story. Genesis 40 and 41 (along with 47:13–26 and 50:26) tell of the remarkable rise and successes of Joseph as an Egyptian courtier. These chapters merit careful attention from several perspectives.

The approach at this point becomes what some scholars have called "diachronic"; we will not only be considering the novella as a whole, but will also note hints regarding its possible growth and development as well as the later utilization and continued shaping of the material as it secured its place in the Torah. It must be stressed that in attempting to sketch a developmental history of the novella, we necessarily deal in hypotheses, for in no manuscript of the Hebrew Bible nor in any ancient version does it appear in other than the form we now have. Evidence will have to be weighed with care, and proper caution exercised. However, even if the sketch of the developmental history of the Joseph novella must be tentative and incomplete, the exercise will allow us to focus on some important aspects of segments of the material and to look at the effect of the novella on its present context as well as the effect of that context on it. We begin with attention to what can be considered as a kernel within the larger novella, the hinge upon which the story of the family turns.

There is a Horatio Alger quality to that part of the Joseph novella telling of his rise to power in Egypt. It is a delightful success story, complete in itself, telling of the incredible rise of a young man who, beginning in the most obscure and hopeless of positions, attains the highest office in the royal court and service of the king of Egypt. This is accomplished by a set of fortuitous circumstances seized through the ready wit and considerable abilities of the hero. It is a story that delights, the story of the poor boy who makes good, who attains great success through the combination of good luck and remarkable skill. It is a story of hopeless beginnings and a happy ending, of ability neglected for a time and then lavishly recognized and rewarded.

Joseph, as we encounter him in chapter 40, is a young man of apparently foreign origins (40:15a) who finds himself in Egypt, in as lowly a position as possible: he is a slave under the authority of the captain of the guard. His master's responsibilities include holding in custody important figures who have fallen from grace with the ruling powers. Into his charge come two important royal officials, accused of unnamed crimes against the state and king. Their position is uncertain at this point; they are in the "custody" or "keeping" of the captain of the guard and are detained in his establishment. The terminology becomes somewhat complex here,[1] but the situation is apparently that of loose detention while the charges brought against the chief butler and chief baker are investigated. In today's terms they are under house arrest. Investigations are apparently carried out (since this is not their story, this process and the charges leveled against them are not detailed) and by the end of the chapter the cases are disposed of as the chief butler is restored and the chief baker executed.[2]

As befits such important persons—who, after all, might be innocent—special attention is given to their personal comforts while they are detained in the establishment of the captain of the guard. Joseph is appointed to wait upon them and to serve their personal needs. Coming to them one morning he finds each visibly distressed over a dream experienced the previous night. While apparently portentous, the dreams cannot be understood, as their present position has cut the men off from the regular avenues of dream interpretation upon which one might normally rely in such a situation. Joseph offers to interpret the dreams for them. When the chief butler recounts his dream, Joseph provides an interpretation that relates it to the case outstanding against the official and the happy disposition of it. In fact, in spite of Joseph's becoming deference (40:8), this dream—and that of the chief baker as well—is quite transparent. The only possible problem is the significance of the number three. That it indicates three days is the critical element disclosed by Joseph. Seizing the moment, Joseph asks that the chief butler intercede on his behalf when he is restored to his former position.[3] The chief baker, taking courage from what has been said, relates his dream as well but receives a quite different interpretation. In three days events transpire as Joseph indicated. However, this episode closes on a note of tension with the observation that the chief butler did not take up the case of Joseph; he forgot him (40:23).

At the end of the first episode the apparent hopelessness of the hero's position has only been reinforced by the forgetfulness of the chief butler.

The second episode has two scenes: in the first Joseph is absent; in the second he is the center of attention. The first opens after two years have elapsed and is set in the court of Pharaoh. Pharaoh also dreams—two wondrous and more complex dreams—and he also is disturbed. The most learned men in Egypt are stumped; not one is able to provide an interpretation. At this moment the chief butler acknowledges that he has been remiss. Reminding Pharaoh as discreetly as possible of the earlier events, he tells about Joseph and his abilities as an interpreter of dreams.

As the second scene opens, Joseph appears washed, groomed, and outfitted in appropriate dress (cf. 2 Kgs. 25:29; Zech. 3:4–5). He is hastened by royal command into Pharaoh's presence, for with unexpected suddenness his moment has arrived. Pharaoh confronts Joseph with what has been reported of him—"you have but to hear a dream to interpret it" (41:15)—and, after Joseph's deferential reply, the dreams are retold with the characteristic additions. Joseph suggests that both dreams indicate the same coming events; they are paired to stress the seriousness of the situation and the determined nature of the divine decree that wills it. And as soon as he interprets the dreams with their warning of seven years of plenty followed by seven years of famine, Joseph goes on to offer sage counsel regarding emergency actions needed to meet the crisis. Not only are the king and his officials impressed by this performance, but Pharaoh suggests that Joseph has just revealed himself to be the very man they need to take the lead in organizing such emergency measures.

Joseph is immediately elevated, with all formality, into what seems to be the highest office in the land next to the king himself, with all the accouterments and honors thereof. With the bestowal by Pharaoh of a new and Egyptian name, and then his marriage into the highest circles of Egyptian society (his new wife is the daughter of the priest of On, the priest of the Sun God), Joseph has become an important, powerful, and integral part of Egyptian political and social order. He becomes an Egyptian and a courtier of Pharaoh. As such he acts with dispatch in initiating measures that will meet the crisis. As a devoted servant of his king he prospers, and produces offspring and heirs (a fitting note of familiar stability in his remarkable rise and success, and a nice counterpoint to the larger family story).

It is an appealing story and well told. The author delights in double and even triple entendre (note the usage of the idiom *nāśā' rô'š*, "to life the head," in 40:13, 19, 20 and of the verb *ḥāṭā'*, "to err, to sin," in 40:1; 41:9). He effectively plays with the reader's patience by making us sit through first his account and then Pharaoh's elaborated retelling of both dreams before we find out whether or not Joseph can successfully seize his moment which has so suddenly arrived. Egypt's best, after all, had failed at the task. Not only are two years effectively passed over without detracting from the intensity of the narrative (41:1), but the tension is heightened in the process (40:23). On the other hand, in one short, staccato burst of verbs (41:14) Joseph moves from rags and a prison cell to an audience with Pharaoh and on to the symbols and substance of power. The narrative then allows the reader to dwell on every detail of Joseph's elevation and new status as each trapping of award, dress, and insignia is recounted. Genesis 40–41 will reward consideration of several of its aspects from different points of view.

GENESIS 40–41 AND ANCIENT WISDOM TRADITION

Gerhard von Rad, who is followed by others, has called attention to a number of possible points of contact between the wisdom traditions and writings of the ancient Near East and Israel and the Joseph material in Genesis.[4] The majority of his specifics that have best withstood criticism are found in Genesis 40–41. It is especially to Egyptian wisdom traditions that von Rad turned when he moved beyond material from ancient Israel. In Egypt the prevailing form is the so-called "Instruction," sage and practical advice given at the close of life by a courtier or king to his son and successor. Instructions have a court setting and sometimes a political as well as a didactic emphasis. The content is wide-ranging and especially well suited for one being trained to enter court service. The Instructions depict an ideal wise courtier, and this motif provides unity to these collections of diverse admonitions. Several aspects of this motif of the wise courtier are often said to be depicted in the character and actions of Joseph.

In Egypt the literary and archaeological evidence indicates particular schools in which Instruction and related materials were created, treasured, and transmitted. During the First Intermediate Period and the Middle Kingdom (2000–1800 BCE) Egyptian literature had its greatest flowering, and this period was later recognized as the golden age of Egyptian language and style. Instruction and other works served as models for schoolboys (sometimes the only existent form is that of a schoolboy's garbled copy), from which the elements of style, syntax, and a style of life were learned. It was through these schools that the would-be courtier received basic training, the first steps on the way to advancement in court service. The Instruction literature, advice of a courtier or ruler to his son and/or successor, imparts the distilled wisdom of his experience in life and the council he himself received.[5] The sayings are cast in a series of short units, using mostly the second-person singular form of address. A conditional "if" clause ("if thou art a leader . . . ") is followed by an imperative ("seek out for thyself every . . . "), and sometimes by the third-person indicative statement of result or situation bearing on the above ("justice is great . . . wrongdoing has never brought its undertaking to port"). Some units begin with the imperative ("guard thyself . . . " "do not carry off . . . " "cast not . . . "), again followed by an objective statement of condition or result ("better is bread when the heart is happy"). Each unit usually deals with one basic theme, but the arrangement of the units themselves shows little pattern. The collections open with a statement about the author in which his titles and credentials are given, and close with a charge to heed and obey.

The major examples are: 1) From the Old Kingdom, the Instruction of Ptah-hotep (ca. 2450 BCE)[6] and the fragmentary remains of the Instruction for Ka-gemni.[7] Legend tells of two wise men of this period who attained fame: Im-hotep and Hor-dedef. From the former nothing remains; from the latter there is a very poorly preserved fragment.[8] 2) From the New Kingdom, the Instruction of Ani[9] and the Instruction of Amen-em-opet.[10] 3) Two other collections, the Instruction for Meri-ka-Re[11] and the Instruction of King Amen-em-het,[12] contain the words of kings, not courtiers, and have a political emphasis. Coming from a period when there were rival claimants to the throne, they seek to shore up particular claims. However, the form is that of the Instructions.

It is also suggested that certain narratives, like the "Tale of Sinuhe," also present instructive models for a pedagogical purpose. A. Gardiner, in his study of the "Tale of Sinuhe," suggests that "to the young student of the XVIIIth and XIXth Dynasties, the adventures of Sinuhe were doubtless as familiar as those of Robinson Crusoe to the English child."[13]

In ancient Israel the situation is much less clear, as the relationship between the royal court, education, and wisdom is more tenuous. Not only is a greater variety of forms preserved in the book of Proverbs—the objective third-person observations and admonitions, short two-line sayings and longer units—but even a cursory reading of Proverbs will reveal that the motif of the wise courtier and court themes play a rather small role.

This motif does not provide the unifying frame of reference for the collection[14] as it does for the Egyptian Instructions.

The material in the book of Proverbs has had a complex transmission history that extends beyond the ancient state of Israel and its royal court.[15] The traditions associated with King Solomon (1 Kgs. 2:6, 9; 4:29–34; 10:1–10, 23–24) must be critically evaluated, as must the headings for the several collections in the book (Prov. 1:1; 10:1; 25:1).[16] Only in proverbs 16:1–22:16 and 22:16–24:22 is material dealing specifically with the courtier and court life present, and even in these collections the number of sayings is quite small. Whatever place and purpose the royal court schools possibly had in the development of ancient Israelite wisdom materials is not as predominant or as central as is often assumed to be the case in Egypt.

With this word of caution concerning the overview of Egyptian and Israelite wisdom material and the life setting of Israelite wisdom traditions, we can turn to the suggested wisdom affinities[17] in Genesis 40–41.

After he interprets Pharaoh's dreams, Joseph immediately offers some practical advice with these words: "Now let Pharaoh select a man discreet and wise (*nābôn uʰḥākām*)" (41:33). While the words *nābôn* and *ḥākām*, are applied to many people in diverse types and kinds of literature, they are especially at home in wisdom literature and are also used of courtiers elsewhere.[18] Of particular interest is the introduction to the book of Proverbs (1:2–6), in which these terms and their cognates recur.

That one may know wisdom (*ḥokmāh*) and instruction,
    may understand (*lᵉhābîn*) words of insight (*bînāh*).
The wise also (*ḥākām*) may hear and increase knowledge,
    and the understanding man (*nābôn*) may acquire skill.
That one may understand (*lᵉhābîn*) a proverb and a clever
    saying, the words of the wise (*ḥākām*) and riddles.

Again, cognates of these attributes as the possession of the wise are found in Proverbs 21:30–31, a theologically significant saying placed in the context of affairs of the royal court and paired with "councel" (*ʿēṣāh*), which, while not so called (of, *dābār* of 41:37), is precisely what Joseph gives to Pharaoh:

There is no wisdom (*ḥokmāh*), there is no understanding
    (*tᵉbûnāh*),
and there is no counsel (*ʿēṣāh*) that can stand before
    Yahweh;

the horse is readied for the day of battle, but victory
is Yahweh's.

The official whom Pharaoh needs must be wise and discerning, and, as
Pharaoh himself observes, Joseph is just the one (41:39). Thus Joseph
becomes a courtier. The climax of this story within the larger story is
reached in his installation; what remains is but denouement, the working
out of the implications of his appointment both for Egypt (41:47–49, 53–
57; 47:13–26) and for the hero's personal life (41:45–46, 50–52; 50:22b,
26).

Particular qualities of the wise courtier, effective self-mastery and
speech, receive notable emphasis in the studies by von Rad. Clever
speech, the apt word, sound counsel given at the proper time, are all elements in the motif of the wise courtier stressed in the Egyptian Instructions and found in the Book of Proverbs as well: "To speak well at the
decisive moment, to give sound advice in any and every contingency of
state affairs, and so if possible to take his place among the king's
entourage, such was the main aim of the education of the scribe."[19] This
ability is especially to be displayed in formal meetings of royal courtiers;
von Rad recalls the words of the Egyptian vizier Ptah-hotep:

> If you are a trusted man who sits in the council of his lord, set your
> heart on excellence. If you are quiet, it will be more profitable than
> *tftf*-plants; speak (only) when you know you can clarify the issue. It is
> the expert who speaks in the council, for speech is more difficult than
> any craft, and it is he who can interpret it who gives it authority.[20]

In the case of Joseph there are two components in this ability. On the one
hand, his speech is carefully cast to fit the situation, to persuade and not
offend, to compel but not alienate. On the other hand, the advice is sound;
it has content and is not empty flattery. Speech of this sort is a powerful
force; it can bring life to one who masters it.

The situation in which Joseph is called to speak is fully illustrative of
the fact that "speech is more difficult than any craft."

> To make an apt answer is a joy to a man,
> an opportune word, how good it is!
> . . .
> Like a golden apple in a setting of silver,
> is a word fitly spoken. (Prov. 15:23; 25:11, author's translation;
> See also 16:21, 23, 24; 17:7; 25:25)

To the chief butler he has good to report, but to the chief baker Joseph has to tell of disaster. And, more importantly, his interpretation of Pharaoh's dreams points to a danger facing the ruler's land. In each instance he begins with a statement that places the matter in a wider context, in which his role as simply a conveyor of messages is clearly established: "And Joseph said to them, 'Do not interpretations belong to God? Tell them [your dreams] to me, I pray you'" (40:8b). "Joseph answered Pharaoh, 'It is not in me; God will give Pharaoh a favorable answer'" (41:16; cf. 41:25, 32). The words to the officials and to Pharaoh represent at one level the customary protocol used by those who interpret dreams in their initial address to the dreamer.[21] It serves as a formal polite and pious wish, but also as a device for detaching the interpreter from the interpretation; the interpreter bears no responsibility but merely announces what is to come. Joseph in each episode shows himself to be a sure master of the complexities of court protocol.

Joseph moves right on, however, into the role of adviser. The speech in which advice is expressed cannot be empty (Prov. 16:23; 26:24–28), and one who speaks must know how to see the matter to conclusion. In both Genesis 40 and 41, Joseph faces the issue. He presents the danger facing the land with clarity and forcefulness, but is immediately able to follow with sound advice on how to meet the danger. His counsel carries immediate conviction: "This proposal seemed good to Pharaoh and to all his servants" (41:37; cf. vv. 38–39). Joseph's very words demonstrate that he himself is the model of the official he describes. It must be stressed that there is no sharp division between the interpretation of the dreams and the advice given on the basis of this. Verse 33, which presents this counsel, introducing it with *weʿattāh* ("Now!"), follows immediately on the dream interpretation. The interpreter and the counselor are one and the same person. Pharaoh observes that Joseph is a man, "in whom is the Spirit of God," and that "God has shown you all this." "All this" refers to all that Joseph has said in 41:25–36. Joseph is thus given the chance to put his words into practice and bring his advice to a successful conclusion. Genesis 41:46–49, 53–57, and especially 47:13–26, tell of the successful outcome of the venture. The story moves from protocol to interpretation to counsel to action in an even flow.

The wise stressed that the apt word is a life-giving force:

Deep waters, such are the words of man,
a swelling torrent, a fountain of life.

(Prov. 18:4, author's translation; see also 13:3; 18:21)

143

The value of Joseph's counsel receives instant recognition, and he who was a foreign slave in a prison is elevated at once to the highest post in the land. He becomes a new man, and he is given a new name expressive of this (cf. Gen. 32:28). His sound and apt counsel brings him new life as he receives new status, a new identity, a wife, and offspring (41:45, 50).

The wise admonished the practice of self-control. Joseph appears as master of himself in all situations. His words and actions are appropriate in whatever context he finds himself (contrast the dreamer of Genesis 37). He not only confronts challenges with coolness and control, but he is a master of his passions, to such an extent that he appears at points almost lifeless in chapters 40–41. For example, the length of time in which he is forgotten by the chief butler seems to be sharply stressed: "Yet the chief butler did not remember Joseph, but forgot him. After two whole years, Pharaoh dreamed" (40:23–41:1). Yet no anger is reported expressed by Joseph, no outraged sense of injustice. He appears in every respect the cool or tranquil person so central in the Instruction of Amen-em-opet:

> The truly tranquil man, he setteth himself aside,
>   he is like a tree grown in a plot;
> . . . .
> Its fruit is sweet, its shade is pleasant,
>   and its end is reached in the garden.
>
> (ch. 6:7–8, 11–12)

In all of this, von Rad stresses that Joseph is the model courtier. Both the outward course of events and the inner bearing of Joseph are illustrative of themes that are developed by the wise of Egypt and of Israel.

The center and focus of the courtier's life is the king. All authority and life itself stem from the ruler. This receives pointed expression in the Instructions of an official of the twelfth-dynasty pharaohs Sesostris III and Amen-em-het III, a popular text that was copied time and again for the next few centuries by schoolboys:

> I have something important to say; I shall have you hear it, and I shall let you know it: the design for eternity, a way of life as it should be and of passing a lifetime at peace.
> Adore the king, Nymaatre, living forever, in your innermost parts. Place His Majesty in friendly fashion in your thoughts . . . .
> He gives nourishment to those in his circle, and he feeds the one who sticks to his path.

The king is Ka.

His utterance is Abundance.

The one whom he brought up is one who will be somebody.

Fight on behalf of his name; be obeisant to his life. Be free and clear of any instance of negligence.

The one whom the king loves shall be a well-provided spirit; there is no tomb for anyone who rebels against His Majesty, and his corpse shall be cast to the waters.

Do this, and your body will flourish, and you will find it (excellent) for eternity.[22]

Joseph's authority and position are determined by royal favor. From Pharaoh he receives the signs of his new life: the titles (ʿal bêt; 41:40; mišneh, 41:43), the royal seal, special dress, the gold chain, and, most important in this regard, a new name. Of this last it is remarked: "The change of his name was aso an important act of court ceremony: by it Joseph was drawn completely into the Egyptian court circle. And this did not happen, furthermore, without Joseph being placed within the protective sphere of an Egyptian deity."[23] He acquires a wife from the highest level of the social and religious orders, and she too is a gift of Pharaoh (41:45). Joseph is in all respects the creation of Pharaoh, and his life is now wholly directed toward his king.

If the distinct unit in 47:13-26 is read as a continuation of the story of Joseph's rise in the Egyptian court, this most characteristic feature of the general motif of the wise courtier is once more and even more fully illustrated. Not only is Joseph successful, able to bring his plans to fruition and to save the land in famine, but in so doing he brings all of the land and people of Egypt into the possession of Pharaoh. Again and again, as a refrain, this is stressed in this unit:

And Joseph brought the money into Pharaoh's house (v. 14c).

And we with our land will be slaves to Pharaoh (v. 19b).

So Joseph bought all the land of Egypt for Pharaoh (v. 20a).

The land became Pharaoh's (v. 20c).

Behold, this day I have bought you and your land for Pharaoh (v. 23b).

And at the harvests you shall give a fifth to Pharaoh (v. 24a).

We will be slaves to Pharaoh (v. 25b).

Rarely has any king been so well served!

This suggests that the relationship of 47:13–26 to chapters 40–41 must now be examined in more detail. In its present context in Genesis 47

the unit stands apart as the center of attention, moving from the relationship between Joseph and his family to Joseph the Egyptian official and the
crisis that confronts the land. This unit seems to offer a fuller development
of a basic theme informing chapters 40–41: effective action by the courtier
is detailed, and the nature of his success and devotion to his king is developed. In 41:33–36 Joseph's counsel on measures to be taken to meet the
crisis is outlined, and in 41:53–57 it is stated broadly that these were carried out by him. In 47:13–26 more specifics are given, and these are
closely linked with the material in 41:33–36. In 41:34 a hapax legome-
non, *wᵉḥimmēš*,²⁴ is found that has traditionally been understood as a
denominative verbal form from the root *ḥmš*, "five." While some have
recently rejected this understanding of the form,²⁵ the tradition seems to
be correct, especially in the light of the related usage of the root *ʿśr*, "ten,"
in 1 Samuel 8:15, 17 to denote a more regular form of taxation in which
one-tenth is taken by the state. Joseph in Genesis 41:34 suggests that a
double tax—that is, one-fifth in place of the usual one-tenth—be collected
in the seven years of plenty to provide a surplus for the following seven-
year cycle of famine when no tax could be collected.

In 47:13–26 two forms of the root *ḥmš* appear: a noun, *ḥᵃmîšît*, in
verse 24, and another hapax, *laḥōmeš*, in verse 26. In verses 23-24 Joseph
commands the Egyptians: "Behold, I have this day bought you and your
land for Pharaoh. Now here is seed for you, and you shall sow the land.
And at the harvest you shall give a fifth to Pharaoh, and four fifths shall be
your own, as seed for the field and as food for yourselves and your house-
holds, and as food for your little ones." The people agree (verse 25), and in
verse 26 the practice becomes a permanent law (*lᵉḥōq*). The expression
lᵉparʿôh laḥōmeš in verse 26 is awkward, and perhaps *lḥmš* is to be read with
the LXX and Genesis 41:34 as a piel infinitive. The word order, with the
mention of Pharaoh in the first position, stresses what has been the thrust
of the whole of 47:13-26: the placing of all of Egypt and its population in
the direct possession of Pharaoh. Thus an explanation is given for what,
especially to the outsider, would appear as Pharaoh's remarkable control
over his people and land and for the comparatively large tax that the
Egyptians seem to pay.

Thus 47:13–26 is linked with 40–41 both verbally and thematically.
The double tax of one-fifth is an emergency measure in 41:33–36; in
47:13–26 the reader is shown how it was transformed by Joseph into a
permanent fixture of the Egyptian economy. The latter unit is a direct
continuation and further development of the former. Carefully, the suc-

cessive stages of Joseph's enslavement of the Egyptians to Pharaoh are outlined; throughout the courtier demonstrates his devotion to his master. This is the capstone of a successful career of royal service.

From the point of view of an ancient Egyptian the only remaining matter of significance to be noted in the life of a courtier is his death. In Egypt a life of such complete service to the ruler must be climaxed by a dignified death at a ripe old age—110 years was the ideal age from the Egyptian point of view—and proper burial as necessary preparation for the afterlife. In 50:26 the Joseph narrative concludes with the notice that "so Joseph died, being a hundred and ten years old; and they embalmed him, and he was put in a coffin in Egypt." The Egyptian Ptah-hotep concludes his Instruction to his son with these words: "I attained one hundred and ten years of life which the king gave me . . . through doing right for the king up to the point of veneration." For the courtier who serves his king well, the pharaoh is the very source of life, both in this world and in the next. Ptah-hotep's words could be set as easily at the conclusion of the story of Joseph the Egyptian courtier.

In summary, the material in Genesis 40–41, with 47:13–26 and 50:26, tells of the remarkable rise of a foreign slave from the depths of servitude to the highest office in the land of Egypt and the success he enjoys in it. It is a story of a very successful courtier. In part, the background traditions against which this story is to be understood are those generally treasured in wisdom circles. Certain admonitions and ideals of the wise find illustration here in a distilled narrative. In a situation in which others have failed, in a situation fraught with danger and yet potent with possibility, Joseph is recalled on the basis of past demonstrations of his ability and is able to best the wise men of Egypt at their own game. He is in all of this the very model of the wise courtier, able to seize his moment, completely in control of himself and of the situation, able to give sound advice and carry it to a successful conclusion. It is not the case that he is always able to shape events, and an element of the fortuitous is clearly present in this story. However, Joseph is shown as always able to seize and make the most of what fortune sets before him. He demonstrates devotion to his king, he lives a long and honored life, sons are born to him, and his death provides a dignified climax for this life. He is in essential ways the ideal courtier, and the story of Joseph as Egyptian courtier can be set nicely in the broad context of the international wisdom traditions and circles that produced and treasured the motif of the wise courtier. The wisdom themes seem so to permeate the material that some close influence from these circles seem probable.

JOSEPH AS A WISE COURTIER

Some criticism has been leveled at this conclusion. J. L. Crenshaw, for example, suggests that there is an etiological thrust in Genesis 47:13–26 that sets it outside the interests of the wise.[26] However, when this is examined in context, this thrust is secondary; furthermore, etiology is not in and of itself alien to wisdom traditions, even if not usually found therein. Crenshaw also suggests that the emphasis on dreams shows that the material is not linked to wisdom. However, as will be demonstrated below, the role played by the dreams and their interpretation is to be understood in the context of the oriental court and its concern for omina of many kinds. It is as an adviser to Pharaoh that Joseph excels; his role is that of courtier, both in the interpretation of dreams and in the giving of counsel, for the two are in no way to be separated. Nor is Joseph's appeal in 40:14-15 for deliverance from his plight separate from his interpretation of the chief butler's dream; it is, in fact, the most propitious moment for such an appeal to be made. Those who mastered the sciences concerned with omina were important figures in most royal courts of the ancient Near East. That the interpretation of dreams and a concern with omina are not present in the Egyptian Instructions and in the biblical book of Proverbs is not surprising. It is to be explained on the one hand, as will be discussed more fully in the next chapter, by position of Pharaoh as god-king in the Egyptian context, and, on the other hand, by the hostility to this sort of thing by certain important Yahwistic circles.

A different objection is raised by L. Ruppert. He interprets the account of Joseph's besting the wise men of the court of Pharaoh as a polemic against foreign wisdom and against magicians, sorcerers, and such in general.[27] But such a polemic would be quite alien to early Israelite wisdom, he suggests, for Israel was open to foreign materials and influences in wisdom circles, if anywhere, and here most clearly and consciously. He cites, for example, Proverbs 30:1; 31:1; 22:17–23:11 and the book of Job. It is rather in the prophetic material that such a polemic is to be found. In this regard he calls attention to Isaiah 19:1-4, 11-15, and also suggests that in Isaiah 19:5-10 there is a virtual commentary on the dreams of Pharaoh; a connection with the Joseph material is even suggested. Thus he suggests that Genesis 41 contains the remnant of a prophetic polemic, and is to be compared to the attitude of Elijah, upon whom the Elohist's material is somehow dependent. It was in material that originated in the north that such men as the *ḥarṭummîm* were condemned (cf. Ex. 22:17 and Deut. 18:10).[28] This merits a closer look, for that there is a polemical element here cannot be denied; but of what sort, and how far-reaching is it?

Joseph is shown as superior to *ḥarṭummîm* in that he succeeds while they all fail. There is indeed none as "wise and discerning" as he. But only in comparison to Joseph are they belittled; they look foolish only when compared to the superior ability of Joseph. They receive, in fact, comparatively little attention. They are not even mentioned after their initial failure and Joseph's introduction except perhaps as among the *ʿabadîm* of 41:37–38, in which they are not at all foolish, for they recognize Joseph's abilities. A comparison with Daniel 2 is instructive here: Joseph's conventional wish of 41:16 does not have the sharp polemical thrust of Daniel's: "Daniel answered the king, 'No wise men, enchanters, magicians, or astrologers can show to the king the mystery which the king has asked, but there is a God in heaven who reveals mysteries, and he has made known to King Nebuchadnezzar what will be in the latter days. Your dream and the visions of your head as you lay in bed are these' " (Dan. 2:27–28).

What Joseph says of the relationship of the deity to dreams and the interpretation of dreams is in accord with the understanding of this throughout the ancient Near East. Joseph beats these Egyptian courtiers at their own game; he interprets the dreams, gives counsel, and takes action based on it. He is superior because he bests all others at the very tasks facing courtiers; the tasks themselves are not subject to criticism, and they cannot be without belittling Joseph. The thrust of this unit is much more like that of the claims made in 1 Kings 4:29–31 (in the Hebrew, 5:9–11) concerning the wisdom of Solomon: "And God gave Soloman wisdom and understanding beyond measure, and largeness of mind like the sands on the seashore, so that Solomon's wisdom surpassed the wisdom of all the people of the east, and all the wisdom of Egypt. For he was wiser than all other men . . . and his fame was in all the nations round about." Here as well the wisdom of the other nations is belittled, if at all, only in comparison that of Solomon (note also the story of the visit of the queen of Sheba in 1 Kings 10). Neither the wise men of the nations nor the Egyptian courtiers of Pharaoh are presented as fools, for indeed that would essentially dilute the force of the comparison in each case. In 1 Kings, as in Genesis 40–41, the harsh religious and nationalistic tone of some biblical polemic is missing (cf. with Dan. 2:27–28 such units as Jer. 10:1–10; Isa. 44:9–20; and even Isa. 19:1–4, 11–15). In fact, the Egyptian "Satirical Letter of Hori to Amen-em-ope" is an example of a very much harsher polemic from within courtier circles, and yet it is often broadly categorized as wisdom.[29]

Thus some elements of the story—etiology, dreams, and polemic—do not play as large a role as sometimes suggested; and, while not found in biblical wisdom literature as that is usually defined, they are not, as here treated, antithetical to it. Their place is defined by their conjunction with other parts of this story which are reflective of wisdom themes. Joseph appears as an ideal wise courtier in Genesis 40–41, and this narrative of his rise and success in the Egyptian royal establishment is illustrative of several motifs associated with that ideal by the wise. While no single instance is determinative, taken as a whole the material cited would seem to point, not just to loose affinities, but to the influence of wisdom traditions and circles upon this story of Joseph the Egyptian courtier that stands as a kernel in the larger Joseph novella. And while such a story of a rise from rags to riches, of small beginnings that climax in unimagined success, has a universal appeal, in this particular case the setting, the characters, and the dynamics of the plot all point to a royal court and its educational/wisdom establishment as a place for its origin and as its primary audience. The tale was composed and treasured by those steeped in court wisdom traditions.

May one then in this instance speak of a "wisdom story"? Certainly the answer must hinge on just how one defines that elusive but useful category "wisdom."[30] There are marked affinities, which are strong enough to point to some influence, with materials generally designated as "wisdom," especially the Instructions of Egypt and limited material in the book of Proverbs. One could even suggest that there is a didactic or illustrative thrust in this story. But the degree to which such a thrust was the intent of an author or was defined by its use is always difficult to determine. Clearly the entertainment value of the story is justification enough for its creation and preservation. And while one may speak of Joseph as illustrative of the model wise courtier, it may go beyond the evidence to say that this story was created with the intention of providing, first and foremost, a model and incentive for future courtiers. In significant ways Joseph shapes his destiny. Yet elements of the fortuitous are focal as well: Joseph just happens to be in attendance on the officials as they have their dreams; he is brought to Pharaoh's notice by the chief baker at the most opportune moment. He shapes his destiny as much by taking hold of what fortune offers as through initiation of events. An examination of this story of Joseph as an Egyptian courtier against the background of what we know of ancient Egypt may provide additional perspectives that enrich our appreciation of it and its place in the larger Joseph novella.

NOTES

1. J. Skinner, *A Critical and Exegetical Commentary on Genesis*, 460 provides details. This complexity and seeming confusion involves, in part, the conclusion of Gen. 39 and the insertion of that unit into the larger narrative.

2. While *tālāh* generally means "to hang" (Esth. 5:14; 7:10), E. A. Speiser (*Genesis*, 307) suggests that here it must be translated "to impale," since a man who is beheaded could not be hanged. Skinner (*Genesis*, 463–64) suggests that the reference is to the exposure of the body, an especially horrid disgrace in ancient Egypt, where proper care and preparation of the body at death was essential. See also Gerhard von Rad, *Genesis*, 367.

On the punning use of the idiom *nāśâ' rô'š*, see Speiser, *Genesis*, 307-8; and "Census and Ritual Expiation in Mari and Israel," *BASOR* 149 (1958): 17-25. As Speiser suggests, three meanings of this idiom are played off against each other in this chapter. First there is the sense of "to poll, to count, to give attention to," which is primary in Gen. 40:20, where it would seem that the results of the enquiry into the matters of the chief butler and chief baker are proclaimed on a public occasion. The second and third meanings are found in Joseph's interpretations of their dreams, which anticipate the results of the enquiry: in the one case the sense is "to pardon, comfort, or restore" (v. 13; cf. 2 Kgs. 25:27; Jer. 52:31), while in the other it is "to execute, to behead" (v. 19). See also Skinner, *Genesis*, 462–164, and von Rad, *Genesis*, 367.

3. The hiphil of the root *zkr* (Gen. 40:14) does not have the sense of "to call to mind or to cause to remember," but rather "to bring to notice, to present a case" (see Gen. 41:9–13). See L. Ruppert, *Die Josephserzählung der Genesis: Ein Beitrag zur Theologie der Pentateuchquellen*, 137.

4. Gerhard von Rad, "The Joseph Narrative and Ancient Wisdom," in *The Problem of the Hexateuch and Other Essays*, 292–300. See W. L. Humphreys, "The Motif of the Wise Courtier in the Old Testament"; George W. Coats, "The Joseph Story and Ancient Wisdom: A Reappraisal," *CBQ* 35 (1973): 285–97.

5. Thus, the vizier Ptah-hotep asks Pharaoh, "Let a command be issued to this servant to make a staff of old age, that my son may be made to stand in my place." The popularity of the several collections of Instructions indicates that they had a wider audience than the single son of the courtier purported to be the author. But the form of father to son, courtier to successor, is maintained by all. For the motif of the wise courtier generally see Humphreys, "Motif."

6. *ANET*, 412-15; A. Erman, *Literature*, 234-42; Z. Zaba, *Les maximes de Ptah-hotep*; R. O. Faulkner, E. F. Wente, Jr., and W. K. Simpson, *The Literature of Ancient Egypt: An Anthology of Stories, Instructions, and Poetry*, 159-76. All quotations are from the last reference.

7. A. H. Gardiner, "The Instruction Addressed to Kagemni and his Brethren," *JEA* 32 (1946): 71-5; Erman, *Literature*, 66-67; Faulkner, *Literature*, 177-79.

8. *ANET*, 419-20.

9. *ANET*, 420-21; Erman, *Literature*, 234-42; E. Suys, *La sagesse d'ani*.

10. F. L. Griffith, "The Teaching of Amenophis the Son of Kanaknt, Papyrus B. M. 10474," *JEA* 12 (1926): 191-231; *ANET*, 421-24; Faulkner, *Literature*, 241-65.

11. Erman, *Literature*, 75-84; *ANET*, 414-18; Faulkner, *Literature*, 180-92.

12. Erman, *Literature*, 72-74; *ANET*, 418-19; Faulkner, *Literature*, 193-97.

13. A. H. Gardiner, *Notes on the Story of Sinuhe*, 164.

14. W. L. Humphreys, "The Motif of the Wise Courtier in the Book of Proverbs," 177-90; J. L. Crenshaw, "Education in Ancient Israel," *JBL* 104 (1985): 601-15.

15. This is certainly true of the Egyptian and Mesopotamian wisdom literature as well. However, the material from these areas is preserved in the form in which it was used by the scribal establishments. See the remark of G. W. Lambert: "The only thought which can be received is that of a small group, presumably the intelligentsia of ancient society" (*Babylonian Wisdom Literature*, 2). This could even more surely be said of Egypt.

16. See R. B. Y. Scott, "Solomon and the Beginnings of Wisdom in Israel,", 262-79. See generally Humphreys, "Motif," 102-20.

17. The terms "parallel," "affinity," and "influence" can be and often are used too loosely. It is one thing to point to a likeness or affinity between two items and quite another to suggest the presence of an influence of one upon the other or the connection of both with a common third item. The term "parallel" is the most abused, and so here avoided.

18. William McKane, *Prophets and Wise Men*, 23-47.

19. von Rad, "Joseph Narrative," p. 294. See also von Rad, *Die Josephsgeschichte*, 11-4; and *Genesis*, 430, 371-2.

20. Faulkner, *Literature*, 68; see also von Rad, "Joseph Narrative," 294.

21. See pp. 74, 121-22 above. See also A. L. Oppenheim, "The Interpretation of Dreams in the Ancient Near East," *Transactions of the American Philosophical Society* 46 (1956): 204-5: "A customary formula in which the professional interpreter of dreams grants permission to a person to report to him a dream for elucidation." cf. Skinner, *Genesis*, 307; E. L. Ehrlich, *Der Traum im alter Testament*, 78.

22. Faulkner, *Literature*, 199-200.

23. von Rad, *Genesis*, 373.

24. There is no need to read the plural as suggested by the LXX, for Pharaoh is the implied subject. In v. 35 the suggested action to be taken by the officials is presented, and it need not stand in contradiction to v. 34, in that *'et kol 'ōkel* cannot be more than a general reference to all the food collected through the tax. Even in the years of plenty the people would have to eat.

25. So Speiser, *Genesis*, 311, 313, who connects this usage with a root *ḥmš* found in Josh. 1:14; 4:12; Judg. 7:11; Exod. 13:18, and the LXX and V of Num. 32:17. However, in all these the form is the *qal* passive participle, and the root is used in each instance of a body of men prepared for war, and not, as in Gen. 41, of the economic reorganization of a land and its people.

26. J. L. Crenshaw, "Method in Determining Wisdom Influence Upon 'Historical' Literature," *JBL* 88 (1969): 129–42.

27. Ruppert, *Josephserzählung*, 74–76.

28. In neither are the *ḥarṭummim* or the *ḥᵃkāmim* referred to expressly. With regard to the latter notice, see Gen. 44:5, 15.

29. See also Donald B. Redford, *A Study of the Biblical Story of Joseph*, 97, n. 6, for a critique of Ruppert along somewhat different lines.

30. J. L. Crenshaw offers a minimal definition in *Old Testament Wisdom: An Introduction*, 11–25.

EIGHT

EGYPTIAN BACKGROUND FOR THE STORY OF JOSEPH THE COURTIER

The material in Genesis 40–41, linked with 47:13–26 and 50:26, comprises a distinct unit complete in itself, the "rags to riches" story of the poor boy who makes good. There are affinities at essential points with traditions found in the materials produced and used by wisdom circles. In this story two closely related elements receive particular stress. Emphasis is placed on the remarkable abilities of the courtier as they are shown in loyal service of the pharaoh, and comparable stress is placed on the rewards and honors he receives for this service. Thus, on the one hand, Joseph's abilities as a dream interpreter and as an adviser and administrator are underscored: "This proposal seemed good to Pharaoh and to all his servants. And Pharaoh said to his servants, 'Can we find such a man as this, in whom is the Spirit of God?' So Pharaoh said to Joseph, 'Since God has shown you all this, there is none so discreet and wise as you are; you shall be over my house, and all my people shall order themselves as you command; only as regards the throne will I be greater than you.'" (41:37–40). His service to the nation and crown in a time of crisis is thus depicted (41:53–57; 47:13–26). Between advice and the execution of it, the elevation of Joseph to high office and the honors he received are detailed. The formality of this ceremony becomes apparent in the recitation of insignia presented—signet ring, linen robes, gold chain, chariot of the second in command (41:42–43)—and in the formula of installation (41:40–45). Clearly, this is the apex of the career of a very successful

154

courtier. The narrative is allowed to move at leisured pace, and the reader is able to savor every detail. It climaxes when Joseph is granted a new name by the king himself, a statement that a new identity has been created for him. It also indicates the gift of life itself, as the name indicates (41:45; cf. 32:22–30). Even his wife and therefore his sons are gifts of the king. He will attain the ideal age of 110 years and, embalmed in the Egyptian manner, have his afterlife assured.

It has been suggested that the story has at points been overly embellished, and it must be admitted that today's reader may feel a degree of impatience at these spun-out descriptions of his honors and awards, which have even been described as "embarrassing."[1] But we must not assume too quickly that this perspective was shared by ancient readers. In fact, there are from ancient Egypt examples of materials that have just these characteristics, which were most popular in the court schools.

This Egyptian material consists of numerous inscriptions of a biographical nature found on the tombs of royal courtiers,[2] and certain literary pieces, such as the "Story of Sinuhe" and the "Story of the Shipwrecked Sailor," that are quite possibly patterned on the tomb biographies. The biographies relate highlights of the courtier's career in service of the pharaoh; attention is at times drawn to the comparatively low origins of the figure in order to highlight all the more sharply his success. Details are given of successful service and of particular activities undertaken at the king's command. Notice is given of the honors and rewards received for this service, especially those presented directly by the royal hand. This material is found inscribed on the courtier's tomb, itself often the final and highest gift and honor granted by the pharaoh.

The nature and specific themes of this type of material can be made clearest through an example. The courtier Uni had a long, varied, and distinguished career, serving under three kings of the sixth dynasty. Of his beginnings he says: "My office was that of supervisor of . . . and I filled the office of inferior custodian of the domain of Pharaoh."[3] Thus, he "entered his official career at the bottom of the ladder."[4] Under Pepi I he was appointed "to the rank of companion and inferior prophet of his pyramid-city."[5] He was also made judge of the Nekhen court, and "he [Pharaoh] loved me more than any servant of his. I heard, being alone with (only) the chief judge and Vizier, in every private matter—in the name of the king . . . because the king loved me more than any official of his, more than any noble of his, more than any servant of his."[6] Pharaoh provided a tomb for Uni, and he was later appointed superior custodian of the domain of Pharaoh. When a court or harem intrigue involving the queen was prosecuted, Uni was selected over all other officials to hear the delicate case.[7] Again, higher officials were passed over when Pharaoh went to war to put down a revolt in Sinai and southern Palestine: "I was the one who made for them the plan while my office was (only) that of Superior Custodian of the domain of Pharaoh."[8] Finally, under Mer-ne-Re he was made "governor of the South," and in that capacity he led expeditions to the southern quarries to provide for Pharaoh's tomb.[9] The number and variety of positions held by this one man are striking. Authority in ancient Egypt was personal in character, stemming from the pharaoh; "officials could be used in whatever function seemed desirable at any moment."[10] Individual qualities and abilities might well be recognized and lead to great success in a range of distinct tasks and roles.

Today historical concerns generally shape scholars' interest in these tomb biographies.[11] It is the specific and atypical that is sought. From the point of view of the ancient courtier, the interest was in the more personal and sometimes stereotypical elements; the official's usefulness to the king and the recognition received from Pharaoh are the focus. This recognition could climax when he was buried in a tomb close to Pharaoh so that his service could continue in the afterlife. Often the points that modern readers find most tedious are those that the ancient reader seems to have considered to be of the essence of these inscriptions: lists of awards, honors, and preparations for the afterlife.

This is also true of certain literary pieces that are similar to the tomb biographies. The best-known example is the "Story of Sinuhe." This is an account of an Egyptian courtier who, for reasons that are not clear, apparently even to himself, fled Egypt at the moment of the succession of Sesostris I. Contained in this recital of his adventures during his self-imposed exile in Syria-Palestine and of his final return to Egypt are long notices of royal favor and concern, such as edicts received and sent. These are always recounted and sometimes repeated in full, and present long descriptions of the courtier's usefulness in former times and his continued place in the affections of the royal court. It is the necessity for the courtier to return to the king, and especially the advantages of a death and proper burial in Egypt, that form the central theme of the tale. Thus, it concludes with an elaborate description of the courtier's warm welcome home and his reinstallation into court service, and finally of the preparations for his death and burial:

I was assigned to the house of a king's son. Fine things were in it, a cooling room in it, and representations of the horizon. Valuables of the treasury were in it, vestments of royal linen were in every apartment, and first-grade myrrh of the king and the courtiers whom he loves. Every domestic servant was about his prescribed task. Years were caused to pass from my body. . . . I was outfitted with fine linen and rubbed with the finest oil. . . . A house of a plantation owner, which had belonged to a Companion, was given to me. Many craftsmen had built it, and all its trees were planted anew. Meals were brought from the palace three and four times a day, in addition to what the royal children gave. A pyramid of stone was built for me in the midst of the pyramids. The overseer of stonecutters of the pyramids marked out its ground plan. The master draftsman sketched it in . . . . Ka-servants were assigned to me, and an endowed estate was settled on me with fields attached, at my mooring place, as is done for a Companion of the first order. My statute was overlaid with gold leaf, its apron of electrum. His Majesty ordered it to be done. There was no commoner for whom the like had ever been done. So I remained in the favor of the king until the day of mooring came.[12]

This courtier, like Joseph, is brought into the ranks of the royal officials, and, among other things, this is signaled by a change of clothing, a putting off of the former status (prison garb/bedouin dress), and the putting on of fine linen. Ideals are here presented—love of the homeland, desire for personal attendance upon the king, the need for a proper burial—that were especially characteristic of the good life for the Egyptian courtier.

It has been suggested, in fact, that in Sinuhe is presented "a prototype of the proper official" of the time and that narratives such as the story of Sinuhe and of the shipwrecked sailor were "pedagogical pieces." The leading figures were models illustrating and inculcating the ideals, characteristics, and values of the wise courtier, as these were developed and treasured in the court schools and as they were expressed in different form in the Instructions.[13] Whether this was the primary reason for the writing of the "Story of Sinuhe" is difficult to determine. Like the unit in Genesis 40–41 the "Story of Sinuhe" does not contain clear didactic tags, such as moralizing summaries, invitation to the reader, or instructional asides. However, sometimes the best instruction is the least obvious. In any case, the fact that the "Story of Sinuhe" was one of the most popular of all pieces of literature among the Egyptians themselves, and was copied time and again by persons in the scribal schools, seems to indicate that it served for centuries in this didactic fashion, as an illustration of the characteristics and ideals of the wise courtier.

The story of Joseph as Egyptian courtier is similar to this material in critical ways, sharing central elements and common characteristics with these Egyptian tales and tomb biographies. Within the frame provided by certain constant or often recurring elements—notice of small beginnings, attention to promotions, titles and other honors received, notice of varied forms of service rendered to the state and crown, preparation for death and burial—a range of themes and situations could be treated. It would seem from the examples of the "Story of the Sinuhe" and of Joseph as Egyptian courtier that, unlike most tomb biographies, the tales would center on some unusual or unfortunate event in the life of the courtier, or on some unusual circumstance in his origins—for example, exile from Egypt, foreign origins, or status as a slave.

Can this be a case of Israelite adaptation of Egyptian material, similar to the widely proposed Egyptian basis in the Instructions of Amen-em-opet for the material in Proverbs 22:16–24:22? The setting for the action in the story of Joseph as Egyptian courtier, is Egypt, and in the course of the narrative traces are found of many characteristics, institutions, and practices that seem at first glance to be peculiar to Egypt. We need not give a detailed analysis of the several Egyptian traces found in the story of Joseph as Egyptian courtier, for comprehensive studies have been presented by D. Redford, and J. Vergote, and to a lesser extent by J. Janssen.[14] All bring a wealth of comparative material to bear on the Joseph narrative, and they seek to demonstrate that there are indeed many genuine Egyptian traces in this part of Genesis. In the summary evaluation of Janssen, "The most astonishing fact is that the story of Joseph, not a scientific history in one sense . . . has a definite Egyptian atmosphere. It has obviously been written by somebody who himself (let us for a moment disregard the tradition) knew and had heard many things about the Nile Valley and its inhabitants."[15]

Beyond this general conclusion, however, far-reaching disagreements are met as specific claims are made about the evidence. The relation of the material in Genesis to Egyptian tradition is not one of simple dependence. There are, of course, a number of differences among scholars on the meaning of this or that detail from Genesis and from Egyptian sources. But there are larger differences as well; if nothing else, these indicate the need for caution. Thus Vergote, on the basis of his study, concluded that almost all signs point to a Ramesside date for the Joseph novella; and, since this is generally agreed to be the period of Moses, the traditional Mosaic authorship of the material must receive fuller consideration in scholarly circles. Indeed, who would have more knowledge of things Egyptian—and especially of life in court—than Moses? Redford, while recognizing the worth of Vergote's analysis, is critical of this conclusion and takes us to another extreme. He turns to the Saite and early Persian period (eighth–sixth centuries BCE) as that to which the evidence points.[16]

This range of conclusions—others fall between these extremes—calls for caution. The question of date seems to have been of overriding concern in these studies, and with it the question of genuineness of the several Egyptian traces in the Joseph novella. We must also keep the larger ancient Near Eastern world before us in an analysis of this sort, for many motifs found in Egyptian materials are found elsewhere as well and need not point to an exclusively Egyptian provenance. And for all periods, and certainly for some more than others, there are lacunae in our reconstructed picture of Egypt's life and culture. One must beware of placing too much weight on arguments from silence. In fact, the period between the suggested date of Vergote and that of Redford—the twelfth through the eighth centuries BCE—is one in which the lacunae are largest in our knowledge of ancient Egypt; this was the very period critical for the development of the literary and religious traditions of ancient Israel.

With this in mind, we can note that further questions must be brought to the data, questions which are usually neglected in the study of the Egyptian traces in the Joseph narrative. One issue relates to the distribution of the Egyptian traces throughout the narrative. The bulk of them are found in Genesis 40–41; 47:13–26; and 50:26. The largest segment of the studies of Vergote, Redford, and Janssen deal with these chapters which treat Joseph as an Egyptian courtier. Furthermore, in this part of the Joseph novella the Egyptian traces are carefully and fully interwoven into the story and function in an essential way in the development of its plot and perspectives. Their removal would tear the story apart; they are much more than just window dressing, designed to give a sense of verisimilitude. In this kernel within the Joseph novella the Egyptian traces are most prevalent and at home.

There are in the Hebrew text of Genesis 40–41, for example, several apparent loan words that have come into Hebrew from the Egyptian language. Along with the expected $par^c\bar{o}h$ (Pharaoh) and $y^{e}\bar{o}r$ (Nile), the word $\bar{a}h\hat{u}$ (reed) is found in the account of Pharaoh's first dream (41:2);

159

the officials first called to interpret the dreams are designated *ḥarṭummîm* (41:8, 24); and Pharaoh commands that the obscure *'abrēk* be called out before the elevated Joseph (41:43).[17] While this is a relatively large number of loan words for a single chapter, all except the last are found elsewhere in the biblical material, and, after all, the setting is Egypt and the subject Egyptian. The meaning of *ḥarṭummîm* in Egyptian is rather precise, denoting the chief lector priest. However, its use in Genesis 41 (see also Exod. 8 and 9), as well as its use in cognate Semitic languages, is much less so, the reference being generally to the wise men of the royal court. As the technical term passed over into other languages, it was generalized, as its use in Genesis 41 with the qualifier *ḥᵃkāmîm* suggests.

Certain elements in the dreams of the courtiers and of Pharaoh have been said to indicate an Egyptian origin. Of course, in the fantastic world of dreams such as these, where vines grow before one's eyes, where cows devour other cows and remain unchanged, where stalks of corn eat other stalks, one must be quite careful when pressing the details. Indeed, these appear to be literary constructions developed to fit the particular situation of the narrative, more elaborate than the earlier pairs of dreams and more in need of interpretation. In regard to the cows in Pharaoh's first dream, while cows are indeed quite prominent in certain Egyptian artistic and literary works, and so perhaps characteristic of Egypt (perhaps especially so from the point of view of outsiders), cows were much too prevalent in the Near East to be considered in any way peculiar to Egypt. Redford indicates that in the Ptolemaic period the Egyptian sign for cow designated the word "year."[18] However, it is doubtful that such a basic identity stands behind the cows in Genesis 41, for there is no such pattern with the other indications of the periods of time represented by the branches of the vine, the baskets of baked goods, or the ears of corn. It has also been noted that vines, as in the chief butler's dream, are in one case said to indicate the quick fulfillment of a dream.[19] But no comparable indication is found in the chief baker's dream, and in neither case is attention called to the rapid outcome of events (cf. 41:32). Nor can much be made of the notice that the grapes in the butler's dream are squeezed by hand, for the dream is a literary construction, carefully tailored to fit the situation of the chief butler and his restoration to office. Certainly he played no immediate part in the actual preparation of the wine, and a man of his rank would not tread upon the grapes himself. The dreams, as baroque and artificial as they appear, seem generally at home in the Egyptian context, but do not reveal an unusual degree of acquaintance with particular Egyptian motifs or customs. They could as well be constructed by one who had even a general picture, shaped from afar, of that remarkable and strange land. In fact, the references to the blasting east wind in Pharaoh's second dream (41:6, 23) seems indicative of a Palestinian setting.[20]

Along with the ḥarṭummîm other officials of the Egyptian court are mentioned. While none that are apparently foreign to what is now known of the Egyptian court is named, the particular offices and titles mentioned seem common to most royal establishments in the ancient Near East. The precise position attained by Joseph has been the subject of special study. The majority of scholars suggest that it was the office of vizier, the highest office in the land next to Pharaoh himself.[21] Janssen suggests that the author of the tale probably thought of Joseph as such, although there are problems with this identification; and while elements in the installation ceremony can point in this direction, the identification is by no means certain.[22] The crisis presented in the story makes the action of the new official difficult to evaluate, for duties which might in normal times fall to others could be placed under the direct authority of a superior official in an emergency. Furthermore, lines of authority were quite fluid in ancient Egypt, especially within the higher reaches of officialdom. Power was the personal grant of the king. The tomb biographies reflect a remarkable range of duties; Uni functioned in administrative, judical, and military roles. While elements of the installation ceremony seem characteristic of Egyptian practice, there has been no real success in pinpointing a particular office to which these necessarily point. Most important, the very nature of this theme of a remarkable rise from rags to riches as it appears in many forms and cultures would demand the hero attain the highest position possible. In Egypt this is the office of vizier. The fact that Joseph is said to ride in the chariot of the second in command (bᵉmirkebet hammišneh, Gen. 41:43) seems to point as well in this direction.[23]

The elements of Joseph's elevation have received careful attention. The author here enters into some detail, for the narrative reaches its climax as the reader and Joseph are allowed to enjoy the moment of triumph in a rapid-fire manner.[24] However, when these details are examined closely, they are once more found to be of a mixed nature. Some seem to represent more widespread ancient Near Eastern court protocol (e.g., the giving of the signet ring, the chariot of the second in command; Esth. 3:10; 6:8; 8:2), while others seem to be more peculiar to but not wholly confined to Egypt. Among the latter are the giving of a fine linen robe, the golden chain, and possibly the peculiar expressions ʿal pîkā yiššaq kol ʿammî and *'abrēk*. The latter seems to be an attempt to render an Egyptian imperative meaning "do obeisance."[25] The former has posed more difficulty. Literally it means "all my people shall kiss upon your mouth." Several emendations have been offered for the text as it now stands. Others suggest that we have here a trace of a misunderstood Egyptian expression that had some such sense as "at your command my people shall kiss the floor."[26]

Redford has shown that the various elements presented in the description of Joseph's elevation are of a mixed nature. In some instances, when compared with Egyptian literary and pictorial evidence, they indicate honors awarded a person, while in other instances they seem to indicate the installation of an official into new office.[27] However, these two are not unrelated: an act of installation into higher office, especially when it follows upon the recognition of demonstrated superior abilities, is itself an honor and could involve elements of this. In the case of the narrative at hand we are at the climax of the story of this courtier's career, the point at which he received the recognition and honor that launch him upon a whole new life as an Egyptian of highest rank. The reversal of his fate is complete as he is effectively born again. Thus, many elements are brought together in a massive ceremony to produce this exaggerated effect, achieved through a loose collection of specifics, some that reflect Egyptian custom and court practice even if drawn from different types of ceremony, others characteristic of wider ancient Near Eastern court protocol. No particular Egyptian court ceremony stands before us. We have a finely designed literary construct. Diverse elements are brought together at this climax to underscore the remarkable turn of events in the life of Joseph.

With his new office and high honor came a whole new life, also the gift of Pharaoh, symbolized in the change of name and the grant of a wife from the highest priestly nobility. All three names in Genesis 41:45 are considered to be Egyptian, and concerning two there has been little disagreement. Potiphera, the name of Joseph's father-in-law and meaning "he whom Re gives," is of a type popular in late Egyptian. The name of Joseph's wife, Asenath ("belonging to Neith"), is not attested, but names of this type are found from all periods, being very popular from the end of the New Kingdom on.[28]

There has been more debate over the meaning of the name Zaphenath-paneah given to Joseph himself by Pharaoh. Redford reviews several suggestions and concludes that probably the name is of the type *gd - NNN - iw.f - ʿnh* when transliterated into Egyptian and has some such meaning as "NNN speaks and he lives." Seeing no particular connection between the narrative and the meaning of the name, for which some translation or interpretation would have to be offered, he suggests that the author simply took an Egyptian name of his period to lend an air of authenticity to his narrative.[29] Names of the type suggested are birth-names, and it is to be noted that this event does mark a complete change in Joseph's status; Joseph is reborn as an Egyptian, and a name that is characteristic of birth in Egypt is selected to underscore this, a name whose meaning and exact form was in time lost.

Other elements of these chapters are occasionally said to reflect Egyptian coloring. Foreign slaves, especially from Syria-Palestine, are known to have been in Egypt in most periods, becoming more and more common in the New Kingdom and later. On occasion foreigners seem to have risen to positions of some authority, if not to the heights and with the speed of Joseph. In Genesis 40–41 the manner in which this slave reached Egypt is left vague; in his petition to the chief butler Joseph claims, "I was indeed stolen out of the land of the Hebrews" (40:15). The account of Joseph as an Egyptian courtier demands no more; he could have reached Egypt through slave trade, military conquest, or whatever. As the story became a kernel utilized in the larger novella, however, this notice became an indirect reference to events in Genesis 37.[30] The celebration of the king's birthday is a custom not well attested in ancient Egypt, nor in the Near East as a whole, and seems to be a general motif that cannot be said to be peculiar to any place or period.[31] The same would seem to be the case with the motif of the seven-year cycles of famine and plenty. These last three items are, however, critical elements in the narrative and function either as turning points in the unfolding of the plot or as essential presuppositions upon which the whole is based. Thus, they reflect Egyptian customs, themes, or coloring less than the need of the author to move the plot along with all due speed and effectiveness. In a story of a dramatic rise from the depths it is very effective to present the hero as one not only foreign (a Hebrew) and, when we first meet him, in prison as a servant, but one brought to this condition through illegal acts (compare *gānab* in Exod. 20:15; Deut. 5:19). Pharaoh's birthday, of course, provides the occasion for Joseph's abilities as a dream interpreter to be recognized, even if he is forgotten by all but the reader, and the seven-year cycles of plenty and famine set the backdrop for Joseph's demonstrated success as a royal official.

Further suggested Egyptian traces are found in the related material in Genesis 47:13–26 and 50:26. To the many attempts made to find in Egyptian sources the conditions reflected in 47:13–36, dealing with the enslavement of the people to the crown, the particular details—such as the rate of taxation, the forms of land-holding, the exemption of the temple estates, etc.—have offered a thin base, and little success has been realized.[32] However, knowledge of the economic conditions in Egypt is not as full as could be desired, and thus the situation with regard to Genesis 47:13–26 must remain uncertain. Janssen notes two large papyri that present relevant information: the Harris Papyrus, which lists temple donations from the time of Rameses III, and the Wilbour Papyrus from the time of Rameses V. The latter has received careful study by A. H. Gardiner. As Janssen notes, Gardiner is most careful in his conclusions with regard to Genesis,[33] suggesting that 47:13–26 reflects more of an ideal than a real situation. In theory the ruler may have owned all the land; but it is doubtful that there ever was a time when the temples were all exempt from taxation, for this was a grant and special privilege of the pharaoh and probably not the permanent situation.[34] The overall tone of 47:13–36 is that of one viewing the situation with less than exact detailed knowledge but with more than a little wonder at the absolute authority and control of the crown in that remarkable land of Egypt. It is difficult to find in this idealized depiction reflections of any particular period in Egypt's history. Once more, it is a basic narrative need that is served through underscoring the remarkable abilities, effectiveness, and authority of Joseph the Egyptian courtier and his use of these to the full benefit of his king. This unit is best understood from a literary perspective.

In Genesis 50:26 we have one of two references to embalming in the Hebrew Bible, the other being in verses 2 and 3 of the same chapter, which deal with Jacob. In the patriarch's case more specifics are given: the work is done by the rōpᵉˀîm, the process lasts 40 days, and the period of mourning is 70 days. Comparative material from Egypt presents a variety of details, reflecting different periods and local customs, but the picture presented in Genesis 50 seems to approximate Egyptian practice in a general way.[35] It is not impossible that the notice in 50:2–3, now applied to Jacob, once applied to the death and burial of Joseph, and was connected to the patriarch in the later development of the novella, especially when it was incorporated into the wider patriarchal traditions of the Torah. In this larger setting the figure of Jacob/Israel is more significant, and his death could not be overshadowed by that of his son. If this is the case, in

an earlier placement the material would have reinforced the impression
that at the conclusion of this courtier's life story the success and honor he
attained in life followed him in death. He received full and proper burial—
an item of critical importance, central in Egypt. We can compare the
extended preparations recounted at the conclusion of the "Story of
Sinuhe" for his eventual death.

Joseph, we are told, died at the age of 110 years. Indications in the
biblical material are that the ideal age was 120 years (see Gen. 6:3 and
Deut. 34:7). In Egypt 110 years was reflective of a good and rich life. Thus
the conclusion of the Instructions of Ptah-hotep states:

> Act until your master says of you: "How good was the teaching of his
> father from whom he issued . . . " Behold, a good son is a gift of
> God. . . . He acts rightly, and his mind has achieved more than his
> actions; according as you reach me, your body will be hale and the
> king will be pleased with all that happens. You will surpass (my)
> years of life, and what I have done on earth is not little. I have passed
> 110 years of life through what the king gave to me, favors over and
> above those who went before, because of acting rightly for the king
> until the blessed state.[36]

The remarkable life of this courtier ended in the proper manner, a fitting
climax and reflection of his whole career.

In summary, in the Egyptian traces considered to this point there is
nothing that can be said to be definitely non-Egyptian. Certain elements
are found throughout much of the ancient Near East, but others seem to
reveal a general knowledge of things Egyptian. The author of this story of
Joseph as an Egyptian courtier was to some degree knowledgeable about
practices and customs of Egypt; yet a certain inexactness, characterized
by exaggeration, generalization, and more than a touch of wonder,
appears in his treatment of the Egyptian setting. This suggests that the
author was not an Egyptian and was not writing for Egyptians. This
impression is reinforced by an element in the tale that seems clearly non-
Egyptian: the depiction of Pharoah and of the king's relationship with the
gods, especially as reflected in the understanding of dreams found in
chapters 40–41.

Several references are made to God or the gods (ʾelōhîm) by Joseph or
Pharoah. Thus Joseph, both in prison and in the royal court, carefully
places dreams and their interpretation within the divine sphere (40:8;
41:16). "God has revealed to Pharoah what he is about to do" (41:25, 28).

The certainty and haste with which it will happen is indicated by the divine doubling of the dream (41:32). As we have seen, 40:8 and 41:16 serve in part as polite disclaimers, as protocol for the proper form of address by a dream interpreter. Yet after Joseph has given the interpretation and presented his counsel on how the revealed danger is to be met, Pharaoh exclaims to his courtiers, "Can we find such a man as this, in whom is the Spirit of God?" (41:38), and to Joseph he remarks, "Since God has shown you all this, there is none so discreet and wise as you are" (41:39). These references in this context demand more attention.

The whole scene is in an essential way counter to what we know of Egypt. That a courtier might receive through a dream a communication from the deity and need to have it interpreted is quite possible from the Egyptian point of view; the pharaoh, however, was divine; he was the god-king, and to suggest that he would need the aid of dream interpreters is markedly out of place. There are instances of communication by other deities with Pharaoh through dreams, chiefly in the cases of Thutmose IV and Marniptah, but also from a later period with the Ethiopian Pharaoh Tanutamon and then with Ptolemy I.[37] These are recorded in royal inscriptions; in the literary and wisdom materials from ancient Egypt there are no such references. In each case the communication is quite direct, the situation is recognized and understood for what it is by the king, and action is taken accordingly. The gods directly address Pharaoh. The example of Thutmose IV, as recorded on the Sphinx Stela, is a clear example:

> One of these days it happened that the King's Son Thutmose came on an excursion at noon time. Then he rested in the shadow of this great god. Sleep took hold of him, slumbering at the time when the sun was at (its) peak. He found the majesty of this august god *speaking with his own mouth, as a father speaks to his son,* saying, "See me, look at me, my son . . . (the dream continues from several lines of the inscription) . . . When he had finished these words, then this King's Son awoke, because he had heard these (words) . . . *and he understood the speech of this god.*[38] [*My italics.*]

In Egypt the king was enveloped within the divine sphere, and he would need no mortal interpreter.

Dream interpretation was practiced in ancient Egypt, and two late copies of dream books are known. The dream book of the Chester Beatty Papyrus III collection, could, its editor proposes, go back to as early as the twelfth dynasty. Both deal with dreams classed as allegoric and hence in need of interpretation (as compared to those called theorematic, which are self-evident, but which may have allegoric elements, like those of Genesis 37).[39] The form of presentation is: "(If a man see himself in a dream,) doing so-and-so: good (or bad)! it means that such-and-such will happen."[40] Often the meaning of the dream is based on a pun, or on catchwords, symbols, or opposites.[41] The editor suggests that this and similar materials were used by and for the less-educated classes.[42] A review of the activity, events, and personages mentioned in the long lists of dreams indicates a range from the lowest classes to the lower levels of officialdom. Pharaoh is clearly not indicated. Moreover, the matters dealt with are of a personal nature entirely; matters of state are absent.

Thus, royal dreams are recorded in Egyptian material, but they are rare and appear in neither the preserved literary nor wisdom materials. The deities could communicate through dreams with the king, but no specialist was needed to interpret them. What is asserted about the deity in Genesis 40–41 by Joseph—that he can in dreams and through their interpretation reveal what is to occur—is not alien in general to the Egyptian. In the late Papyrus Insigner, it is noted that "He [the god] . . . has created dreams to guide him who experiences them—if he is blind (i.e., he cannot see his way through life)".[43] From the total evidence preserved, this could be said of the Egyptian understanding of dreams in all cases but that of Pharaoh, between whom and the gods no mortal intermediary would stand.

Those first called by Pharaoh to interpret his dreams are designated *harṭummîm*, and are further defined as *hᵃkāmîn* (Gen. 41:8). The word is usually translated as "diviner," or "magician"; it is also used of men in the court of Egypt in Exodus 7–9, and again of Babylonian courtiers in Daniel 1:20 and 2:2. The term is a loan word, based on the Egyptian *hyr tp*, and is also found in Akkadian (*hartibi*) and in Greek as well as in Hebrew. Vergote states that in Egypt the word is usually used of the chief lector priest[44] linked with the so-called "House of Life," where some suggest texts like the dream books were copied and composed. Oppenheim suggests that they were particularly concerned with the dreams of Pharaoh, but no specific evidence for this survives.[45] Thus, in the Egyptian sources the connection between the *harṭum* and dreams is tenuous at best. It is in the Hebrew Bible that this connection is made. Most striking is a late text, usually described as a "pious fraud," in which it is related how an ancient king was distressed because of a seven-year famine in the land.

He sent for the *hyr tp*, none other than the famed and revered Vizier Imhotep, who consulted the archives and gave advice on how to meet the danger. The text is late and the advice of a different order, but the vizier's connection with the role of adviser in Joseph's case is striking.[46] A royal dream is involved in this instance, but it occurs after the advice of Imhotep has been given and acted upon, and it needs no interpretation.

The root used in Genesis 40–41 for dream interpretation is *ptr*, which is found in a range of Semitic languages.[47] In Akkadian materials a *ša'ilû*-priest is mentioned as one who interprets (*pašarû*) through different means of enquiry of the deities as to a dream's meaning. Oppenheim describes the duties and role of this figure: "The interpretation of 'symbolic' dreams by means of divination techniques which aim to make the deity convey his meaning through another and unequivocal medium is but one of the many functions of the diviner-priests called *ša'ilû*, 'he who asks (the gods) questions.'" He has further noted that in "omen-conscious and portent-ridden Mesopotamia dream-omina never reached the popularity of the other methods of divination."[48] However, they are present, as Oppenheim's study itself indicates, and dreams are closely associated with other omina. In Mesopotamia the term "wisdom" (*nemequ*) and the adjectives used for wise (*enqu, mudu, hassu, etpesu*) are generally used to refer to "skill in cult and magic lore, and the wise man as the initiate." While in Mesopotamia and Palestine the "interpretation of dreams was considered the highest and the typical achievement of Egyptian divination techniques,"[49] the particular attitude toward Pharaoh's dreams shown in Genesis 41 is more characteristic of Mesopotamia with its consciously detailed omen sciences and its theology of kingship. A remarkable mixture of elements appears in Genesis 40–41. The general attitude and understanding of dreams and their means of interpretation are within what is known of dreams throughout the ancient Near East, including Egypt. However, when the dream is that of the king, the attitude is that revealed most characteristically in Mesopotamia; it is not that of ancient Egypt.

Joseph thus acknowledges that both dreams and interpretations are from God (or the gods), who controls the future and determines events. Joseph then proceeds to best the Egyptian *ḥarṭummîm* by interpreting Pharaoh's dreams. This is immediately followed (41:32–36) by advice on how to meet the danger that is thus revealed. No line is drawn between the interpretation and the advice. And it is on the basis of interpretation and advice that Pharaoh finds Joseph is just the man he needs to deal with the crisis that is coming. This observation by Pharaoh, which embraces both the interpretation and advice, is best comprehended through the understanding of the importance of royal dreams as matters of state, which is reflected in materials from Mesopotamia. Examples of Gudea and Gilgamesh come to mind, in that both, as kings, had dreams that they could not understand and thus sought interpretation (the first from the deities directly; the latter from his mother).[50] Pharaoh is not, as here presented, a divine king, and in this matter Genesis 40–41 is decidedly not Egyptian. He is a figure held in respect and even awe by his courtiers, and not a figure of fun; he is not a bumbling or rash fool at his wit's end, making hasty pronouncements and frantically searching for a solution to his problems (cf. the figure of the king in Daniel 2), nor is he the dull-witted and malleable figure found in the book of Esther. He seeks aid and recognizes sound advice when it is presented, and he acts to see that it is put into effect. However, he is clearly a mortal, not a deity.

It is in this context that notice must be taken once more of Redford's criticism of suggested links between the Joseph material and wisdom themes:

> Good speech before kings and competent work in one's office recall us to chapter 41, and suggest that at least here the writer has in mind the paragon of the Wisdom Literature, when he speaks of Joseph. But the unmistakable fact is that nowhere in this chapter is Joseph's excellence of speech or superior counsel held up as an object of admiration. Both the Butler and Pharaoh are impressed by one thing, viz. that by virtue of *divine inspiration* Joseph can interpret dreams and thus forecast the future. Joseph's suggestions are extremely valuable, and are characterized by wisdom, but *only* because God has revealed it all to him (compare verse 39). Divine inspiration takes us out of the practical world of the wisdom school, and into the realm of the storyteller. By its very nature it is miraculous, a gift of god, not a cultivated virtue. A man so gifted cannot be emulated.[51]

However, it is both the interpretation and the counsel that are held up for admiration. Nor need divine inspiration be antithetical to the world of the wise. To speak of the practical world of the wise as a sphere in which the divine has no place is artificial and contrary to the evidence. The wise men of the book of Proverbs speak not only of the deity's support of the orders and patterns that govern life and of which the wise are aware (e.g., Prov. 16:3, 4, 5, 7, 11; 20:23, 27: 21:3), but also of an area of experience outside of this order and thus mysterious. Here the wise plunge into the sphere of the divine freedom and miracle.[52]

The plans of the mind belong to man,
    but the answer of the tongue is from Yahweh. (16:1)
A man's mind plans his way,
    but Yahweh directs his steps. (16:9)
The lot is cast into the lap,
    but the decision is wholly from Yahweh. (16:33)
Many are the plans in the mind of a man,
    but it is the purpose of Yahweh that will be
    established. (19:21)
No wisdom, no understanding, no counsel,
    can avail against Yahweh.
The horse is made ready for the day of battle,
    but the victory belongs to Yahweh. (21:30–31)

Of these sayings von Rad observes:

> It is affecting to see how such a vital art of mastering life is aware that is must halt at these frontiers—indeed it even contrives to liquidate itself there. . . . It combines two things—man's confidence in his ability to master life and at the same time, with all the wisdom in the world, an awareness of the frontiers and a preparedness to fail in the sight of God.[53]

Here divine freedom breaks through all human insight and initiative. All of these citations are from that collection in the book of Proverbs showing greatest connection with the motif of the wise courtier.[54] In Mesopotamia, as noted above, there is a close connection between wisdom and the ability to reveal the hidden purposes and guidance of the deities (see also Prov. 2:1–8).

    We must ask whether the wisdom school and the realm of the story-teller need be set over against each other to the extent that Redford would seem to suggest. Certainly a good story can serve as an effective pedagogical tool; the use made of the "Story of Sinuhe" in the Egyptian court schools testifies to this. Surely a wise man might spin a story in which many of his ideals and values are incorporated. Yet Redford's remarks can serve as a caution, for the presence of wisdom motifs and ideals cannot automatically lead to the supposition of a didactic intent. Joseph is not present here in each and every detail of his character or career as a model for future courtiers. The element of the unexpected, be it perceived as fate, chance, or the providential action of the god(s), plays an important role in this tale and cannot be overlooked. Joseph's career, in its sudden and complete reversal of fortune, is not that of most courtiers; just this makes his story so engaging. We can still discover in the person and character of our hero ideals illustrated that were of special concern to the wise. Clearly this is not simply a wooden illustration of wisdom teaching but first and foremost an engaging tale of a sudden change of fortune in one man's life and his ability to capitalize on it. The general model is the tomb biography and especially stories developed on the pattern these biographies set, with their particular motif of faithful service rewarded in this life and in preparation for the next.

In conclusion, it would seem that, in spite of the several Egyptian traces in Genesis 40–41; 47:13–26; and 50:26 an origin for the story outside Egypt is indicated. The rather general nature of many of the traces, their sense of wonder and remoteness, and especially the picture presented of the pharaoh and his relationship to the divine sphere, all suggest this. We should consider as well that the hero is of foreign origin. Yet this story of Joseph as an Egyptian courtier reveals links to the royal court and wisdom circles; those influenced and trained therein would treasure it, and here we might seek its origins. In Syria-Palestine, in the Late Bronze Age, Egypt held sometimes greater and sometimes lesser sway, with its control centered chiefly in the major city-states. These enclaves were under Egyptian influence on many levels, and were in close contact with it. Influences from Mesopotamia were also present, and the Amarna correspondence reveals that Akkadian was the language of diplomatic and commercial affairs. Canaanites from these city-states were found in Egypt, as slaves, as merchants, as scribes, and even from the upper classes as hostages; all would be to a significant degree Egyptianized. Even after political domination had waned, the cultural influences of Egypt continued in Palestine, especially in the larger city-states such as Jerusalem, which were not under the influence of the new peoples moving into the area. Major urban areas in Syria-Palestine were focal points for a rich and complex blend of cultural influences. The story of Joseph as an Egyptian courtier (possibly with the hero originally having another name) could be one of the fruits of this meeting of traditions and cultures.

In Syria-Palestine in the late second millennium the story of Joseph as an Egyptian courtier would find a natural home. The several Egyptian traces in the narrative would be explained, as would the attitude toward the pharaoh, which, while not uniquely characteristic of Egypt, holds him in highest respect and even awe. He is in no way made to appear foolish. We can again contrast with this the depiction of King Ahasuerus in the book of Esther or of the several kings in the book of Daniel; Joseph is lavishly praised by the pharaoh, but he is not worshiped by him (cf. Dan. 2:46). Pharaoh is the focus of the courtier's life and activity in our story, the source of his authority, position, and his life, as well as the goal of all his actions. Even with our very partial knowledge of the royal courts of the Palestinian city-states of the Late Bronze Age (Ugarit had a scribal school, and the literary and nonliterary remains has revealed influence of both Egypt and Mesopotamia) it seems quite possible that this story of the remarkable rise of a foreign slave in the great court of Egypt could have its origins and been treasured in a Canaanite royal center. To say more requires a consideration of the larger unit into which the story of Joseph as an Egyptian courtier is now incorporated; that is, the Joseph novella as a whole.

NOTES

1. Donald B. Redford, *A Study of the Biblical Story of Joseph*, 87: "But the embellishment in the remainder of the chapter is more embarrassing. In describing Joseph's elevation to power, the writer keeps returning to the scene of investiture, after ostensibly closing his description of it, no less than four times (verses 41, 44, 45, 46)! A similar repetitive style is unmistakable in the account of Joseph's measures to ensure the grain supply (verses 47–49), and, especially, in the description of the famine (verses 53–57), Thereafter, in chapter 42, the reticence and brevity of the 'normal' style returns." If this means these embellishments are extraneous, I must disagree; I suggest that rather they are precisely the central focus and climax of this part of the Joseph novella—hallmarks of just this type of narrative.

2. See J. H. Breasted, *Ancient Records of Egypt*, passim.; H. H. Schmid, *Wesen und Geschichte der Weisheit*, 16, 44, 54, and the studies listed on p. 16. See also W. L. Humphreys, "The Motif of the Wise Courtier in the Old Testament," 10–16, 56–58.

3. Breasted, *Records*, # 294.

4. *Records*, # 292.

5. *Records*, # 307.

6. *Records*, # 307.

7. *Records*, # 308–10.

8. *Records*, #312. See also *ANET*, 227–28.

9. *Records*, # # 319–24.

10. H. Frankfort, *Ancient Egyptian Religion*, 35; see pp. 33–46 generally. As authority was from the person of the pharaoh, "this left great scope to energetic individuals" (36).

11. This shapes the selection of the material on Uni given in *ANET*, 227–28.

12. R. O. Faulkner, E. F. Wente, and W. K. Simpson, *The Literature of Ancient Egypt: An Anthology of Stories, Instructions, and Poetry*, 73–74.

13. Faulkner, *Literature*, 6, 57.

14. Redford, *Study*; J. Vergote, *Joseph en Égypt: Genèse chap. 37-50 à la lumière des études égyptologiques récentes*; J. M. A. Janssen, "Egyptological Remarks on the Story of Joseph in Genesis," *JEOL* 5 (1955–58): 63–72. See the references there for further studies.

15. Janssen "Remarks," 72. See also Gerhard von Rad, "The Joseph Narrative and Ancient Wisdom," 299: "Can assume Egyptian literary influence and models, even specific literary sources." See also von Rad, *Genesis*, 429–30; E. A. Speiser, *Genesis*, 292, 316, et passim.; O. Eissfeldt, "Genesis," 376; Vergote, *Joseph*, 2–3 et passim. Redford is less sure: "The Hebrew writer was not so well acquainted with Egypt as has often been imagined" (*Study*, 241–42).

16. Vergote, *Joseph*, 207–13 and the last chapter generally; Redford, *Study*, 241–43 and ch. 8 generally.

17. Vergote, *Joseph*, 59–66, 80–94, 135–41; Janssen "Remarks," 67–68; O. Wintermute, "Joseph Son of Jacob," 985; J. Skinner, *A Critical and Exegetical Commentary on the Book of Genesis*, 470; T. O. Lambdin, "Egyptian Loan Words in the Old Testament," *JAOS* 73 (1953): 146–55.

18. Redford, *Study*, 205. See Janssen, "Remarks," 66. There is little to support his suggestion that the reference in the dream is a "malevolent allusion" to sacred cows and the grain god of Egypt.

19. Redford, *Study*, 203–5.

20. So Janssen, "Remarks," 66.

21. So Roland de Vaux, *Ancient Israel*, 130, and "Titres et fonctionnaire égyptiens à la cour de David et de Solomon," *RB* 48 (1939): 401; von Rad, *Genesis*, 372; Speiser, *Genesis*, 316.

22. Janssen, "Remarks," 66–7. So also Vergote, *Joseph*, 102–12, who gives a detailed analysis of several elements of the installation ceremony and suggests that they indicate the office of vizier. A full discussion of the titles of Joseph in this material is given by W. A. Ward, who takes a different view, in "The Egyptian Office of Joseph," *JSS* 5 (1960): 146–50; see also his "Egyptian Offices in Gen, 39–50," *BSac* 114 (1957): 40–59. He treats six titles that he believes are assigned to Joseph and suggests that none can be shown to belong solely to the vizier. He suggests that Joseph was "appointed to serve as Overseer of the Granaries of Upper and Lower Egypt and as Great Steward of the Lord of the Two Lands" (*BSac* 50). Ward's study is useful, but he assumes that here one is dealing with an accurate historical account and fails to consider the questions of the literary nature of the work and the purpose and setting of the author.

23. This is so understood with Speiser, *Genesis*, 314. He suggests that the reference is not to the "second (best) chariot" (so RSV; cf. NEB's "Viceroy's Chariot"), but to Joseph as second in command, and he cites 2 Chr. 28:7. He also notes that the analogous Akkadian term, *terdennû*, is used both as an adjective and as a title. Joseph is to ride in the chariot set apart for the second in command.

24. See generally Vergote, *Joseph*, 95–141; Redford, *Study*, 208–26.

25. See Vergote, *Joseph*, 135–41; Redford, *Study*, 226–28, and the further references given by them. For a different suggestion see J. S. Croatto, "Abrek 'Intendant' dans Gen. XLI 41, 43," *VT* 16 (1966): 113–15.

26. Syriac reads *yspt*, and the LXX seems to read *yqsb*. *Biblia Hebraica*, Kittle edition, and Speiser, *Genesis*, 313–14, propose *yāsōq*, and Speiser offers the translation: "All my people shall submit to your orders," or possibly, "be managed at your orders." Vergote,

Joseph, 96–97, followed by L. Ruppert *Die Josephserzählung der Genesis: Ein Beitrag zur Theologie der Pentateuchquellen.*

27. Redford, *Study*, 226–28.

28. Janssen, "Remarks," 67–68; Vergote, *Joseph*, 146–52; Redford, *Study*, 228–29 and references there.

29. See the discussion by Redford, *Study*, 230–31.

30. Note that *gānab*, "to steal," is not used in Gen. 37.

31. Redford, *Study*, 205–6. He notes that "in Archaemenid Persia the celebration of a king's birthday was so fashionable that the festivities to mark the occasion became for the Greeks proverbial of luxury." On the Rosetta Stone the birthday of Ptolemy is noted on which a general amnesty was proclaimed. But contrary to suggestions that here are parallels to Gen. 40, in the latter the amnesty is not general—witness the baker—and it is not even clear that amnesty is involved at all. It rather seems to be the case that the charges against the two courtiers are investigated and the matters dealt with accordingly. The details are of no concern in this tale and are left out.

32. See Redford, *Study*, 236–39 and references there.

33. Janssen, "Remarks," 71.

34. W. F. Edgerton, "The Government and the Governed in the Egyptian Empire," *JNES* 6 (1947): 156–57. Vergote, *Joseph*, 190–92 agrees, but stresses the positive side of the evidence, suggesting, e.g., that Gen. 47:13–26 deals not with taxes but with rental of the land.

35. Against Redford, *Study*, 238–39, who sees reflected in a general manner the conditions of the Saite period and later. See Redford, *Study*, 240–41; Vergote, *Joseph*, 199–200. Redford (240, n. 3) is rightly critical of Vergote's suggestion that Joseph calls the *rōp'im* as opposed to the "embalmers" in order to avoid any contact with foreign religious rites. There is no such abhorrence of things foreign in this narrative, which is, in fact, one of its most striking features and which sets it off from other Hebraic materials.

36. Faulkner, *Literature*, 175–76.

37. A. L. Oppenheim, "The Interpretation of Dreams in the Ancient Near East," *Transactions of the American Philosophical Society* 46 9 (1956): 187, and # # 15, 16, 17, 21 in the group of relevant texts. Of an even later tradition see # 22.

38. *ANET*, 449. Compare also Oppenheim, "Interpretation," 188.

39. A. H. Gardiner, *Hieratic Papyri in the British Museum*, 9ff. See also Vergote, *Joseph*, 48–52; Janssen, "Remarks," 64–66; Oppenheim, "Interpretation," passim.

40. Gardiner, *Papyri*, 10–11. The first phrase is written just once over the full page.

41. E.g., "(If a man see himself in a dream) fetching vessels ('*in hnw*) out of the water; Good: finding increases life (n h3w) in his house." Gardiner, *Papyri*, 21.

42. Gardiner, *Papyri*, 21–25.

43. Cited by Oppenheim, "Interpretation," 239. See also E. L. Ehrlich, *Der Traum im Alten Testament*, 67–68, 78–79.

44. Vergote, *Joseph*, 66-73, esp. 72–73. See also Janssen, "Remarks, 65–66; Redford, *Study*, 204–7; Lambdin, "Loan Words," 150–51. Contrary to BDB, which relates the word to the root *hrt*, "stylus."

45. Openheim, "Interpretation," 238.

46. *ANET*, 31–32; Oppenheim, "Interpretation," # 19; Redford, *Study*, 206–7; A. H. Gardiner, *Egypt of the Pharaohs*, 76.

47. See Dan. 5:12, Aramaic *pšr*; Arabic *pšr*; Akkadian *pašîrû*. See Oppenheim, "Interpretation," 217–20. He suggests that the best translation is not "to interpret," but "to solve," and that the term is used with omina of several kinds. There is an Egyptian term *wḥʿ*, which means "to untwine a rope, to explain a difficult passage," and it is later used of dreams as well.

48. Oppenheim, "Interpretation," 220–25. Joseph does not use any mechanical means, but it is interesting to note that in the Hymn to Shamash the *šaʾ ilû* priest used a cup, and of Joseph it is said later that he used a silver cup when he practiced some form of divination (Gen. 44:5).

49. Oppenheim, "Interpretation," 238.

50. S. N. Kramer, *The Sumerians: Their History, Culture, and Character*, 138–39; *ANET*, 75–77.

51. Redford, *Study*, 103.

52. R. E. Murphy. "The Concept of Wisdom Literature," 49; von Rad, *Old Testament Theology*, 1: 438–41. H. Gese, *Lehre un Wirklichkeit in der alten Weisheit*, 38–44, has indicated that at times, as in Egyptian literature, one must speak of "the incomprehensibility of the cosmos." This is no denial of the laws of order, but a recognition of the limits of man's ability to comprehend this (Prov. 14:12; 20:9). Thus there is a dual attitude reflected toward the poor: on the one hand, poverty is to be scorned and avoided while wealth is praised (Prov. 10:4, 5, 12; 19:4); on the other, one is admonished to pity the poor (Prov. 14:21, 31; 17:5; 19:17). It is in this context, as in the Egyptian traditions, that one is to understand the admonition to self-control and mastery and the avoidance of appetite, passion, rash words, and anger. Thus the wise, at times, capture in a single saying the limits of man's ability to comprehend the order and the need for humility in the face of this:

> Boast not about tomorrow,
> for you know not what a day may bring.

With this one might compare Ptah-hotep, ll 327–28, and Amen-em-opet 22:5–6. Yet there is a confidence here, a certainty that, however unknowable, there is an established order, and that one is to orient his life on this.

53, Von Rad, *Theology*, 440; see senerally 438–41.

54. W. L. Humphreys, "The Motif of the Wise Courtier in the Book of Proverbs," 177–90.

NINE

THE DEVELOPMENT OF THE
JOSEPH NOVELLA

In contrast to the independence of the story of Joseph as an Egyptian courtier, the larger Joseph novella is markedly dependent on this kernel. We have seen that the story of Joseph as an Egyptian courtier could stand alone as a unit that is complete in itself. There is no need in Genesis 40–41 (and the brief related sections) for any account of how Joseph came to be in Egypt as a slave of the prison master. Even the brief notice in 40:15 appears gratuitous, except to underscore the injustice he suffers being confined as he now is. Yet some account of his rise to power, in fact of his very preservation, is necessary to link the novella's initial complications developed in chapter 37 with their eventual resolution in chapters 42–50. Not only do Joseph's own words in 45:8, 9, 12 assume what transpired in chapter 41, but the heart of the novella in chapters 42–50—the famine as motive for the brothers' trips to Egypt, Joseph's authority to order events and to act as he does, his ability to deliver his entire family from the crisis—requires the material presented in the story of Joseph as an Egyptian courtier. Genesis 40–41 is set in the royal establishment, and all the trappings of court life are fully on display. The larger novella is a family's story. However, once the royal establishment is introduced with all its protocol and trappings, it is never allowed to recede fully (note the effective reminder in 42:23). Dimensions of the kernel are skillfully woven into the entire novella as it is developed in chapters 42–50.

As we begin chapter 42 we find a shift in the major characters, returning to those introduced in chapter 37. But now Joseph is a courtier, the highest official in Egypt, and encounters with his brothers take place in his establishment. The larger court of Pharaoh recedes until 47:1–6; 50:4–6, but in the person of Joseph regular hints of the larger court establishment are ever present: he is "ruler" over the land (42:6), one whose power the brothers must fear (42:8–25); he speaks through an interpreter (42:23), works through a chief steward who is over his household (43:16, 19; 44:1), and has a large household establishment (43:32; 45:1). Through him access is gained to Pharaoh (45:17; 47;1). In this regard a small but striking detail in the narrative, which is illustrative of a passage from the Instruction of Ptah-hotep, is characteristic of the special court protocol and of Joseph's ability to make particular use of it in his manipulation of his brothers. In the Instructions of Ptah-hotep it is said: "As for the great man when he is at meals; his purposes conform to the dictates of his *ka*. He will give to the one whom he favors" (lines 136–8). All events involved in formal court occasions have great portent: the table becomes the symbol and scene of significant events in court and in the life of the courtier. The general statement of Ptah-hotep is nicely illustrated in the Joseph novella as Joseph prepares to dine with his brothers: "Then he washed his face and came out, and controlling himself he said, "Let food be served. . . ." And they sat at his direction,[1] the oldest in accord with his seniority and the youngest in accord with his youth, and the men looked at each other in astonishment. Portions were taken from his table to them, and Benjamin's portion was five times larger than any of theirs,"(Gen. 43:31–34, author's translation). Joseph so arranged his table that at this dramatic meal the enigmatic quality and strange significance of all that has happened to the brothers is reinforced (cf. 1 Sam. 9:22–24).

While through the person and establishment of Joseph the novella remains in the larger sphere of the royal Egyptian court, it cannot be understood as a courtier's story, as can Genesis 40–41. We are no longer dealing with the success or failure of a figure in the royal service. We rather refocus on the inner dynamics of one family, one member of which happens to be a courtier, a position he uses to good effect. Attention centers on the working out of personal issues, not matters of state. It is only in 46:31–47:6 that once again the setting is the court of Pharaoh, as Joseph, ever the skilled courtier, prepares his brothers in what they are to say in their meeting with Pharaoh to ensure that the king will grant their wishes.

At this point a consideration of details in the larger Joseph novella which von Rad cites as reflective of wisdom themes is appropriate. His discussion takes in all of Genesis 37–50; and while the majority of his examples are found in the material in chapters 40–41, some examples are drawn from the remaining material as well.

The effectiveness of the apt word is illustrated with examples found in several parts of the novella. Von Rad has noted that along with Joseph, Judah and even Joseph's steward are cast in the role of the forceful and persuasive speaker. Genesis 44:16–34 is an extended model of how one should address a superior in correct court style. Judah's words are introduced with a full flourish (44:18–19); he is even able to interpret Joseph's earlier demand to see Benjamin in a favorable light, as a desire to show him kindness, for this is one sense of the phrase "to set one's eyes on" in court parlance.[2] Especially for a man who has seen events slip wholly from his comprehension and control, the speech is a tour de force. Joseph, as before, speaks as befits the situation, with a bluntness and directness before inferiors and petitioners (42:9–20; 44:15) and with all respect before Pharaoh (47:1–6). He carefully arranges the meeting of his brothers with Pharaoh, giving detailed attention to all aspects of the encounter. Thus the outcome is as desired and foreseen (46:31–34; 47:1–6). In fact, the account of the meeting (reading with the LXX) is a copy of the account of the preparations made beforehand.[3] This short unit is again a striking picture, in capsule form, of life in the royal court. And earlier even Joseph's steward's speech is a gem, both reassuring and distracting the brothers, yet introducing a note of hidden mystery with his reference to 'God" and "the God of your father" and to the ambiguous "treasure" (43:23).[4]

But even beyond this particular set of speeches and events, from the point at which Joseph first encounters his brothers in his new and exalted office until the conclusion he is in complete control of himself and the situation. He carefully structures the conditions under which they meet, the course which events then follow, and he prepares the situation so as to provide at the very least a test of his brothers' attitudes. In all this he is found to be the model of the "cool spirited" and patient man:

> He who restrains his words has knowledge,
>   and he who has a cool spirit is a man of
>   understanding.
> He who bridles his anger is better than a warrior,
>   and he who rules his spirit than he who captures
>   a city. (Prov. 17:27; 16:32, author's
>   translation)

Noting these examples, von Rad states: "In his relationship with his brothers, Joseph is the very pattern of the man who can "keep silent," as described in Egyptian wisdom-lore. He is the prudent man who conceals his knowledge (Prov. 12:23) and who restrains his lips (Prov. 10:19)."[5] Particularly notable is his ability to master his emotions, to retain control over his feelings. Not only does he hold back any desire to identify himself before he has exposed the change in his brothers' attitude toward their father's favorite, the moment with most telling effect, but he refrains from any display of anger or feeling, even in the first unexpected meeting, of which it is simply stated: "Joseph saw his brothers and knew them, but he treated them like strangers and spoke roughly to them. . . . Joseph knew his brothers, but they did not know him" (42:7–8). Throughout the narrative this same control is shown; Joseph is always one who masters his spirit (Prov. 16:32).[6] Perhaps this is most apparent when he first sees Benjamin: "And he lifted up his eyes, and saw his brother Benjamin, his mother's son, and said, "Is this your youngest brother, of whom you spoke to me? God be gracious to you, my son." Then Joseph made haste, for his heart yearned for his brother, and he sought a place to weep. And he entered his chamber and wept there. Then he washed his face and came out; and controlling himself he said, 'Let food be served'" (43:29–31). He then proceeds to arrange the meal with the care that gives it special significance.

In the final reconciliation scene further admonitions of the wise are said to be illustrated:

Do not say, "I will repay evil";
    wait for Yahweh, and he will help you.
Hatred stirs up strife,
    but love covers all offenses.

                (Prov. 20:22; 10:12; see also
                14:17, 29; 15:18; 17:13; 24:29; 25:12–22; 29:22).

Say not, "Find me a strong chief,
    for a man in thy city hath injured me";
Say not, "Find me a redeemer,
    for a man who hateth me hath injured me."
Sit thee down at the hands of God;
    thy tranquillity will overthrow them.

                (Amen-em-opet 22:1ff.)

Such an attitude is shown by Joseph toward his brothers: "But Joseph said to them, Fear not, for am I in the place of God? . . . Do not fear; I will provide for you and your little ones.' Thus he reassured and comforted them" (50:19, 21; see also 45:4–15). In his entire attitude and bearing, always in complete control of himself and of the situation, in his coolness of spirit and forgiveness, Joseph is, von Rad suggests, the very model of the wise man.

In this light it is difficult to agree wholly with Redford's analysis of the figure of Joseph presented in chapters 42–50. He may indeed be a "presumptuous dreamer" in chapter 37; and no doubt the sort of person who "blurts out meaningful dreams to jealous brothers" is not the "prudent man who conceals knowledge" held up as an ideal in Proverbs 12:23 and elsewhere. Indeed, he suffers for just this brashness and presumption, as the wise suggest one must. But one might question if Redford has given a balanced and accurate description of Joseph after his elevation when he goes on to ask:

> Is the stubborn, bullying "man, the lord of the land" of chapters 42–44 a model of friendliness or good manners? Is this brow-beating tyrant who plays with his victims like a cat with a mouse, and boasts of his power to divine and of his relationship to Pharaoh, a man of modesty? And how can we apply a term like "self-controlled" to a man who becomes violently angry one minute, runs out to cry the next, and finally breaks down completely when he can no longer continue the sham?[7]

Is this the Joseph whom we meet in chapters 42–45? It leaves out of consideration all possibility of carefully designed purposes behind the actions and words of Joseph. He is, to be sure, a man with absolute authority and with knowledge that others do not share, and he does carefully order events; but there is none of the rashness, the arbitrary or mindless quality of the bully, none of the senselessness of a cat with a mouse. And it is a shallow reading of the wisdom Instructions to suggest that modesty rules out a realistic assessment and understanding of one's position and powers. A knowledge of one's place, of both the possibilities and limitations found therein, and the ability to move and function effectively within these, is what was sought and admired. The wise did not value any form of false humility. Joseph's words are not, for that matter, idle boastings, but carefully tailored to fit the overall situation which he has created. In this regard his words on the "fear of God" (42:18) can be as well read, in line with the admonitions of the wise (Prov. 1:7; Job 28:28), as a recognition of one's place and limitations within the scheme of things (far from being in a position to act in a completely arbitrary manner, the successful and wise man recognizes his bounds), and still serve to provide an ironic thrust within the larger situation of this confrontation. The assessments of von Rad and Redford, in fact, provide poles within which it is possible to appreciate the rich and ambivalent qualities in the very subtle depiction of Joseph and his development. One of the most complex figures in the Hebraic literary tradition emerges in this novella, as we have already seen.[8] Like the figure of David, much is reported about what he did and said while very little is reported of his motive for his deeds and words.

There is a marked difference between the presentation of Joseph in chapters 42–45 and that of chapters 40–41. It is a difference, however, that is appropriate to the change of scene and refocusing of our attention back to the family of Jacob. The courtier of 40–41 used his skill and authority to save a land facing crisis and in the service of his king (with a degree of harshness, for that matter, in the events depicted in 47:13–26). With chapter 42, however, his attention is directed once again toward more personal concerns. Certainly the degree to which he manipulates his brothers and even his father, the span of time during which they are forced to stew in agony over a fate that looms so strangely over them, and the manner in which he plays upon their guilt must not be overlooked. There seems an element of ruthlessness here that can even be compared to that demonstrated by the faithful courtier in service of his king in 47:13–26, when in the face of the famine all of Egypt is bound over for Pharaoh. On the other hand, the situation at the end of chapter 37 is one of complete dissolution and of utter disharmony; protracted and extreme measures, it can be argued, are needed to heal it. We can recall the earlier discussion in which we saw that the figure of Joseph, who knows so much, is in essential ways the least known to the reader in that we receive fewest indications from the narrator of what motivates him. We must judge him by his words and deeds, for no narrative asides offer us directions, nor are we allowed until well along to enter into his own emotions. He is in the full novella neither a straightforward illustration of wisdom tenets—a "type" of the ideal wise courtier—nor the crass antithesis of this ideal that Redford's counter to von Rad would make of him.

Emotions play a role in these chapters; in fact, they take the characters and the readers to an emotional climax that is rarely surpassed in Hebraic narrative. In this emotion-charged context—in which the person who felt nothing would be a ruthless bully—Joseph is the very model of the self-controlled man. It is the control of emotion, and not its denial, that the wise valued. They sought men who were self-possessed and not empty or shallow. Emotion must not be allowed to block effective action nor blind one to a situation, leading to haste or rashness that sets aside well-laid plans (we might contrast this with the figure of Haman in the book of Esther, who sets aside his plans at a critical point in order to seek the immediate destruction of Mordecai, thereby setting in motion the forces leading to the dissolution of his plan, career, and existence). The emotion displayed in Genesis 45:1–15 and 46:29 is just what the situation calls for.

Whether these elements and themes noted by von Rad and others can be said to point to possible wisdom influence, and if so, to what degree, will be considered below; but first other items in the novella must be considered. First of all, we can give attention to apparent Egyptian traces in those parts of the Joseph novella outside the material considered in the last two chapters. While the bulk of such traces are to be found in the segments dealing with Joseph as an Egyptian courtier (40–41; 47:13–26; 50:26), several are located in the material dealing with Joseph and his brothers as well.[9]

A number of those cited by scholars do not point to an exclusively Egyptian origin, even if they are reflective of general conditions in Egypt. Thus, in spite of some difficulties in understanding the details, the several factors associated with the trade between Syria-Palestine and Egypt in Genesis 37:25–28 (the identity of the traders, the items traded, the means of transportation, and even the sale of slaves) are all quite general. Knowledge of these matters would be common not only in the place of destination, but also among those with whom such trade originated and through whose hands and lands it passed.[10] Redford's caution with regard to Joseph's designation of himself as "father to Pharaoh" (45:8), even though it parallels somewhat the Egyptian *it-ntr*, "God's father"—which, for example, Ptah-hotep applies to himself in the introduction to his Instructions—is well taken in the light of the biblical usage of the designation "father" for "someone who exerts paternal influence over others."[11] In 42:15–16 Joseph swears an oath "by the the life of Pharaoh" (*hey par^{c}ōh*), which is found, if rarely, in some Egyptian texts.[12] The general nature of the form, however, and its identity with Israelite forms of oath-taking suggest that it is less a reflection of Egyptian customs than a conscious attempt to give an Egyptian coloration to the narrative.[13]

Of particular interest are two additional notices. Twice mention is made of situations in which Egyptians separate themselves from Hebrews. In 43:32, as Joseph prepares to dine with his brothers, it is noted in explanation of the fact that the Egyptians present separated themselves that "Egyptians might not eat bread with the Hebrews, for that is an abomination (tô‘ēbāh) to the Egyptians." Later, in the course of the preparations for the audience between his brothers and Pharaoh, and in line with his desire to have his brothers settled in Goshen, Joseph instructs them to explain that they are shepherds, for "every shepherd is an abomination (tô‘ăbat) to the Egyptians" (46:34). While Egypt may broadly have been characterized by an exclusiveness, especially revealed in an enmity—tempered by some fear—to Asiatics who threatened at times to cross into Egypt from Palestine, both of these observations are difficult to substantiate in any specific and concrete manner from Egyptian sources.[14] It might be suggested that the second note plays on a popular understanding of the term "hyksos," foreign rulers held later in contempt, as "shepherd kings." More to the point, both notices, and especially the first, if pressed to their logical outcome would create an impossible situation within the structure of the narrative. Joseph has made no attempt before chapter 43 to conceal his foreign origins, and makes none later. Clearly one could not function as the highest official in the land and as an integral part of the Egyptian social and political structure if one were cut off from contact with the natives on such an essential level as eating with them. Then, as often now, little of political, economic, social, or cultural import took place without the sharing of food, and meals become thereby the primary locus for much that is fundamental to life in its broader senses. Surely, with such an intense hatred of shepherds as suggested in 46:34—tô‘ēbāh is as strong a term for taboo as Hebrew allows—Joseph's intimate association with them would at best compromise his position in Egypt, and certainly it would not help further his immediate plans.

But these notices are not pressed to this extent; they are passed over before they can interfere with the flow of narrative, and they serve no essential purpose in the development of its plot. Unlike the many Egyptian traces found in the story of Joseph as an Egyptian courtier, which have at least some ring of genuineness and which function literarily in an unobtrusive and sometimes essential manner, these notices could easily be omitted. In chapter 44 it is perhaps best to have Joseph and his brothers alone (his dismissal of the Egyptian retainers in 45:1 heightens both the parallel and contrast with the scene in chapter 37: once more the brothers are alone, but the power relationships are now reversed). Yet in 43:32 and 46:34 this seems an awkward way to clear the stage of all but essential figures. Nor are these simply unassuming details naturally mentioned in the course of the narrative. They have the ring of hearsay, of the exaggerated and even false impression of one whose knowledge of others is both limited and colored by a sense of wonder and awe. These notices appear simply to give the novella an added degree of verisimilitude as reminders of the exotic setting of this story. Thus, once mentioned, they are passed over as quickly as possible and not allowed to intrude on the inner logic of the narrative.

There is nothing new here that is genuine and unique to Egypt. Rather we have clear indication of a knowledge of that land that is indirect, inexact, and characterized by a popular sort of bias that mixes dislike and distrust with awe and some respect. Since major segments of the novella are set in Egypt, these notices represent further attempts to give it local color. While these two notices may strike us as awkward and forced, we must recognize that this is clearly an Israelite tale about an Israelite family. And any notice that indicates Egyptian abhorrence of Israelites, and at the same time holds Egyptians up as odd, might have special impact on an Israelite audience and be particularly savored by those whose traditions elsewhere spoke more directly of unfortunate encounters with Egyptians.

How might we then characterize the novella? Affinities exist with elements and themes developed in wisdom circles and with certain characteristics of the motif of the wise courtier treasured by them. And while this is not narrowly a courtier's story, the setting of the royal court of the Egyptian king remains ever present if in the background, and much of the action is set in the establishment of Joseph, who appears as an Egyptian official. Futhermore, some knowledge of court protocol is found in 46:32–47:6 as well as 43:33–34 and 44:18–34. The novella reveals a delight in things foreign, in the strange characteristics and customs of the people of Egypt among whom the tale is set, even if this knowledge is indirect and characterized by hearsay and exaggeration. Most important, at the heart of the novella of Joseph and his brothers appears an older narrative about the remarkable rise of a young man in the Egyptian court, which can be designated a courtier story. The story of Joseph as an Egyptian courtier is at the heart of the larger novella as a point on which the events and tensions of the latter hinge. It provides the sequel to chapter 37 and is the necessary basis upon which chapters 42–45 proceed. Joseph in chapter 37 is a spoiled and pampered youth; this boy becomes in chapters 40–41 a man who will effectively govern events from this point on. Joseph remains the courtier throughout the later chapters (42:6, 23; 43:33 34; 44:15;

45:8–9; 46:31–47:6). The story of Joseph as an Egyptian courtier can stand alone. The novella of Joseph and his brothers could not exist without this kernel. The author of the novella seems to have been within the broad range or effective reach of wisdom circles, and has skillfully utilized the older courtier tale as the vital center for his own larger narrative. Moreover, while the novella is clearly Israelite in origin, the kernel need not have been.

Beyond this, it is difficult to say much about the nature and background of any additional traditions upon which the author drew in the construction of this work. As it now exists, the individual episodes are so carefully interlocked and so clearly scenes within a whole that it is not possible to define a *Vorlage* for any of them. Even if one could say with Gunkel that "the earliest period knew only individual tales,"[15] it seems now impossible, given the tight construction of the novella, to recover any individual stories. Thus, older hypotheses as to this nature, and to the possibility of their having reference to intertribal historical events, let alone the suggestion that Joseph was originally a king, appear extremely tenuous today.[16]

It seems more likely that there were no independent sources behind the now carefully integrated and interlaced episodes of the Joseph novella, beyond the story of Joseph as Egyptian courtier and Genesis 38, 39, 48, and 49 discussed in the next chapter. The author of the novella may have simply reached into the traditional lore of ancient Israel to draw upon the various members of the large family of Jacob and then constructed the story around them, using such universal and popular motifs and types as jealousy between brothers, the pampered youngest son of a loving father, the ascent of a younger brother to a position of authority over his older siblings, fulfillment of boyish dreams of grandeur, and the salvation of an entire family by the least likely member. These and other motifs are carefully integrated into an artfully constructed novella that cannot be broken down any further into once independent separate parts.

While the entertainment value of the novella is more than enough to ensure its popularity and preservation, certain emphases can be isolated that can help us characterize it further. The discussion in chapter 6 above can serve as a basis upon which to build. If the analysis of the context of the story of Joseph as an Egyptian courtier given in chapter 8 is correct, it is apparent that references there to the god or gods are to be understood primarily in the context of divine control over the future and indications given by the gods of what the future holds in store. Royal dreams are a matter of the state; they are a part of the business of the court in sections of the ancient Near East. In the larger novella into which this old story is woven there are further references to the deity. These have received careful attention from von Rad, who has suggested that Genesis 45:5–12 and 50:19–20 recall material found in both Egyptian and Israelite sources.[17] Manifestly in the Instructions of Amen-em-opet, and even earlier in Ptah-hotep, the statement is made that events are in the hands of the deity, even when mortals are unaware of this:

> One does not know what may happen, so that he may
>   understand the morrow. (Ptah-hotep l. 343)

> Lay thee not down at night fearing the morrow;
>   when day appears, what is the morrow like?
> Man knoweth not how the morrow will be.
> The words which men say are one thing,
>   the things which God doeth are another.
>   (Amem-em-opet 19:11–15)

In the book of Proverbs there are also a number of statements that reveal the belief that there is a divinely established order in life, which the deity spins out and sustains (Prov. 16:3, 4, 5, 7, 11; 20:23, 27; 21:3, to cite just those from a collection in which the motif of the wise courtier plays a large role). Other sayings have a tone much like the material from Amen-em-opet and stress the limits to human ability to understand that order (Prov. 16:2, 25). Still others, having no real counterpart in Egyptian material, stress the freedom of the deity with regard to this order:

> The plans of the mind belong to man,
>   but the answer of the tongue is from Yahweh. (16:1)
> The lot is cast into the lap,
>   but the decision is wholly from Yahweh. (16:33)
> Many are the plans in the mind of a man,
>   but it is the purposes of Yahweh that will be established. (19:21)

With these statements von Rad and others have compared Joseph's reassurance to his brothers in the resolution of the novella's plot: "And now do not be distressed, or angry with yourselves, because you sold me here; for God sent me before you to preserve life. . . . And God sent me before you to preserve for you a remnant on earth, and to keep alive for you many survivors. So it was not you who sent me here, but God" (Gen. 45:5, 7, 8a). This reassurance has been paired with Joseph's additional reassurance as the brothers petition him once more after their father's death: "Fear not, for am I in the place of God? As for you, you meant evil against me; but God meant it for good, to bring it about that many people should be kept alive, as they are today" (Gen. 50:19–20). In each reassurance, it has been suggested, we have a consciously formed wisdom saying.

> In each case the human purpose is expressed in the first sentence, the divine action in the second. And in view of this similarity of form and content . . . it may well be asked whether the latter is not in fact a wisdom saying which has been adopted to the purpose of the story: "You meant evil against me, but God meant it for good."[18]

In a summary evaluation of the narrative it is thus said that the "hidden realization of God's purpose in human affairs" is affirmed. And, as this is an Israelite tale, this god, while not so designated in the novella, is Yahweh. This same summary goes on to state: "The story affirms that affairs were not governed by the evil designs of men, or by the economic stress that led to Jacob's migration to Egypt, but by the overruling providence of God, who makes all things serve his purpose."[19]

Yet, in appreciation of the complexity and level of indeterminacy of this novella, we must stress that human activity and motives are not rendered meaningless through recognition of God's overruling providence, and the characters do not become merely unknowing automatons in some divine game. Redford is correct in asserting that here is the "supreme irony of the narrative . . . . God has brought about the entire affair as part of a preconceived design, and it was he who had contrived to turn to good the evil the brothers had intended." Yet it is not possible to take the next step with Redford and claim that with this revelation "the motivation of the actors themselves" becomes "trivial."[20] An ambiguity is here attained, between the purposeful and meaningful quality in human motive and actions on the one hand, and the absolute sovereignty and control of the deity over the course of affairs on the other. Both are to be affirmed, and the tension between them is unresolved. It is to this cutting edge of human theological insight into the complex interaction of the divine and human in history that the author brings the reader of the Joseph novella, and it is within the tensions set by these poles that one remains.[21]

Within this tension developed in the Joseph novella, as in the Egyptian Instructions and in the biblical book of Proverbs, lies the basis for the humility and forgiveness finally displayed by the powerful Joseph. Looking over the course of events, Joseph cannot but exclaim at the life-sustaining order revealed therein; nor can he through any anger toward his brothers, or through any desire for revenge, stand in the place of the deity. As the one to recognize and state this, Joseph once more acts on superior knowledge: "The will of God is hidden from evil men, and the wicked schemes are thwarted . . . . The secrets of God are revealed to Joseph, the favorite of God."[22] Yet it is important to note just how much is revealed to Joseph, and at what point. There are the dreams in the opening episodes. Those in chapters 40–41 make known only a specific and limited course of future events in which the family plays no part. In 42:9 the narrator remarks that Joseph remembered his former dreams, and it is stressed more than once that the brothers do in fact bow down in homage before Joseph (42:6; 43:26; 50:18). This occurs, however, after those events to which Joseph's words in 45:5–8 and 50:19–20 refer have taken place, after the critical reversal in Joseph's fortunes, and with only the working out of details of the denouement left to be accomplished. It is especially to the course of events recited in the kernel dealing with Joseph as an Egyptian courtier, as well as the effect of this on the relationship between Joseph and his brothers, that his statements in Genesis 45 and 50 refer. In these charged theological recognitions of a divine providence that can catch up human initiatives and intentions in some larger life-sustaining course, much more is taken in than specific events "foretold" in Joseph's own dreams. As we have seen, Joseph has the advantage over his brothers in what he knows, and he makes effective use of this knowledge. But he too has something fundamental to learn, and in these critical statements his own lessons are mastered: "Am I in the place of God?"

Von Rad concludes his analysis of this aspect of the narrative in this way:

> What place, then, ought we to assign to the Joseph story, both spiritually and with regard to the ancient traditions? It displays no historico-political interests, nor any cultic, aetiological motive. It is equally devoid of any specifically theological interest in redemptive history. We can only say that the Joseph story, with its strong didactic motive, belongs to the category of early wisdom writing.[23]

This last statement claims too much, and is indicative of the looseness with which the category "wisdom" is at times employed. Crenshaw is certainly correct when he observes that within Israelite religious traditions and circles the theme of the hidden providence of God is too common to be designated as a sure sign of wisdom material.[24] Yet it is a theme that is developed in material that on other grounds can be designated "widsom." Furthermore, important similarities with the so-called Succession Narrative of 2 Samuel 6–20; 1 Kings 1–2 have been noted. Both units have a complex overarching structure and unity, reveal skill and a developed narrative technique, and show a psychological interest and depth of character development. In each there are very few references that call specific attention to a theological theme (in the Joseph novella these are all placed in speeches by one of its characters), yet there are key references to the providence of God who works quietly but effectively behind the human scene. In each case we have extended narratives that appear at first glance remarkably secular, especially when contrasted with other early Israelite material in which the deity seems always present and directly active in the course of human lives, often in dramatic ways. Yet at key points, in the words of the central protagonist in the Joseph novella and in the narrator's own asides in the Succession Narrative (2 Sam 11:27b; 12:24b; 17:14b), our perspective is enlarged to take in at least partial vision of a divine guidance of the course of human affairs that takes up but does not void human motives and acts. Men and women are not in this vision simply pawns in the hand of the deity; they are not puppets playing out in an unthinking way lives already scripted by the god. Human beings count for more than that. Yet their lives are caught up and played out in the sustaining context of a drama that is the handiwork of a creator who wills life and good for mortals, even if that will is not always or often apparent to men and women in their daily struggle, and even if it seems that they often struggle against it. This is a vision found in, but not confined to, material that is clearly "wisdom." It is a vision especially honed in material developed in Israel's first flower of monarchy and the rich cultural, literary, and religious development and experimentation it fostered.[25]

It is helpful to make a distinction between an author who writes as a wise man and whose work can be called "wisdom literature" and one who, whether he would be designated as a wise man or not, writes about and possibly under the influence of themes and ideals treated by the wise. The Joseph novella can be fruitfully studied against the background of wisdom themes and theology. However, it does not show any signs of having been composed for and by the wise for use within their educational establishments. There are no lessons specifically underscored or applications drawn. We can here think rather of the wider circles who came within what H. J. Hermisson calls the "effective reach" of the wise. He describes a larger and highly cultured circle for whom literature such as this novella would have especially appealed.

> The traces of wisdom which are discovered in a certain part of the literature of the Old Testament seem to be best explained through direct or indirect influence of the wisdom schools, and in part just so that we have to reckon with authors who had once participated in the instruction of these schools.[26]

On several grounds, as we have seen, the Joseph narrative has been compared with the Succession Narrative, and both have been assigned to Israel's early monarchy as products of the so called "Solomonic Enlightenment."[27] This would seem, in light of the several characteristics of the narrative discussed, to be the earliest point at which a novella as this could appear in ancient Israel. It is thus suggested that it was in the Jerusalem-centered united monarchy that the author of this work drew upon the older story of Joseph as an Egyptian courtier to form this novella about the family of Jacob.

A critical shift in the use made of the motif of the wise courtier has occurred in the formation of the Joseph novella. When the older courtier story is incorporated as the kernel of the novella, the focus of the courtier's life changes. No longer is he centered simply on the pharaoh; now the center of his activity is his family. The figure of Pharaoh still demands great respect, but he is a part of the background, the one by whom Joseph makes his oath (42:15) or defines his position in Egypt (45:8). But in the larger novella the attention of the courtier focuses on his family, and their story as seen in the context established by the life-ordering power of the deity. Joseph the courtier is here an instrument in the working out of the divine will for good. The climax is now reached, not as earlier with the elevation of the courtier to high position and honor in royal service, but as the family is reunited, brother with brother and father with son, the whole clan delivered from the dangers of the famine into a land of security, and this acknowledged as God's work.

A possible tension within the larger novella is carefully avoided. The inclusion of the older courtier tale in the larger context has given a double focus to the hero's life and action, and it is important that any real conflict between these be blunted. Pharaoh's will must not conflict with that of the deity. He is therefore depicted as in complete acquiescence with the desire of Joseph to settle his family in Egypt, and in this he even seems to seek the initiative. This sets this narrative about an Israelite in the royal court of a foreign monarch apart from later developments of this motif in such biblical works as the stories of Esther and Daniel, which otherwise show links with the Joseph narrative. Ahasuerus and the several rulers in Daniel 1–6 seem for a time set at cross purposes with the welfare of the protagonists and their people. The resolution of these stories comes as foreign kings and Israelite/Jewish courtiers at last work together for their common good.

In the Joseph novella there is never a hint of divorce between the good that comes to Joseph and his family and royal benefit. Indeed, the brief account of Joseph's securing the land and people of Egypt for Pharaoh is set at the climax of his arrangements for his father and brothers in Egypt. This incorporation of the older courtier story within the novella also underscores the harmony between Israelite and Egyptian and their mutual benefit throughout. Egypt is the land of life for Israelites in this novella, secured through the action of Joseph, behind which is finally perceived a divine design for life for all people. Around the kernel provided by the older story of Joseph as an Egyptian courtier was formed the Joseph novella. The fortunate and skilled courtier became foremost a son and brother, and his story became that of his family. The kernel provided the needed transformation of his status, and it was carefully absorbed by the larger novella. Segments of it were transported to later parts of the novella (47:13–26; 50:26) to bind the two as well as for apparent chronological reasons. Clearly Joseph could not bind the Egyptians over to Pharaoh's control until the famine had run part of its course, and notice of his death could only conclude the novella. From this kernel was to develop in creative hands a rich novella set in the land of Egypt, a land in which the family of Joseph finds life. This is in marked contrast to the role of Egypt in Israelite narrative tradition. It may further indicate a setting for the novella in the royal establishment of Solomon when relations with Egypt, while not without tension (1 Kgs. 11:18–22, 40) were as good as they would ever be (1 Kgs. 9:16; 11:1). It also suggests something of the distinctive quality of this piece within Israel's literary corpus.

NOTES

1. For this sense of $l^e p\bar{a}n\bar{a}yw$ see Speiser, *Genesis*, 329.
2. Von Rad, *Genesis*, 388–90; see also his *Die Josephsgeschichte*, 13.
3. Von Rad, *Genesis*, 399–401.
4. Von Rad, *Genesis*, 383–84.

5. Von Rad, "The Joseph Narrative and Ancient Wisdom," 295.

6. See generally von Rad, *Josephsgeschichte*, 10–13; "Joseph Narrative," 296–97; *Genesis*, 432 et passim.

7. Redford, *A Study of the Biblical Story of Joseph*, 103.

8. See above, pp. 86–92.

9. J. Vergote, *Joseph en Égypt: Genèse chap. 37–50 à la lumière des études égyptologiques récentes*, 10–20, 159–76, 183–92; Redford, *Study*, 191–200, 204, 232–35; J. M. A. Jannsen, "Egyptological Remarks on the Story of Joseph in Genesis," *JEOL* 5 (1955–58): 64ff.

10. Vergote, *Joseph*, 10–20; Redford, *Study*, 192–200. Further references will be found in these two basic works.

11. See Redford, *Study*, 191, n. 7 for examples and further references. See also von Rad, *Genesis*, 394; Speiser, *Genesis*, 339.

12. Janssen, "Remarks," 68; Vergote, *Joseph*, 162–70; Redford, *Study*, 233.

13. See Speiser, *Genesis*, 322, for relationships with Hebrew oath forms. Janssen, "Remarks," 68, suggests that the repeated use of *par^c ōh* serves to give an Egyptian flavor to the narrative and was so intended by the author.

14. See Vergote, *Joseph*, 188–89 and Redford, *Study*, 235, for what slight evidence there is. With regard to Gen. 43:32 Speiser, *Genesis*, suggests that it was a matter of rank, since "the cultic and social taboo . . . against taking food with Hebrews would scarcely include the Vizier, who bore a pious Egyptian name." See also von Rad, *Genesis*, 384, who suggests that this does reflect Egyptian customs and cites a notice from Herodotus on "the exclusive ritual ideas of purity among the ancient Egyptians." J. L. Crenshaw ("Method in Determining Wisdom Influence Upon 'Historical' Literature," *JBL* 88 [1969]: 137) suggests that Gen. 43:31–34 deals with "kosher food."

15. H. Gunkel, "Die Komposition der Joseph-Geschichte," *ZDMG* 76 (1922): 64–67, 71.

16. H. Gressmann, "Ursprung und Entwicklung der Joseph-Sage," offers one of the most careful attempts, but it is not compelling. See also the earlier study of W. F. Albright, "Historical and Mythical Elements in the Story of Joseph," *JBL* 37 (1918): 111–43; and H. G. May, "The Evolution of the Joseph Story," *AJSL* 47 (1931): 83–93.

17. Von Rad, "Joseph Narrative," 296–300; *Genesis*, 422ff.

18. Von Rad, "Joseph Narrative," 297.

19. B. W. Anderson, *Understanding the Old Testament*, 185–86.

20. Redford, *Study*, 74.

21. Redford must finally judge that the irony that "lies in Joseph's revelation of the underlying divine plan" appears to be "debilitating to the plot" (*Study*, 74). He elsewhere speaks of Gen. 50:15–20 as a "secondary creation" and of 45:5–8 as "later embellishment" (*Study*, 104). Both units "smack of overstatement and the obvious, and . . . are unavoidably denigrating to the story as a whole." However, the debilitating effect is present even if they are removed, especially if the statements are as obvious as he suggests. Rather, and this is most remarkable for a Hebraic narrative, the author avoids the temptation directly to underscore the divine plan in the novella.

22. Crenshaw, "Method," 136.

23. Von Rad, "Joseph Narrative," 298–99.

24. On this see Crenshaw, "Method," 129–37, for the need to give careful consideration to the designations applied by scholars and the basis on which they are made.

See also R. E. Murphy, "Form Criticism and Wisdom Literature," *CBQ* 31 (1969): 475–83; Crenshaw, *Old Testament Wisdom: An Introduction*, 11–26.

25. See W. L. Humphreys, *The Tragic Vision and the Hebrew Tradition*, 43–52, and the literature cited there.

26. H. J. Hermisson, *Studien zur israelitischen Spruchweisheit*, 128–29; see generally 125–29.

27. Von Rad, *Josephsgeschichte*, 5–7; "Joseph Narrative," 292–93.

TEN

THE JOSEPH NOVELLA AND
THE TORAH

As we today encounter the Joseph novella it is only part of a much larger narrative that relates the history of ancient Israel. It is integrated into a complex of traditions sometimes designated the sacred story of the ancient Israelites, telling of their origins and formation as a nation through the activity of the deity Yahweh. In this large and varied collection of carefully ordered traditions of many distinct types and points of origin that make up the narrative frame of the Torah, the Joseph narrative stands at a critical juncture. While a sensitive reading of the novella uncovers evidence that it can be set apart on literary and formal grounds from the material dealing with Abraham and Jacob (Isaac seems hardly to stand alone) and with the deliverance from Egypt, it also appears as a continuation of the traditions dealing with the patriarchs in Genesis 12–36, taking their story on to another generation. On the other hand, it brings the ancestors of the tribes of Israel into Egypt, and looks forward to Egyptian bondage and beyond to deliverance. This narrative thus appears as an elaborate transition piece between the patriarchs and the exodus, two basic themes within the sacred story: Jacob and his son are brought to Egypt, and the stage is set for the exodus, that most basic element in Israel's theological self-understanding.[1] In the linking of these themes Israel is transformed from a family into a people and potential nation.

While the novella may provide an extended transition between these two themes that treat Israel's ancestors in Canaan and then in Egypt, as it now stands in relation to them it is not quite a perfect fit. On the one side, there is a considerable difference in both time and situation between the sons of Israel at the end of the Joseph novella, settled in harmony in Egypt at the invitation of Pharaoh with one of their own in a position of full authority in this alien land, and the Israelites in ever more severe bondage in the first part of the book of Exodus. We pass from at most an extended family of seventy persons (Gen. 46:27) to a people so numerous that they pose a threat to the internal security of Egypt. Some time has clearly passed and the context altered before there arose a Pharaoh "who knew not Joseph" (Exod. 1:6–14).

On the other side, and even more striking, the Joseph novella seems to function with its own chronology within the book of Genesis, with a different order of events than the Jacob complexes with which it is linked. In Genesis 37 Joseph is the son of Jacob's old age, and there is no mention of any younger full brother (37:3; cf. 35:16–18), and 37:10 appears to indicate that Joseph's mother is still alive, even though the larger context of the book of Genesis states that she had earlier died while giving birth to her second son, Benjamin (35:18–20).[2] Within the framework of the Joseph narrative it would appear that Benjamin's birth and Rachel's death occur during the extended period in which Joseph is on the rise to power in Egypt and before the famine brings his brother to him. Benjamin is still a youth, while Joseph is a man with a family of his own, in the latter part of the novella, indicating a gap of some years between the birth of the two full brothers (43:29). While it might appear odd that Joseph, in his eagerness to learn of the condition of his brother and father (43:27–29), makes no mention of his mother and her fate, we have already observed that this is the story of men, of the complex relationships of a father and his sons, of brothers in relation to each other and to their father. Within the tightly woven matrix of intense emotions that link these several figures the cast is carefully circumscribed. It appears that the complexity that the presence of Joseph's mother would have brought to this matrix is avoided.

The original independence of the Joseph novella from the larger traditions that comprise the sacred story and the freedom exercised by its author in his utilization of the figures from those traditions seem a more natural explanation of the place of Benjamin (and of Rachel) in this material than Noth's suggestion that Benjamin was, on the one hand, too small to have any part in the brothers' feelings and activity, and, on the other, that "he appears in such especially close association with Joseph that he is not counted as an independent member in the circle of the brothers."[3] The Joseph novella required both that at the outset Joseph appear as the youngest son, the only child of his mother, and that later he have a younger brother, who, like him, appears as a youth, in relation to the others. This alone might account for the author's selection of Joseph from among the sons of Jacob as the hero of the novella, and thus not necessarily indicate that the tale had its origins within Joseph tribes of northern Israel. We find here a creatively free use of traditions that, by the time of the monarchy, were the property of all Israel and available to one who wished to tell of the complexities of family ties.

In spite of these and other indications that the Joseph novella is but loosely fit into its context, there are elements that integrate it into this setting as well. Several links are found, the most explicit being the notice that now concludes the novella, in which Joseph declared to his brothers what will befall them and their seed in the future: "And Joseph said to his brothers, 'I am about to die; but God will visit you, and bring you up out of this land to the land which he swore to Abraham, to Isaac, and to Jacob.' Then Joseph took an oath of the sons of Israel, saying, 'God will visit you, and you shall carry up my bones from here' " (50:24–25). He even arranges for his future burial in the land of promise (cf. Josh. 24:32). With the exception of chapters 48 and 49, this is the one clear reference to themes of the larger sacred story within the novella, and it looks very much like a linking device. It not only looks forward to the events of the oppression and the exodus, but looks back to the central theme in the patriarchal traditions of the promise made to Abraham, Isaac, and Jacob. However, we have also seen that Joseph is able to speak now of the family's future and of his own, and to link them. This effectively underscores the harmony that has at last been attained in the speech of reconciliation just a few lines above (50:19–21).

Like 50:24–25 there are other units which have generally been considered traditio-historically as secondary additions to the Joseph novella, but which also serve to link this story with its larger context—for example, chapters 48 and 49 and the shorter unit in 46:1–4. The tight narrative integrity of the plot is interrupted through the introduction of originally extraneous elements into its conclusion. With the introduction of the novella into the larger context of the account of Israel's origins the focus of attention at the conclusion moves from Joseph to Jacob, who, as the last of the three patriarchs and as the recipient of the promise made earlier to

Abraham and Isaac (see Gen. 48:16), is in this larger setting the more significant figure. The notice of his death naturally and of necessity attracted several once independent elements. We have here the first of what will be a whole series of pronouncements by formative figures in Israel's history at or near the point of their death: Moses in Deuteronomy 33; Joshua in Joshua 23 and 24; Samuel in 1 Samuel 12; David in 2 Samuel 23. So here Jacob orders the future life of the Joseph tribes who will be so important in the later history of the nation Israel (Gen. 48) and of all those units which ideally were constituents of later Israel (Gen. 49).

More implicit links between the novella and its context can be suggested as well. The central characters, Jacob and his sons, are all figures encountered earlier in the book of Genesis. Implied points of irony, linking the Joseph novella with the larger story of Jacob, have been recognized. Thus, Jacob once deceived his father through a legal ruse involving special garb: "Then Rebekah took the best garments of Esau her older son, which were with her in the house, and put them on Jacob her younger son; and the skins of the kids she put upon his hands and upon the smooth part of his neck" (27:15–16). Just so he is now deceived by his sons in another legal ruse involving the use of a special garment. "Then they took Joseph's robe, and killed a goat, and dipped the robe in the blood; and they sent the long robe with sleeves and brought it to their father, and said, "This we have found; see now whether it is your son's robe or not.'" (37:32–33). The ironic thread of the garment has already been noted as stitched through the Joseph novella, and this larger linkage with the context has not been missed by sensitive readers.

The Jacob who deceived his father and brother, and who thereby won what was not by right his, is now deceived by his sons and deprived of the one he treasures most. Jacob, the old man of the Joseph narrative, is in many ways the further development of the earlier figure in the cycles that center on him—sometimes chastened and accepting the apparent retribution that has overtaken him; still excessive in emotion; yet at points at least able to act with craft and decisiveness to meet a crisis (43:11–14). The one who, as a younger man, could love Rachel so fully at first sight (29:9–20) now finds that it is an excessive love for one son then another that brings grief down upon his gray head. And, on the highest level, the Joseph novella shows affinities with the cycles about the patriarchs in which, again and again in the face of apparent sure destruction and extinction of the line of promise, the deity acts, if earlier more openly, to preserve his chosen. Thus, in spite of seams and minor incongruities, the

Joseph novella, through both internal themes and through additions to it, is woven into the rich fabric of the sacred story of ancient Israel. This stage in the development of the Joseph novella was of decisive importance and had a pronounced influence on the reader's perspective on it.

It is at this point that our study of the Joseph novella comes up against what has stood, at least until recently, as one of the solid results of critical study of the Hebrew Bible. The Pentateuch, the five books that comprise the Torah, sometimes linked with Joshua to form a Hexateuch, are said to represent the results of complex interweaving of distinct sources or strata to form the complex whole that now confronts us. The documentary hypothesis has largely won the day in all but very conservative circles of biblical scholarship, and recent attacks on it have not generally been very successful. Traditionally the Joseph material in Genesis has provided some illustrative set pieces for source critics who attempts to distinguish the serveral sources in the Pentateuch. They point to the fact that the father is sometimes called Israel (e.g., 37:3, 13) but at other points called Jacob (37:34); that two different brothers, Reuben and then Judah, attempt to save Joseph from death; that the pace and order of events in 37:21–30 is complex to the point of confusion; that the brothers twice discover their silver in their sacks (42:26–28 with the word ʾ*amtaḥāh* used for sack; 42:35–36 with *śaq* used for sack). And yet it is precisely the Joseph novella that has provided a base for some recent attacks on the documentary hypothesis—at least as it is applied to the novella itself, for these critics have not moved beyond the material in Genesis 37—50 to take on the theory as applied to the rest of the narrative portions of the Torah.[4]

The direction of our study of the Joseph novella would lend credence to these more recent suggestions that the traditional formulations of source critical analysis are not applicable to the last chapters of the book of Genesis. This is not the place for a detailed analysis of the documentary hypothesis as applied to the Joseph material in Genesis, or for a careful critique of this. Yet the analysis of the novella on a synchronic plane in the first part of our study suggests that, with the exception of Genesis 48, 49, 46:1–4, and 38, the novella is in so many ways an artfully constructed fabric that to pull at bits of thread here and there is to unravel its balanced texture. The second part of this study proposed a thesis concerning the development of the novella, based on the recognition that in Genesis 40–41 we find a story that seems complete within itself, with a number of characteristics that set it apart from the material that envelops it, and which serves as a kernel around which the larger novella is constructed.

This kernel originated in Late Bronze Age Canaan, in the context of courtly circles of one of the city-states (Jerusalem?) which had links with and was generally under at least the nominal sway of Egyptian rule. Most likely it emerged and was cherished in circles that comprised the bureaucracy of such a city-state, one that would be especially under the influence of Near Eastern wisdom traditions. It was then suggested that the larger Joseph novella was constructed by someone within the establishment of the Israelite united monarchy, someone able to draw upon both this older story as a kernel and upon older Israelite tradition for the cast of characters from the family of Jacob to construct the novella.

That such a work would then come in time to be preserved in two distinct forms, one as part of the Yahwist's theological-historical epic of Israel's history and the second as a part of the Elohist's version of that history, seems improbable. Even more improbable would be the combination of these two versions of the narrative when the Elohist material was brought into the Yahwist's work, as, at a later point, a redactor, according to the standard documentary hypothesis, combined J and E. It is certainly unlikely that the resulting combination would result in a work as extensive and yet as carefully and tightly constructed as we have found the Joseph novella to be. It must be noted that this is not to be taken as a basic critique of the larger documentary hypothesis or of the value of the work of the source critic on the Pentateuch as a whole. It simply suggests that the Joseph novella is not fruitful ground for this effort, and that the developmental history of this unit is different than that of other material preserved in the books of Genesis and Exodus. That the novella came to be part of the Pentateuch cannot be denied, but the route it took must be in some ways distinct.

It appears most probable that the novella, once formed, was treasured and enjoyed as a distinct work for an extended period of time before it was incorporated into the Torah. Possibly it was preserved in Davidic court and bureaucratic circles in Jerusalem; possibly, with it focus on the figure of Joseph, in northern Israel as well, following the division of the kingdom of David and Solomon. Yet too much emphasis should not be placed on the fact that the novella centers in critical ways on Joseph, for it cannot be said to manifest a clear critical perspective toward Judah, and, most important, it is simply not colored by a strong political polemic of any sort. A point came when the novella was drawn into the confluence of streams that were drawing together to form the Pentateuch. Possibly this would be at the time when the Elohist traditions were being woven into the basic epic of the Yahwist. The novella would address the question: How did the people of Israel, the children of Jacob, come to be in Egypt? It was not created to deal with this question, but it could be used to address it if drawn into the larger collection of materials about Israel's history. In the process not only would the narrative about Judah and his daughter-in-law Tamar, found in Genesis 38 and drawn from J, have been set in the position it now occupies in the Joseph novella, but material dealing with the patriarch Jacob and his last days (46:1–4; 48; 49), would have been brought in as well.

In this way what had been an independent story became now one extended element in a much larger whole: the story of Israel from creation to conquest and kingship, a story of promise and fulfillment, and an extended witness to Israel's belief in the guidance of Yahweh, both in particular events and in the course of all history. Genesis 50:24 is an explicit expression of just this new orientation: "And Joseph said to his brothers, 'I am about to die; but God will visit you, and bring you up out of this land to the land which he swore to Abraham, to Isaac, and to Jacob.'" This one sentence has the decisive effect of reorienting much of the material in the novella.

In the story of Joseph as an Egyptian courtier the object of the courtier's attention and service is the pharaoh. This is blunted to a degree in the novella. Pharaoh, when present, is held in awe, but the center of Joseph's activity is his family, and he is unknowingly the instrument of divine providential care. The story becomes more personal; the events related involve not primarily a courtier, but a man and his brothers and father. The characteristic focus of the wise courtier is blunted. When the novella is included in the still larger framework of the Torah, this change is underlined. Now the rule of Yahweh, demonstrated in the history of Israel and in Joseph's role as an instrument of that divine governance, is stressed. The center of attention is on the people of Israel, the people of Yahweh's promise and guidance, who are ever again placed in danger and ever again delivered. Pharaoh, his court, and all therein, and even Joseph as a royal courtier, become instruments of this God. Von Rad concludes his commentary on Genesis with the following observation:

> This incorporation of the Joseph story into the body of the patriarchal narratives, which we perhaps must attribute to the Yahwist, is of great theological significance; for what was a general belief in providence in wisdom literature and the formerly isolated Joseph

story has now become the testimony to God's special rule in sacred history. The "many survivors" . . . of which Joseph spoke in chapter 45:7 now means much more than the saving of a few shepherds from famine; and the statement about God's good plans, which change evil into good, now comprises the mystery of all the gracious acts of Israel's God.[5]

Here the motif of the wise courtier is completely reoriented; the principal concern is no longer the king, in the sphere of whose authority and interest he lived and acted. Now it is the deity Yahweh and his activity for this chosen people on the way to nationhood. Statements about Joseph receive new emphasis; in this new frame of reference even Pharaoh's remarks in 41:38 have new meaning. In this context further depth and added meaning is given to the words of both Joseph and Pharaoh in 40:8 and 41:16, 25–32, 38–39. Now *elōhîm* is clearly Yahweh, the God of Israel, and the events leading to this courtier's rise are Yahweh's doings. Now, with an irony that the Israelites would not miss, even the Egyptian king, representative of the later oppressors of people of God, acknowledges Yahweh's power and control over events in his own way, and he even cooperates in this god's plan. Set in the context of the sacred story as a whole, these remarks take on new depth.

The tension in the double focus of the courtier's life is underscored as well. All are now subject to the deity. For a Yahwist there is but one center for his life, and the only part of the Joseph novella in which the courtier's action and plans are firmly fixed on the king is in material that is pre-Yahwistic in origin, the story of Joseph as an Egyptian courtier. The tension is still not destructive to the narrative, for the king is presented working toward the furtherance of the divine plan. But the potential for conflict is there, and the irony that the words of Joseph and Pharaoh now bear in this larger perspective is a trace of this.

Joseph has now become first official in the land, not because he won the respect and recognition of the king, but because "Yahweh was with Joseph." This claim takes us at last to Genesis 39, in some ways the best-known episode in the novella.

At first glance it would seem that the episode involving Potiphar's wife would be included as part of the adventures of Joseph as an Egyptian courtier. As in chapters 40–41, the setting of this part of the novella is Egypt, while his home in Canaan and his brothers and father are forgotten. Here is a short episode that gives a foretaste of Joseph's later rise to greatness as well as an indication of certain aspects of this hero's character. It is, however, a false start on his road to success. The basic motif used here, that of the rejected woman who turns on the desired paramour, is a common one in the folklore and literature of the world, and, most striking from the perspectives of study of the Joseph novella, it is found in the first part of the Egyptian "Tale of Two Brothers."[6]

As the story is told in Genesis 39, Joseph is purchased by an Egyptian named Potiphar, who is identified as an official of Pharaoh and captain of the guard.[7] Perhaps first serving as a personal attendant of this official, Joseph soon becomes his favorite and is appointed to a position of charge over all the estates and affairs of his master. It is stressed repeatedly that this is because Yahweh is with Joseph. He also finds favor—if for very different reasons—with his master's wife. He rejects her and, when finally trapped in the most compromising of positions, flees, leaving his outer garment in her grasp. With this most incriminating evidence in hand, she easily convinces her husband that her lies are the truth. He is enraged, but instead of having Joseph summarily executed, he has him placed in prison. This is surprising, but it is, of course, essential for the further development of the novella. But even in prison Yahweh is with Joseph, and in an almost verbatim parallel to the first part of the chapter we are told that again he prospered, and was given charge over the entire operation of the prison. The fate of Potiphar's wife is not mentioned, but this is, after all, not her story.

Yet, upon closer reading, the conclusion of chapter 39 at this point in the narrative line, and as a preface to chapter 40–41, does not seem smooth. Joseph's position at the outset of chapter 40 does not quite correspond with that at the end of chapter 39. In the latter he holds a position of authority: "The keeper of the prison committed to Joseph's care all the prisoners who were in the prison; and whatever was done there, he was the doer of it; the keeper of the prison paid no heed to anything that was in Joseph's care, because Yahweh was with him; and whatever he did, Yahweh made it prosper" (39:22–23). This forms a frame with the opening of the episode: "So Joseph found favor in his sight and attended him, and he made him overseer of his house and put him in charge of all that he had. From the time that he made him overseer in his house and over all that he had Yahweh blessed the Egyptian's house for Joseph's sake; the blessing of Yahweh was upon all that he had, in house and field. So he left all that he had in Joseph's charge; and having him he had no concern for anything but the food which he ate." (39:4–6).

Joseph's position at the end of chapter 39 is not that of an attending servant, who is waiting upon two officials charged with crimes against the king and state. Yet in chapter 40 he is presented as personally attending to the needs of the chief butler and chief baker. In fact, the joins that link this chapter with the narrative as a whole are apparent at both ends. Both 39:1 and 40:1–5 are often said to be overloaded and, therefore, composite in character. Potiphar, while named in 39:1 and identified as captain of the guard, is not so named again, and there is no further hint of his acting in this capacity; certainly he is not the official with that title in 40:3–4.

Moreover, we must note that the episode does not appear to be complete and that the conclusion seems artificial. While no notice is given of any punishment suffered by Potiphar's wife—and convention demands that she not escape—this is not her story, and to follow her fate further would detract attention from the hero. Yet Joseph's punishment is too light for his alleged crime; and while he must, of course, live on for the novella to continue, he would be expected at least to face the threat of death.[8] The conclusion of chapter 39 seems to have been blunted by being forced to fit into a context with which it was not originally in harmony.

The style and general tone of the unit also set it apart from the material in chapters 40–41. Repetition and some redundancy leap out. Three times the reader is told of the final fateful encounter between Joseph and his master's wife. This serves in part to seal Joseph's fate and to underscore the evil yet crafty character of this woman, and perhaps also to provide some suspense as the reader must await the outcome. The effect is well crafted. But the exposition and conclusion seem especially wordy and drawn out, a flat narration of Joseph's success as he takes full authority of his master's estate (39:2–6a) and over the prison (39:21–23). Most important, only here in the Joseph novella is the divine name "Yahweh" used, and here repeatedly—seven times in all—to stress that the hero's success is due to Yahweh's activity on his behalf. This overt theological emphasis stands in sharp contrast to the tone of chapters 40–41 and the larger novella.

Von Rad has also found in Genesis 39 elements that he believes are illustrative of wisdom themes linked with the motif of the wise courtier.[9] Chief among these is the role of the "strange women" in wisdom circles:

> The narrative about Joseph and Potiphar's wife leads to the narrower field of morality, and with it we find ourselves again in very close proximity to an important subject of wisdom literature, namely the warning against "strange women" (Prov. 2:16; 5:3, 20; 6:24; 22:14; 23:27f.). Thus the temptation story in chapter 39 reads like a story composed ad hoc to illustrate these admonitions of wisdom.[10]

Ruppert has criticized this analysis. He correctly notes that the most explicit statements in this respect in the Israelite wisdom materials are found in Proverbs 1–9. However, this theme is also found in older Egyptain materials, and the date of the several units found in Proverbs 1–9 is a matter of uncertainty. Ruppert also notes that in the book of Proverbs it is the dull-witted who is brought to ruin by the strange woman (Prov. 7:6–23), while in Genesis 39 it is the hero who suffers misfortune precisely because he rejects the advances and lures of this dangerours person; that is, "he falls into the woman's clutches *because* he resists."[11] While in the larger course of the life of Joseph a "retribution schema of wisdom," to which Ruppert refers, is satisfied, this paticular episode would serve as a poor incentive to avoid the evil woman, even if it does illustrate the danger of her wiles. Ruppert suggests that behind this theological narrative, with its repeated emphasis on the divine guidance in Joseph's life, might be certain narratives that served as examples of the admonitions of international wisdom, and that one of these might have provided the inspiration or source for this unit.[12]

Taken together these observations would suggest that the episode related in Genesis 39 entered the Joseph novella at a later stage. It utilizes a theme common in folklore and literature, and one that was especially developed in the Egyptian "Tale of Two Brothers." It is the Egyptian form of the theme that may have made its use particularly appropriate for the account of Joseph as an Egyptian courtier. The theme was tailored to fit its context, however, and was joined to the novella through an extended exposition and conclusion. It is in these that the theological emphasis is so bold, with the repeated use of the name Yahweh and the repeated stress that Yahweh was with Joseph and was the source of all his remarkable success. This addition to the novella would thereby serve boldly to underscore what is expressed more indirectly in the larger work. In this episode providential guidance is not the work of an invisible hand, largely seen only in hindsight. The statement in Genesis 39 is clear: Yahweh ensures success in all that the hero undertakes, even if the road to this success must pass through dangers. And in its way the episode also serves to highlight a nobility in the character of Joseph, especially as he is set over against the evil of his master's wife and the blindness of his master. There is a clarity of character here and a simplicity that is in contrast to this central figure as we have encountered him in chapter 37, and will encounter him again when his brothers rejoin the narrative. He is more a type here, a model of the upright even when things seem not to go well for him.

This episode seems designed to bring into the Joseph novella a motif, perhaps especially linked with Egyptian heroes, to direct our assessment of the figure of Joseph away from ambiguity and complexity toward idealization (with this we might compare the presentation of him in Psalm 105:16–22), and to underscore early on the theological point that Yahweh, God of Israel, stood behind the good fortune of Joseph, a point that gains in urgency as the novella assumes a place within the larger narrative line of the Torah. Comparison with the case of Genesis 38 is instructive. Both chapters 38 and 39 are here suggested to have entered the Joseph novella at later stages. Chapter 38, when the novella was incorporated into the larger Torah narrative, took its place between the opening episode of the story of the family of Jacob and the continuation of that story as it traces the fate of the youngest son in Egypt. It serves in its present position to retard the action, to keep the reader in some suspense regarding the fate of the family and the youngest son, and also to underscore certain themes (deceit, different reactions to death, retribution, and acknowledged unfairness) in the larger novella. This is done through setting the Judah and Tamar episode and the opening of the novella side by side, asking the reader to make the links that will thereby play a role in shaping the reading of the novella. Chapter 39, by contrast, seems to have been constructed especially to take its place in the novella. Alone it is incomplete: tradition demands at least that the hero not be left in prison even if he is successful there; and in the larger novella he of course does not remain jailed. This chapter also serves to underscore theological themes, as we have just seen. Here, however, this is done through the direct presentation of the figure of Joseph as an ideal and in contrast to Potiphar and his wife, and in extended theological observations by the narrator on what Yahweh was about in the life of this young man—the only observations of this sort made by the narrator directly in the novella. Thus both Genesis 38 and 39, each in its own distinct way, appear to be later additions to the novella, and each serves to shape or direct the reader's experience of it.

Genesis 38 entered the Joseph novella when the story of this family was incorporated into the Torah; quite likely it was already an element in that larger narrative. It, along with 46:1–4 and chapters 48 and 49, would have been an element in the Torah's body of traditions dealing with Jacob in his last days and his family. The Joseph novella became the latest and largest of units dealing with these themes. Chapter 39 was most likely added after this. The virtual repetition of 37:36 in 39:1 with regard to Potiphar's identity serves to resume the line that traces Joseph's story after the interruption. Both chapter 38 and especially chapter 39 serve to accent essential elements in the Joseph novella. The later additions, especially chapters 48 and 49, seem by contrast rather to refocus the story back on the last days of Jacob as the third patriarch. Therefore, in a variety of ways the novella was expanded when, and after, it took place in the larger context of the Torah.

A few elements in the Joseph novella are generally assigned by source critics to the latest of the strata or stages in the Torah that developed in priestly circles (P). These are not extensive and are not found in the core of the novella. In large part they deal with Jacob and with the last days of the patriarch,—that is, with the wider context into which the Joseph novella is set in Israel's sacred story. Genesis 37:1–2; 41:46; 46:6–27; 47:7–12, 27–28; and 50:12–13 are generally assigned to P.

Several[13] would construe 37:1 and possibly verse 2a[14] with 36:1–8, and therefore consider it to be the priestly introduction to its own version of the Joseph narrative. There is, in fact, no indication that such a version ever existed, as a brief consideration of the few P notices shows. Verse 2b is not to be seen as a last remaining vestige of some different P version of the narrative that has, but for this notice, vanished, but rather as an editorial introduction to the Joseph narrative, possibly produced by priestly circles. The mention of the half brothers Dan, Naphtali, Gad, and Asher, the sons of Bilhah and Zilpah, might well be intended to exclude the other brothers, and especially Levi, from at least an initial involvement in the tension with Joseph, and thus from primary responsibility for the scenes that follow. Redford suggests that the word order of the phrase "shepherding the flock with his brothers" (*hāyāh rō^{c}eh 'et-'eḥ āyw baṣṣōn*) indicates an intended double entendre, in which, while the primary sense of the root $r^c h$ is in this usage clear enough (i.e., tending the herds), a secondary sense of this verbal root and the Hebrew particle *'et*, that of ruling over as a king, is also implied. This would suggest that the Joseph narrative as a whole stood before the author of this notice and, thus, that this introduction contained a proleptic summary of the novella.[15] The tale-bearing motif, which is not mentioned again, could either serve simply to develop further the picture of a spoiled younger son, or this last clause in the verse could be an initial element in the exposition (37:3–4) to the novella itself, and thus a third cause of the brother's hatred. As such it is possibly to be removed from possible priestly notices in Genesis 37:1–2.[16] But if 37:1–2 is from a late hand, it is fully joined with 37:3–4 to provide an effective introductory exposition for the novella.[17]

Genesis 41:46a is generally assigned to P simply for the reason that this source is said to be interested in such matters as the ages of leading figures in Israel's past (cf. 37:2a). This would set Joseph's period of enslavement at thirteen years. We have already seen that the Joseph narrative as a whole follows its own chronology and, with the exception of the repeated seven-year pattern, is quite general in its designation of the passage of time (cf. 41:1; 3:1–2). Clearly since Joseph is the youngest son of Jacob at the outset and Benjamin is born only after Joseph is lost, a span of some years is assumed to separate the two brothers (see 43:29); thus the narrative is not bound to the patriarchal chronology of P, and there is slim reason to regard 41:46a as secondary.

Genesis 46:6–27 is a list of those who went down to Egypt with Jacob, and is not only a secondary element in the Joseph novella but probably within the P source as a whole as well.[18] The remaining notices deal with the last days and death of the patriarch and have no direct relationship with the Joseph novella. As with other traditions concerning Jacob's death, these have been set in here only after the narrative found a place in the sacred story. Genesis 47:7–12 presents the brief encounter between Pharaoh and the patriarch in which Jacob blesses the king of Egypt. The unit presents the figure of Jacob in a nice contrast to the earlier grieving father, as the dignity of this encounter depicts a development from the earlier figure of emotional extremes. Genesis 47:27–28 is summative and betrays certain lexical and stylistic characteristics of P. Genesis 50:12–13 is again summative of what had just taken place, the burial of Jacob in Canaan by his sons, and adds the notice that this was in the cave of the field at Machpelah. This is a clear reference to the earlier account of Abraham's purchase of this place for the burial of Sarah found in Genesis 23, a unit generally assigned to P. None of these proposed priestly additions to the narrative is overly intrusive, and most seem sensitive to and even enrich the literary context into which they are placed.

Outside of Genesis 37–50 there is remarkably little reference in the Hebrew Bible to the figure of Joseph and the story told in the Joseph novella. When a reference is found, it is the figure of Joseph that commands the center of attention. There are, of course, the lists of the sons of Jacob, in which Joseph is named, in Genesis 30:22–25; 35:22–26; Exodus 1:1-6; and elsewhere. Beyond these lists there are but two references to Joseph as a person and not a group within Israel: Joshua 24:32 and Psalm 105:16–22.

Joshua 24:32 is an isolated notice referring back to Genesis 50:25, which serves to link the novella to the larger context in the Torah. "The bones of Joseph which the people of Israel brought up from Egypt were buried at Shechem, in the portion of ground which Jacob bought from the sons of Hamor the father of Shechem for a hundred pieces of money; it became an inheritance of the descendants of Joseph." In the brief notice in Psalm 105, not only is the rags to riches quality of the Joseph story stressed (vv. 17b–18 and 20–22), and the whole series of events clearly presented as the work of Yahweh (v. 19), but the whole is set firmly in the sacred story:

> When he had summoned a famine on the land,
>   and broke every staff of bread,
> he had sent a man ahead of them,
>   Joseph, who was sold as a slave.
> His feet were hurt with fetters,
>   his neck was put in a collar of iron;
> until what he had said came to pass
>   the word of the Lord tested him.
> The king sent and released him,
>   the ruler of the peoples set him free;
> he made him lord of his house,
>   and ruler of all his possessions,
> to instruct his princes at his pleasure,
>   and to teach his elders wisdom.

Verse 19 is difficult and may have more than one reference. The phrases *dᵉbaro* and *imrat YHWH* clearly refer to the interpretation, here seen as Yahweh's word, given by Joseph in Genesis 40 to the dreams of the courtiers of Pharaoh, for it was the outcome of these events that led in time to Joseph's being called to Pharaoh's presence and his success there. They could, however, also have a wider reference, including not only the dream interpretation of Genesis 41, but also the indications regarding the future found in Joseph's own dreams in Genesis 37. The notice in Psalm 105:22, in which Joseph is said to instruct the officers and elders of the Pharaoh (reading *lᵉyassēr* with the LXX for MT *leʾsōr*) finds no counterpart in the novella. Yet this reversal of roles among courtiers, in which the successful hero of a court tale alone succeeds where all others fail and is then placed in a position of authority over them, is a characteristic element in a developed form of tales of this sort. One might compare the sudden and ironic reversal of roles between Haman and Mordecai in Esther 6:10–11 or between Daniel and his companions and the wise men of several Eastern royal courts (Dan. 1:20; 2:48–49; 3:30; 5:29; 6:28). Here a matter that is left rather undeveloped in the story of Joseph as an Egyptian courtier is given characteristic emphasis.[19] The Joseph traditions, somewhat freely used, are woven into the psalm's larger theme of the fulfillment of the deity's promise in spite of small beginnings and great obstacles, a theme already found in the Joseph novella.[20]

With the exception of these two passages all other uses of the name Joseph have reference to the northern tribes or the separate nation of Israel. This can be seen as indicative, not only of the novella's secondary position in the sacred story, but also of a certain incompatibility between it and the perspectives of circles that produced other major segments of the Hebrew Bible. The openness to a foreign court and its personages, the ease with which the story moves in this international and pagan context, especially the setting in Egypt, as well as certain specific items such as the interpretation of dreams and the use of divination by the hero, set this material apart from other traditions in ancient Israel (note the usage of the root nḥš, "to divine," in Gen. 44:5, 15 and the attitude toward such divination in Lev. 19:26; Deut. 18:9–14; and 2 Kgs. 21:6).

Further brief reference to Joseph is found in Sirach 49:15, in what seems to be an appended unit to the long hymn of praise to past worthies:

No one like Enoch has been created on earth,
    for he was taken up from the earth.
And no man like Joseph has been born,
    and his bones are cared for.
Shem and Seth were honored among men,
    and Adam above every living being in the creation. (Sir. 49:14–16)

In 1 Maccabees 2:53, as part of a long speech by Mattathias on firmness in the face of oppression, Joseph is presented as a model of the steadfast Jew who, on the pattern of Daniel, observes the commandments in the face of all difficulties. While Joseph is not named, Wisdom 10:13–14 seems to be a reference to the Joseph narrative. Attention might also be called to 4 Maccabees 18:11, where once more Joseph is an idealized model. In the New Testament the references in Hebrews 11:21–22 develop themes that are secondary to the Joseph novella: "By faith Jacob, when dying, blessed each of the sons of Joseph, bowing in worship over the head of his staff. By faith Joseph, at the end of his life, made mention of the exodus of the Israelites and gave directions concerning his burial." In the speech of Stephen in Acts 7:9–16 reference to Joseph is part of a long reveiw of Israel's story and its God's action:

> And the patriarchs, jealous of Joseph, sold him into Egypt; but God was with him, and rescued him out of all his afflictions, and gave him favor and wisdom before Pharaoh, king of Egypt, who made him governor over Egypt and over all his household. Now there came a famine throughout all Egypt and Canaan, and great affliction, and our fathers could find no food. But when Jacob heard that there was grain in Egypt, he sent forth our fathers the first time. And at the second visit Joseph made himself known to his brothers, and Joseph's family became known to Pharaoh. And Joseph sent and called to him Jacob his father and all his kindred, seventy-five souls; and Jacob went down into Egypt. And he died, himself and our fathers, and they were carried back to Shechem and laid in the tomb that Abraham had bought for a sum of silver from the sons of Hamor in Shechem.

All of these notices are clearly based on the Joseph novella as now found in the Torah.[21]

Our study can close with a brief consideration of the development of a motif from the Joseph novella in the much later tales of Esther and Mordecai and of Daniel and his companions. As early as 1895 L. Roenthal suggested that there are several literary links between the Joseph narrative and the books of Esther and Daniel.[22] In each case we have narratives set in a foreign royal court, in which Israelite/Jewish courtiers move from positions of obscurity to the heights of authority and riches. In their fully developed forms these court tales all result in either the deliverance of the family and people of the courtier from some danger, or in the acknowledgment of the authority of the God of the courtier, or both. This similarity in the form of each story, together with striking literary similarities, suggests that there is a direct link between the Joseph novella, the tale of Esther and Mordecai, and stories dealing with Daniel and his companions. The authors of the latter were aware of a relationship in their theme with this older part of their heritage, and they used it, in part, as a model.[23]

It was observed earlier in this study that in the story of Joseph as an Egyptian courtier the focus of the courtier's activity is the king. This is characteristic of the model courtier developed in the Egyptian Instruction literature and is characteristic of Joseph in the earlier level of the tradition. In Genesis 47:13–26 this is developed most forcefully with the several repetitions of *ləparʿōh*. In return, it is from the hand of the king that a new authority and position—in fact, a new identity and life—is given to the courtier. In the utilization of the courtier tale in the larger Joseph novella this focus is blunted to a degree, as the center of the courtier's attention, and that of the story, move to the family of Jacob and the divine action taken to preserve them. Yet even here the actions of Joseph the courtier and of Joseph the son and brother are not brought into any final tension: Pharaoh himself seeks to settle Joseph's family within his land and grants their every request. Yet in this fuller narrative, and explicitly in its incorporation into the larger sacred story, the focus of the courtier's action has moved. There is a double focus in the courtier's life and action, even if within the Joseph novella the two are kept together without real tension.

In the tales of Esther and of Daniel 1–6 there is, at heart, an affirmation of the possibilities of a rich and creative life in the context of the foreign court that has affinities with that expressed in the Joseph narrative and is in marked contrast to the attitude of other ancient Israelite and early Jewish traditions. One can function, it is affirmed, within the social, political, and economic world of the diaspora, within this foreign environment, and yet remain a devoted member of one's religious community and a servant of his God.[24] The courtier can serve both king and kinsmen; he can be both a servant to a pagan ruler and a Yahwist. Thus the tale of Esther ends with this notice: "For Mordecai the Jew was next in rank [*mišneh*, cf. Gen. 41:43] to King Ahasuerus, and he was great among the Jews and popular with the multitude of his brethern, for he sought the welfare of his people and spoke peace to all his people" (Esth. 10:3). With a change of names this could stand at the conclusion of the Joseph novella.

And yet as developed in these later Jewish tales, the motif of the wise courtier undergoes some stress, for the double focus on the king, on one hand, and the people and deity, on the other, is not easily held. Tensions develop in the relationship. In the tale of Esther and Mordecai there is a danger to the courtier's people, not from some external source like the famine that is a danger to all humanity, but from an element within the foreign world in which the courtier moves, from within the court itself, and the conflict centers on just this. Esther and Mordecai triumph and rise to new levels of power and royal favor, but the potential for destructive conflict and divided loyalties within this pagan environment is recognized. When this material is then utilized as a festal legend for Purim, this element receives even more accent, and the tale is almost turned over against itself.[25]

This recognition is also found in the tales of Daniel 1–6, accounts of court contests or court conflicts. Here again the dangers to the Jewish courtiers rise from within the pagan environment in which the courtier must live. And here the tension between service to the king and service to one's God and loyalty to one's religious heritage nearly reaches the breaking point. Not only do the courtiers appear more passive and lifeless, tossed about by forces beyond their control, but elements of the miraculous are called upon to deliver the courtiers at moments of apparent destruction. In fact, the real hero of these accounts of Daniel and his companions seems to be the deity who fights for his people and who is glorified at the end of each. And the possibility of death in this pagan and often hostile environment is clearly acknowledged (Dan. 3:16–18). This was about as far as Israelite and early Jewish tradition could utilize and develop this motif of the wise and successful courtier in a foreign court. Historic tensions, both within Judaism and with the world at large, were such that this thread of ancient tradition—reaching back to pre-Israelite Canaan and the story of Joseph as an Egyptian courtier—was submerged, and ceased to play a creative role in the emerging normative traditions of Judaism in the Common Era.

NOTES

1. Martin Noth, *A History of Pentateuchal Traditions*, 208; Gerhard von Rad, "The Form-Critical Problem of the Hexateuch," 60. This analysis does not agree with the further suggestion of Noth (209, 212–13) that the Joseph narrative had its origins in the element in the sacred story summed up in the phrase "Jacob and his sons went down to Egypt" (cf. Josh. 24:4 and Deut. 26:5). Noth suggests that the narrative is the result of "the imaginative powers of a gifted narrator" who asked "how might this have come about?" (209). I suggest that the author of the tale of Joseph and his brothers simply drew upon the family group from Israel's traditions and, in a free and creative way, used them to develop his narrative, which illustrates the all-present, if hidden, mystical power and control of his God. Certainly he knew and used the tradition of the descent to Egypt by Jacob and his sons, but his purpose does not seem to have been simply to elaborate on this. Cf. George W. Coats, *From Canaan to Egypt*.

2. The earlier Genesis tradition itself seems to imply some span of time between the birth of Joseph and of Benjamin. The latter is not included in 29:31–30:24, and his birth is linked with the death of Rachel. See Noth, *Traditions*, 210, n. 567.

3. Noth, *Traditions*, 209.

4. See esp., R. N. Whybray, "The Joseph Story and Pentateuchal Criticism," *VT* 18 (1968): 522–28; Coats, *From Canaan to Egypt*, 55–79.

5. Gerhard von Rad, *Genesis*, 434.

6. See H. Gunkel, "Die Komposition der Joseph-Geschichte," *ZDMG* 76 (1922): 62–63, and Theodore Gaster, *Myth, Legend and Custom in the Old Testament*, 217–18, for the presence of this theme elsewhere in the folklore of different peoples. Note esp. Gaster's suggestions on a possible Canaanite utilization of this theme (218). For the Egyptian "Tale of Two Brothers" see A. Erman, *The Ancient Egyptians, A Sourcebook of Their Writings*, 150–61; *ANET*, 23–24; R. O. Faulkner, E. F. Wente, and W. K. Simpson, *The Literature of Ancient Egypt: An Anthology of Stories, Instructions, and Poetry*, 92–107. Because of the widespread presence of this narrative theme von Rad (*Genesis*, 361), Ruppert (*Die Josephserzählung der Genesis: Ein Beitrag zur Theologie der Pentateuchquellen*, 56–57), and Donald B. Redford (*A Study of the Biblical Story of Joseph*, 93) suggest that there can be no direct relationship between Gen. 39 and the Egyptian tale. For a general discussion of the Egyptian background in Gen. 39, cf. Claus Westermann, *Genesis 37–50*, 28, and J. Vergote, *Joseph en Égypte: Genèse chap. 37–50 à la lumière des études égyptologiques récentes*, 22–28.

7. The designation *sᵉris* for Potiphar is a general one denoting an official. The author of this unit need not have had a specific Egyptian usage in mind, and certainly it need not presuppose a "period of history in which there was little difference between the make-up of the court of Egypt and the composition of those of Asia, and in which this fact was common knowledge" (Redford, *Study*, 200–201; one might note Redford's own remarks on pp. 191–92). The title *śar haṭṭabāhîm* is a link taken over from Gen. 40.

8. Redford, *Study*, 92–93. See the fate of the adulterer and unfaithful wife in the tale recited in the unit called "King Cheops and the Magicians," Faulkner, *Literature*, 16–19. In the "Tale of Two Brothers" only a divinely sent miracle (talking cows and the sudden appearance of a lake) save the younger brother.

9. *Genesis*, 359–62, 430–31. See also "The Joseph Narrative and Ancient Wisdom," 295–96, and *Die Josephsgeschichte*, 10–12. In this context von Rad recalls 1 Sam. 16:18: "The narrator of 1 Samuel 16:18 also draws a very similar ideal picture of such a young man of good standing and good upbringing, whom 'Yahweh was with.' One can almost say that here is expressed the educational and cultural ideal of definite exalted stations with which our narrator is familiar. (*Genesis*, 359.)

10. Von Rad, *Genesis*, 431.

11. Ruppert, *Josephserzählung*, 58.

12. Ruppert, *Josephserzählung*, 59. J. L. Crenshaw ("Method in Determining Wisdom Influence upon 'Historical' Literature," *JBL* 88 [1969]: 136) also objects, on the one hand suggesting that "the theme of evil women is a common one, far too ubiquitous to demand wisdom influence." However, even von Rad ackowledges this (cf. *Genesis*, 361); it is the treatment and context in which the theme is used that von Rad underscores. And, furthermore, Joseph's statement in 39:8–9 (the two parts are to be read together) is not antithetical to wisdom traditions, and an "anthropological tone" does not require exclusion of all reference to the deity.

13. Von Rad, *Genesis*, 341–42; E. A. Speiser, *Genesis*, 278; Ruppert, *Die Josephserzählung*, 30–31; Redford, *Study*, 3.

14. The question depends, in part, on the meaning assigned to the term *tōlᵉdōt*. See Speiser, *Genesis*, 280–81; Redford, *Study*, 3–14; von Rad, *Genesis*, 345; Martin Buber, *Kingship of God*, 195, n. 29. See Redford for further references and for possible links with Gen. 46:8–27.

15. Redford, *Study*, 15–16.

16. The term *dibbāh* is said, however, to be a sign of P; so J. Skinner, *A Critical and Exegetical Commentary on the Book of Genesis*, 443. On its meaning here see also J. Peck, "Note on Genesis 37:2 and Joseph's Character," *ExpTim* 82 (1970/71): 342–43, who suggests that we have here a "subjective genitive," and translates the phrase "Joseph brought their slander against him to their father." If this is the sense of this usage, then this might further seek to place the initial blame for the tensions within the family on the half brothers.

17. See above, pp. 33–34.

18. On this see von Rad, *Genesis*, 397–98; Skinner, *Genisis*, 492–95; Speiser, *Genesis*, 344–45; Ruppert, *Josephserzählung*, 130–31, 136–39. Also see these for references and consideration of the relationship of this to the lists in Exod. 1:1–5; Num. 26; 1 Chr. 1:1ff.

19. W. L. Humphreys, "A Life-Style for Diaspora: A Study of the Tales of Esther and Daniel," *JBL* 92 (1973): 211–21.

20. A. Weiser, *The Psalms*, 674–76.

21. For further development of the Joseph tradition in Jewish and early Christian literature see A. W. Argyle, "Joseph the Patriarch in Patristic Teaching," *ExpTim* 67 (1955/56): 199–201.

22. L. A. Rosenthal, "Die Josephsgeschichte mit den Büchern Ester und Daniel verglichen," *ZAW* 15 (1895): 278–84; "Nochmals der Vergleich Ester, Joseph, Daniel," *ZAW* 17 (1897): 125–28. Jewish tradition has long suggested links between Joseph and Esther and Daniel. See Rosenthal, "Josephsgeschichte," 284, and Theodore Gaster, *Purim and Hanukkah in Custom and Tradition* 71–72. More recently this has been developed by M. Gan, "The Book of Esther in the Light of the Story of Joseph in Egypt," *Tarbis* 31 (1961): 144–49 (Hebrew with English summary), and S. Talmon, " 'Wisdom' in the Book of Esther," *VT* 13 (1963): 419–55.

23. In the case of Esther, see Gen. 41:42–43 and Esth. 6:11; Gen. 44:34 and Esth. 8:6; the use of the hithpael of *'pq* in Gen. 43:31 and 45:1 and Esth. 5:10; Gen. 41:34–37 and Esth. 2:3–4. In the case of Daniel see Gen. 41:42 and Dan. 5:29; Gen. 41:8 and Dan 2:1, 3; Gen. 41:25, 28 and Dan. 2:28; Gen. 41:38 and Dan. 5:11, 14; Gen. 41:15 and Dan. 5:15–6. For further cases see the articles of Rosenthal cited in note 22 above. See also P. Reissler, "Zu Rosenthal's Aufsatz, Bd XV, S. 278ff.," ZAW 16 (1896): 182; W. L. Humphreys, "The Motif of the Wise Courtier in the Old Testament," 288–91, 311–15; G. Gerleman, *Studien zu Esther*, 11–12, for some criticism of individual examples.

24. See Humphreys, "Life-Style," 211–23, for more details on the nature and form of these tales and for considerations on their later reutilization in connection with the feast of Purim and with the apocalyptic speculation of the period of Maccabees.

25. Humphreys, "Life-Style," 211–23. See also Humphreys, "The Story of Esther and Mordecai: An Early Jewish Novella."

BIBLIOGRAPHY

Albright, W. F. "Historical and Mythical Elements in the Story of Joseph." *JBL* 37 (1918): 111–43.

Alter, Robert. *The Art of Biblical Narrative*. New York: Basic Books, 1981.

Anderson, B. W. *Understanding the Old Testament*. Englewood Cliffs, NJ: Prentice-Hall, 1966.

Argyle, A. W. "Joseph the Patriarch in Patristic Teaching." *ExpTim* 67 (1955/56): 199–201.

Barton, J. *Reading the Old Testament*. Philadelphia: Westminister, 1984.

Becker, Ernst. *Denial of Death*. New York: Free Press, 1973.

Berlin, A. *Poetics and the Interpretation of Biblical Narrative*. Sheffield: Almond, 1983.

———. "Point of View by Biblical Narrative." In *A Sense of Text: The Art of Language in the Study of Biblical Literature*. Winona Lake, WI: Eisenbrauns, 1983. 71–113.

Breasted, J. H. *Ancient Records of Egypt*. 5 vols. Chicago: University of Chicago Press, 1906–1907.

Buber, Martin. *Kingship of God*. New York: Harper, 1967.

Coats, George W. *From Canaan to Egypt: Structural and Theological Context for the Joseph Story*. CBQMS 4. Washington: Catholic Biblical Association of America, 1976.

———. "The Joseph Story and Ancient Wisdom: A Reappraisal," *CBQ* 35 (1973): 285–97.

———. "Redactional Unity in Genesis 37–50." *JBL* 93 (1974): 15–21.

Crenshaw, James L. "Education in Ancient Israel." *JBL* 104 (1985): 601–15.

———. "Method in Determining Wisdom Influence upon 'Historical' Literature." *JBL* 88 (1969): 129–42.

———. *Old Testament Wisdom: An Introduction*. Atlanta: John Knox, 1981.

Croatto, J. S. "Abrek 'Intendant' dans Gen. XLI 41, 43." *VT* 16 (1966): 113–15.

de Vaux, Roland. *Ancient Israel: Its Life and Institutions*. New York: McGraw-Hill, 1961.

———. "Titres et fonctionnaire égyptiens à la cour de David et de Solomon." *RB* 48 (1939): 394–405.

Edgerton, W. F. "The Government and the Governed in the Egyptian Empire." *JNES* 6 (1947): 152ff.

Ehrlich, E. L. *Der Traum im alten Testament*. Berlin: Topelmann, 1953.

Eissfeldt, O. "Genesis." *Interpreter's Dictionary of the Bible*. Nashville: Abingdon, 1962.

Erman, A. *The Ancient Egyptians: A Sourcebook of Their Writings*. New York: Harper, 1966.

Faulkner, R. O., Wente, E. F., and Simpson, W. K. *The Literature of Ancient Egypt: An Anthology of Stories, Instructions, and Poetry*. New Haven: Yale University Press, 1972.

Frankfort, H. *Ancient Egyptian Religion*. New York: Harper, 1948.

Gan, M. "The Book of Esther in the Light of the Story of Joseph in Egypt." *Tarbis* 32 (1961): 144–49.

Gardiner, A. H. *Egypt of the Pharaohs*. New York: Oxford University Press, 1966

. *Hieratic Papyri in the British Museum, Third Series. Chester Beatty Gift*. London: British Museum, 1935.

. "The Instruction Addressed to Kagemni and His Brethren." *JEA* 32 (1946): 71–75.

. *Notes on the Story of Sinuhe*. Paris: Recueil de Travaux, 1916.

Gaster, Theodore. *Myth, Legend, and Custom in the Old Testament*. New York: Harper, 1969.

. *Purim and Hanukkah in Custom and Tradition*. New York: Henry Schuman, 1950.

Gerleman, G. *Studien zu Esther*. BibS 48. Neukirchen: Neukirchener Verlag, 1966.

Gese, H. *Lehre und Wirklichkeit in der alten Weisheit*. Tubingen: J. C. B. Mohr, 1958.

Gressmann, H. "Ursprung und Entwicklung der Joseph-Sage." FRLANT 36. Göttingen: Vandenhoeck & Ruprecht, (1923), 1–55.

Griffith, F. L. "The Teaching of Amenophis the Son of Kanaknt, Papyrus B. M. 10474." *JEA* 12 (1926): 191–231.

Gunkel, Hermann. "Die Komposition der Joseph-Geschichte." *ZDMG* 76 (1922): 55–71.

. *The Legends of Genesis*. New York: Schocken, 1967.

Hermisson, H. J. *Studien zur israelitischen Spruchweisheit*. WMANT 28. Neukirchen: Neukirchener Verlag, 1968.

Holman, Hugh C. *A Handbook to Literature*. 3d ed. New York: Odyssey, 1972.

Humphreys, W. L. *Crisis and Story: Introduction to the Old Testament*. Palo Alto: Mayfield, 1979.

. "Joseph Story, The." *Interpreter's Dictionary of the Bible, Supplementary Volume*. Nashville: Abingdon, 1976.

. "A Life-Style for Diaspora: A Study in the Tales of Esther and Daniel." *JBL* 92 (1973): 211–23.

. "The Motif of the Wise Courtier in the Book of Proverbs." In *Israelite Wisdom: Theological and Literary Studies in Honor of Samuel Terrien*, edited by John Gammie. Missoula, MT: Scholars Press, 1978. 177–90.

. "The Motif of the Wise Courier in the Old Testament." Dissertation; New York: Union Theological Seminary, 1970.

. "The Story of Esther and Mordecai: An Early Jewish Novella." In *Saga, Legend, Tale, Novella, Fable: Narrative Form in Old Testament Literature*, edited by George W. Coats. JSOT Series 35. Sheffield: JSOT Press, 1985. 97–113.

. *The Tragic Vision and the Hebrew Tradition*. OBT. Philadelphia: Fortress, 1985.

Janssen, J. M. A. "Egyptological Remarks on the Story of Joseph in Genesis." *JEOL* 5 (1955–58): 63–72.

Keegan, T. J. *Interpreting the Bible*. New York: Paulist, 1985.

Kramer, S. N. *The Sumerians: Their History, Culture, and Character*. Chicago: University of Chicago Press, 1963.

Lambdin, T. O. "Egyptian Loan Words in the Old Testament." *JAOS* 73 (1953): 146–55.

Lambert, G. W. *Babylonian Wisdom Literature*. Oxford: The Clarendon Press, 1960.

McKane, William *Prophets and Wise Men*. Naperville, IL: Allenson, 1964

. *Studies in the Patriarchal Narratives*. Edinburg: Handsel, 1979.

Mann, Thomas. *Joseph and His Brothers*. New York: Knopf, 1981.

May, H. G. "The Evolution of the Joseph Story." *AJSL* 47 (1931): 83–93.

Murphy, R. E. "The Concept of Wisdom Literature." In *The Bible in Current Catholic Thought*. New York: Herder and Herder, 1962. 46–54.

. "Form Criticism and Wisdom Literature." *CBQ* 31 (1969): 475–83.

Noth, Martin. *A History of Pentateuchal Traditions*. Englewood Cliffs, NJ: Prentice-Hall, 1972.

Oppenheim, A. L. "The Interpretation of Dreams in the Ancient Near East." *Transactions of the American Philosophical Society* 46 (1956).

Peck, J. "Note on Genesis 37:2 and Joseph's Character." *ExpTim* 82 (1970/71): 342–43.

Polzin, R. *Moses and the Deuteronomist*. New York: Seabury, 1980.

Pritchard, James B. *Ancient Near Eastern Texts Relating to the Old Testament*. Princeton: Princeton University Press, 1955.

Redford, Donald B. *A Study of the Biblical Story of Joseph* (Genesis 37–50). VTSup 20. Leiden: J. Brill, 1970.

Rosenthal, L. A. "Die Josephsgeschichte mit den Büchern Ester und Daniel verglichen." *ZAW* 15 (1895): 278–84.

. "Nochmals der Vergleich Ester, Joseph, Daniel." ZAW 17 (1897): 125–28.

Ruppert, L. *Die Josephserzählung der Genesis: Ein Beitrag zur Theologie der Pentateuchguellen*. Munich. Kosel-Verlag, 1965.

Sanders, J. A. *Canon and Community: A Guide to Canonical Criticism*. Philadelphia: Fortress, 1984.

Schmid, H. H. *Wesen and Geschichte der Weisheit*. Beihefte zur *ZAW* 101. Berlin: Topelmann, 1966.

Schmitt, H.-C. *Die nichtpriesterliche Josephsgerschichte*. Beihefte zur *ZAW* 154. Berlin: Walter de Gruyter, 1980.

Scott, R. B. Y. "Solomon and the Beginnings of Wisdom in Israel." VTSup 3. Leiden: J. Brill, 1960. 262–79.

Skinner, J. *A Critical and Exegetical Commentary on Genesis*. ICC. Edinburgh: T. & T. Clark, 1930.

Speiser, E. A. "Census and Ritual Expiation in Mari and Israel." *BASOR* 149 (1958): 17–25

———. *Genesis*. AB1. Garden City, NY. Doubleday, 1964.

Suys, E. *La sagesse d'Ani*. Rome: Biblical Institute, 1935.

Talmon, S. "'Wisdom' in the Book of Esther." VT 13 (1963): 419–55.

Trible, Phyllis. *God and the Rhetoric of Sexuality*. OBT 2. Philadelphia: Fortress, 1978.

———. *Texts of Terror*. OBT. Philadelphia: Fortress, 1984.

Vergote, J. *Joseph en Égypt: Genèse chap. 37–50 à la lumière des études égyptologiques récentes*. Louvuin: Publications Universitaires, 1959.

von Ran, Gerhard. "The Form Critical Problem of the Hexateuch." In *The Problem of the Hexateuch and Other Essays*. New York: McGraw-Hill, 1966. 1–78

———. *Genesis*. OTL. Philadelphia: Westminster, 1959.

———. "The Joseph Narrative and Ancient Wisdom. In *The Problem of the Hexateuch and Other Essays*. New York: McGraw-Hill, 1966. 292–300.

———. *Die Josephsgeschichte*. BibS 5. Neukirchen: Neukirchener Verlag, 1954.

———. Old Testament Theology 1. New York: Harper, 1962.

Ward, W. A. "Egyptian Offices in Gen. 39–50." *BSac* 114 (1957): 40–59.

———. "The Egyptian Office of Joseph." *JSS* 5 (1960): 146–50.

Weiser, A. *The Psalms*. OTL. Philadelphia: Westminster, 1962.

Wellhausen, J. *Prolegomena to the History of Israel*. Meridian Books; Cleveland: World, 1957.

Westermann, Claus. *Genesis 37–50*. Minneapolis: Augsburg, 1986.

Whybray, R. N. "The Joseph Story and Pentateuchal Criticism." *VT* 18 (1968): 522–28.

Wintermute, O. "Joseph Son of Jacob." *Interpreter's Dictionary of the Bible*. Nashville: Abingdon, 1962.

Zaba, Z. *Les maximes de Ptah-hotep*. Prague: Editions de l'Academie Tchecoslovaque des Sciences, 1956.

INDEX
AUTHORS

BIBLICAL PASSAGES

221

SUBJECTS

INDEX OF SUBJECTS

WESTMAR COLLEGE LIBRARY

165736

RE OTE BS 1235.2 .H86 1988 / Joseph and his family

BS 1235.2 .H86 1988
Humphreys, W. Lee.
Joseph and his family
                    (88-429)

DEMCO